Unauthorized Versions

José Lanters

Unauthorized Versions
Irish Menippean Satire, 1919–1952

The Catholic University of America Press
Washington, D.C.

For my mother, and in loving memory of my father.

The paper used in this publication meets the minimum requirements of
American National Standards for Information Service—Permanence of
Paper for Printed Library Materials, ANSI z39.48-1984. ∞

Library of Congress Cataloging-in-Publication Data

Lanters, José.

Unauthorized versions : Irish Menippean Satire, 1919–1952 /
José Lanters.

p. cm.

Includes bibliographical references (p.) and index.

1. Satire, English—Irish authors—History and criticism.
2. English fiction—Irish authors—History and criticism. 3. Figgis,
Darrell, 1882–1925—Criticism and interpretation. 4. O'Duffy, Eimar,
1893–1935—Criticism and interpretation. 5. Clarke, Austin,
1896–1974—Criticism and interpretation. 6. O'Brien, Flann,
1911–1966—Criticism and interpretation. 7. Wall, Mervyn, 1908–1997
Criticism and interpretation. 8. Satire, English—Irish authors—
Classical influences. 9. Ireland—Intellectual Life—20th century.
10. Ireland—In literature.

PR8815 .L36   2000

827′.912099417—dc21

99-089814

ISBN 0-8132-0986-2 (cl : alk. paper)

Contents

Acknowledgments

I would not have been able to realize this project without the generous assistance of the University of Oklahoma: two Junior Faculty Summer Research Fellowships in 1992 and 1993, a Humanities Center Fellowship in the Spring of 1996, and a Sabbatical Leave of Absence in the Fall of 1997 provided me with valuable time to think and write. Two University of Oklahoma Research Council Grants and a President's International Travel Fellowship enabled me to carry out research in Dublin. Travel assistance was also provided by a Grant from the South Central Modern Language Association. Portions of this book were completed with the assistance of the Oklahoma Foundation for the Humanities and the National Endowment for the Humanities.

James MacKillop and Rüdiger Imhof read the manuscript and provided useful comments. A version of the chapter on Darrell Figgis's *The Return of the Hero*, entitled "Darrell Figgis, *The Return of the Hero*, and the Making of the Irish Nation," was published in *Colby Quarterly*, 31, 3 (1995): 204–13. A version of the chapter on Austin Clarke's *The Singing-Men at Cashel* appeared in *New Hibernia Review*, 1, 2 (1997): 134–51, under the title "'To Keep Body and Soul Together': Austin Clarke's *The Singing-Men at Cashel*, 1936." I thank the editors of these journals, Douglas Archibald and Thomas Dillon Redshaw, respectively, for their helpful suggestions, and for permission to use material from these essays here. I would also like to express my appreciation to the staffs of the Harry Ransom Humanities Research Center in Austin, Texas, and in particular the National Library of Ireland in Dublin, for their helpfulness and courtesy.

On a personal note, I thank my colleagues in the Department of Classics and Letters of the University of Oklahoma, particularly the department's chairman, John Catlin, for allowing me to indulge professionally in my love for Irish studies, and for providing moral support. I owe a tremendous debt of gratitude to Pat Burke for his encouragement, friendship, and generosity, as well as to Marion McEvoy, Patrick, Cathy, and Denis for their hospitality over the years. Finally, I would like to thank Keith Busby, who understands the demands of scholarship, and whose love has sustained me over the years and during the writing of this book.

Introduction

When Irish independence finally became a reality in 1922, it did not manifest itself in the shape of a jubilant young nation confidently striding into the future. The Civil War of 1922–1923 between, on one side, the armed forces of the Irish Free State that had been created by the signing of the Anglo-Irish Treaty and, on the other, the Republican wing of the Irish Republican Army (IRA) led by Éamon de Valera, who violently opposed the Treaty, made sure of that. Rather, the fledgling state under the leadership of W. T. Cosgrave's Cumann na nGaedheal found itself from its violent beginnings onward in "a condition of permanent emergency" and "on the defensive from the outset; its overriding concern was the protection of the new order against internal attack."[1] In fact, as Declan Kiberd has argued, "[T]he leaders of the new state remained painfully uncertain of its legitimacy. This was a condition calculated to generate endless crises of self-legitimation, and with them a nervously patriarchal psychology."[2] Although Church influence, at least in an official capacity, had initially appeared to be diminished in the new state, in practice the new, insecure government proved more than willing to enforce the Catholic moral code prescribed by the Irish bishops. Divorce was made impossible almost as soon as the nation came into existence, and the Censorship of Films Act of 1923 was only the first of many censorship laws to be passed in the 1920s. When the Republicans, who had at first refused to take their seats in the new parliament, entered the Dáil in 1927 in the form of the Fianna Fáil Party led by Éamon de Valera, the latter's Catholic, conservative views reinforced further the state's already strong tendency to protect the nation's moral values, a

---

1. Donal Ó Drisceoil, *Censorship in Ireland, 1939–1945: Neutrality, Politics, and Society* (Cork, Ireland: Cork University Press, 1996), 1.

2. Declan Kiberd, *Inventing Ireland: The Literature of the Modern Nation* (London: Jonathan Cape, 1995), 406.

1

tendency, moreover, that received the support of the great majority of the population. The first decade of independence, then, "did not bode well for the development of a democratic political culture or a functioning civic culture in the new state. Political insecurity, and the conservative impulses of moral and cultural protectionism, led to a closed, overcentralised and authoritarian political system and a sense of cultural and intellectual isolation."[3]

In this postindependence Ireland, where fear and lack of imagination were narrowing the minds of those in authority, the energy was lacking to envision the nation in ways that would satisfy the cultural and intellectual élite. The mood of the country had changed: whereas the writers and artists of the Celtic Revival had played an active part not just in reflecting but in actually creating a vision of the future of Ireland, the Free State, with its narrowly defined moral and cultural code, fearful of independent and creative thought, forced its literary figures into an oppositional and increasingly marginalized role. The Celtic Revivalists of the turn of the century, with W. B. Yeats prominent among them, had used medieval Irish mythology and literature as a source of inspiration to establish the idea of a national identity that was ancient and noble: if people could but identify with the old gods and heroes of Ireland, the future of the nation, once it finally emerged, would be bright indeed. In the wake of such idealism, the somewhat grimmer reality of Irish independence could only lead to disillusionment, on the part of the writers as well as the political leaders and the population at large. Writers could no longer expect their works to be read and debated widely and enthusiastically: literature was increasingly regarded with suspicion, while enthusiasm—for anything—was in short supply. Partly in response to this newly antagonistic mood, the writers themselves soon began to express their own frustration, first with the new country's lack of political daring and imagination, but increasingly with the more serious side effects of national insecurity, censorship, and repression. The climate was right for satire.

Satire is broadly defined as the literary art of discrediting a subject by making it appear ridiculous. The different forms of satire as a literary mode date back to classical antiquity: Horace (65–8 B.C.) and Juvenal (A.D. ca. 60–ca. 130) refined the art of verse satire, while Varro (116–27 B.C.) and

---

3. Ó Drisceoil, *Censorship*, 2.

Lucian (A.D. ca. 120–ca. 180) perfected a narrative, often overtly dialogical, form of satire, commonly referred to as *Menippean satire*, because it was purportedly first developed by the Greek writer Menippus (active in the third century B.C.). Whatever the degree of their familiarity with the classical tradition, the modern Irish satirists who are the subject of this book also write under the influence of a great Irish satirical tradition. Vivian Mercier, in his important study of Irish literary wit, *The Irish Comic Tradition*, stresses that one of the most striking facts "about Irish literature in either Gaelic or English is the high proportion of satire which it contains."[4]

Satire was an important element in early Gaelic literature, where it was considered a form of verbal magic with which poet-seers cursed and disabled enemies and trespassers of the law. In the Irish tradition, satire thus came to be strongly associated with attack and denunciation. Mercier argues that the reason why Irish satire frequently takes the form of "personal lampoon or even invective" is its origin in the belief that "satire had the power to inflict actual physical harm on its victim."[5] Of the Anglo-Irish writers, Swift is one of the earliest satirists, and by far the greatest. Mercier proposes that "Swift added a new element, sustained irony, to the Gaelic comic tradition,"[6] but also argues that he was at the same time very much a part of that tradition of denunciation. Although Mercier states that *irony*—writing one thing and meaning another—rather than mere invective is the basic device of all true satire, he is nevertheless uncomfortable with the implications of this double-voiced device, given his view that it is the purpose of satire "to deflate the foolish and the evil,"[7] and given his assumption that it is the satirist's wish "to change or transcend" the world.[8] For this reason, he finds it hard to place a writer such as James Joyce comfortably within his definition of satire, because Joyce's vision is ultimately too accommodating of the world's imperfection.

Mercier's reading of Swift connects the latter's "intemperate rage" with the spirit of Irish satire, and detects parallels between Swift's work and that of his Gaelic counterparts, for example, between the imaginary journey of *Gulliver's Travels* and the fantastic voyage tales of the Irish tradition.

---

4. Vivian Mercier, *The Irish Comic Tradition* (Oxford, U.K.: Oxford University Press, 1962), 105.

5. Ibid., 145.   6. Ibid., 186.

7. Ibid., 184.   8. Ibid., 207.

However, while it *may* be the case that Swift knew *some* Irish material, he ultimately has more in common with a writer like Lucian, whose satirical account in *A True Story* might equally, and perhaps more plausibly, have served as a model for the fantastic journey in *Gulliver's Travels*. Indeed, Northrop Frye argues that "the literary ancestry of *Gulliver's Travels* . . . runs through Rabelais and Erasmus to Lucian," that Menippean satire as a form has its own distinct traditions, and that these have often been misidentified and misunderstood.[9] Menippean satire is essentially a genre of ideas, and "presents people as mouthpieces of the ideas they represent" rather than as individuals.[10] Such satire "relies on the free play of intellectual fancy" and "presents us with a vision of the world in terms of a single intellectual pattern. The intellectual structure built up from the story makes for violent dislocations in the customary logic of narrative, though the appearance of carelessness that results reflects only the carelessness of the reader or his tendency to judge by a novel-centered conception of fiction."[11]

Frank Palmeri has argued convincingly that a distinction should be made between the perspective of narrative (Menippean) satire and that of verse satire. The latter is properly a vehicle for invective, as the verse satirist "closely resembles the prototype of the satirist as lay preacher, acting as a moral authority to excoriate contemporary practices or individuals."[12] Narrative satire stands apart from other satirical forms in that it adopts a questioning, critical stance toward other authoritative discourses as well as toward its own pronouncements. After querying a prevailing perspective, narrative satires "go on to parody their own parodic inversion, without reverting to the original point of departure. . . . Through repeated parody and self-parody, such satire counterpoises multiple frames of understanding without assenting to the authority of any single perspective."[13] Menippean satire is defined by these repeated inversions in that it typically depicts a struggle between opposed views without reaching a satisfactory conclusion or synthesis, "leaving meaning indefinite and suspending the

9. Northrop Frye, *Anatomy of Criticism: Four Essays* (Princeton, N.J.: Princeton University Press, 1957), 308–9.

10. Ibid., 309.

11. Ibid., 310.

12. Frank Palmeri, *Satire in Narrative: Petronius, Swift, Gibbon, Melville, and Pynchon* (Austin: University of Texas Press, 1990), 6.

13. Ibid., 3.

reader uncomfortably between alternate and opposed interpretations of the work."[14] Whereas verse satire acknowledges "the validity of social and cultural distinctions between high and low,"[15] narrative satire contests hierarchies and questions rather than enforces cultural authority.

In theoretical terms, the dialogic, unresolved nature of Menippean satire has been discussed most extensively by Mikhail Bakhtin, in *Problems of Dostoevsky's Poetics,* as well as in other works. Bakhtin identifies fourteen characteristics of Menippean satire; while some of these attributes overlap with each other to a certain extent, and while not all of them need to be present for a text to be characterized as "Menippean," the categories provide helpful guidelines in establishing the satirical potential of a narrative text. (1) There is generally an increased comic element. (2) Menippean texts are not hampered by demands for realism or verisimilitude: consequently, (3) their plots are often extraordinarily fantastic. (4) They juxtapose extremes of "high" and "low": baseness and vulgarity rub shoulders with lofty symbolism and philosophy; on the textual level, this hierarchical leveling translates into (5) the widespread use of inserted genres and parody, and (6) the mixing of many different styles and registers. (7) Often Menippean texts feature a three-planed construction analogous to heaven—earth—hell (8) in order to ask "ultimate questions" about existence. (9) They present unusual viewpoints as well as (10) abnormal moral and psychic states, (11) scandal scenes, and inappropriate behavior as a way of presenting experiences from unexpected angles and perspectives. (12) For this reason, too, they contain sharp contrasts, abrupt transitions, and incongruous juxtapositions. (13) They feature elements of social utopia; (14) and they show a concern with current and topical issues.[16]

In Menippean satire, the purpose of creating extraordinary situations, borrowing and parodying all kinds of existing texts, and bringing together sharply contrasting themes, characters, and styles is to provide a fantastic setting within which a philosophical or ideological idea or "truth" can be tested. Menippean satire is a dialogic literary expression that subverts both the official voice of public authority and, ultimately, that of its opponents:

14. Ibid., 5.

15. Ibid., 6.

16. See M. M. Bakhtin, *Problems of Dostoevsky's Poetics,* trans. and ed. Caryl Emerson (Minneapolis: University of Minnesota Press, 1984), 114–19.

"[T]he Menippean forms are based on man's inability to know and contain his fate. To any vision of a completed system of truth, the menippea suggests some element outside the system. Seriocomic forms present a challenge, open or covert, to literary and intellectual orthodoxy, a challenge that is reflected not only in their philosophic content but also in their structure and language."[17] Narrative satire questions not any particular version of the truth, but the nature of "truth" itself; it undermines all ideological positions—its own included—by presenting them as polarized and untenable extremes.

Darrell Figgis, Eimar O'Duffy, Austin Clarke, Flann O'Brien, and Mervyn Wall, the satirists who are the focus of this study, all work within the tradition of Menippean satire. They use medieval Ireland as a setting for discussing contemporary concerns and/or borrow characters and motifs from early Irish texts (such as the *Táin Bó Cúailnge*, "Aislinge Meic Con Glinne," *Buile Suibhne*, the Fenian Cycle, and various mythological tales), which they frequently place in a modern context along with new characters whose attitudes and beliefs create an incongruous contrast with the early Irish material; the Old and Middle Irish texts, moreover, are more often than not satirical in nature to begin with. The use of the Middle Ages as a setting, combined with stylistic and anachronistic "lapses" to create references to contemporary Ireland, is a Menippean technique: it creates a double vision in which the satirist both *is* and *is not* criticizing the present conditions in his country. Such ambiguity, apart from providing the Menippean satirist with a safe vantage point from which to fire his arrows with relative impunity, is a characteristic feature of this type of satire. Each writer creates a series of dialogues: between the past and the present; between characters who represent opposing values and ideologies, whereby the ancient characters are generally used to show up the weaknesses and inconsistencies in modern ideologies; but also between the older texts from which the satires borrow and their modern reworkings, and hence between his ancient counterparts and the contemporary author himself. This underlying textual dialogue—especially the reference within several of these satires to the existence of multiple manuscripts, fragments, and versions

---

17. Philip Holland, "Robert Burton's *Anatomy of Melancholy* and Menippean Satire, Humanist and English," Ph. D. dissertation, University of London, 1979; quoted in Bakhtin, *Dostoevsky's Poetics*, 106–7, note b.

of the text—paradoxically sabotages the criticism of contemporary attitudes implicit in the characters' dialogue by questioning the authority and reliability of the epistemological foundation (text, language, meaning) on which their criticism is based.

The importance and popularity of satire as a critique of social and cultural values and as a tool for questioning cultural authority are to a high degree dependent on the nature of that society. The greater the extremes prevalent in that society, the more its literature will tend toward satire. Bakhtin argues that Menippean satire "was formed in an epoch when national legend was already in decay, amid the destruction of those ethical norms that constituted the ancient idea of 'seemliness' ('beauty,' 'nobility'), in an epoch of intense struggle among numerous and heterogeneous religious and philosophical schools and movements, when disputes over 'ultimate questions' of worldview had become an everyday mass phenomenon among all strata of the population and took place whenever and wherever people came together."[18] In general, certain moments in history, especially periods of cultural turmoil and political change (such as civil war) involving the dismantling of established institutions and the formation of new norms and values, appear to be conducive to the writing of narrative satire. This explains the prevalence of Menippean satire in Ireland following the signing of the Treaty, for the first decades after the declaration of the Irish Free State reflect many of these characteristics. From the early 1920s onward, Ireland faced the division of the country, civil war, political insecurity, and economic depression, culminating in the policy of neutrality and isolationism during World War II (in Ireland euphemistically referred to as the "Emergency"). The works of the satirists writing during these decades reflect the economic, moral, and artistic climate in Ireland during this period.

While the focus of the satires written in the 1920s is predominantly on the turbulent nature of internal Irish politics, by the 1930s this focus has shifted to a concern with the increasingly precarious position of the individual, especially the artist himself, in a conservative, even repressive society. Increasingly, writers have to deal with the privileged position of the Catholic Church in Ireland as a moral authority, with state censorship (especially after the passing of the Censorship of Publications Act in 1929), and

18. Bakhtin, *Dostoevsky's Poetics*, 119.

with other restrictive legislation. In this transition from political to moral concerns, the role of the Church appears to have been pivotal. Richard Kearney argues that, after independence,

and particularly during the Civil War, the Church found itself divided against a significant portion of what she considered to be her own people. With the alien oppressor gone from the scene, the violence that exploded in the Civil War between Irishman and Irishman could no longer be attributed to an *external* cause (i.e., the colonial British occupation). It had to be acknowledged as "our own," that is, as a rupture *within* the Catholic nationalist community itself. So that with the setting up of the Irish Free State after the Treaty of 1921, the Church found itself in the ambiguous position of being at once the representative of the ideals of the Catholic nationalist population and at the same time of siding with one "legitimate" portion of that population (the Free State) against another "illegitimate" portion (those Republicans who rejected the Treaty in the name of the still unrealized ideal of a United Ireland).[19]

Even after these differences were straightened out once Fianna Fáil had entered the Dáil, the problem remained that the new, independent, Catholic Irish state was a far cry from being a utopia. To circumvent this disturbing reality, "[B]etween the twenties and the fifties, 'sexual immorality' became something of an ideological scapegoat in this regard," so that "the former *political* threat to our national integrity was now replaced by a *moral* threat. And since it was continually asserted in these rather insular years, that this threat to our 'Faith and Morals' came principally from 'abroad' (that is, from the liberal licentiousness of 'foreign' countries), the presumption could be sustained that the root cause of our evils came once again from *without.*"[20]

Under such circumstances, the epic vision created by Yeats and other Celtic Revivalists of an ideal Irish state built on the foundations laid by the ancient Celtic gods and heroes became subject to criticism and satirical ridicule. To be sure, Yeats's use of Gaelic subject matter to create a "national literature" had its detractors early on—for example, John Eglinton and Frederick Ryan in their magazine *Dana* (1904–1905)—and satirists such as Gerald MacNamara had effectively shown, in plays like *Thompson in Tír-*

---

19. Richard Kearney, *Transitions: Narratives in Modern Irish Culture* (Manchester, U.K.: Manchester University Press, 1988), 243.

20. Ibid., 245.

na-nÓg (1912), that the mythological perspective can be as culturally confining as it is potentially liberating. James Stephens, who added a strong blend of comedy and fantasy to his borrowings from mythology in such works as *The Crock of Gold* (1912) and *The Demi-Gods* (1914), can be regarded as an intermediary figure between Yeats and the postindependence satirists: his messianic vision is comical, but the comedy, rather than being negative, is an aspect of its overriding optimism. Only the creation of an independent state could put this optimism to the test, and in 1921 at least one commentator had a premonition of the direction literature and politics would take in the immediate future: "It is scarcely surprising, in the present national mood of almost religious exaltation, that certain visionaries have begun to foretell a kind of Irish Messiah. They appear to take for granted that he will come of Gaelic stock, feeling justified, I suppose, in ignoring to this extent the lesson of human experience, that fixed preconceptions are liable to disappointment. Perhaps he will come as a jester, causing a ripple of oblivious laughter to pass over the countenance of the Ireland of the Sorrows: a whimsical Cachullin [*sic*] of whose beneficent prowess Mr James Stephens might in his extreme old age be the devout St John."[21] Eglinton proved to be right: disappointment was just around the corner, and the jesters were waiting in the wings, ready to expose the hollowness of any Celtic idealism that might still prevail by writing against the grain of the national legend.

21. John Eglinton, "Dublin Letter," *Dial*, March 1921, pp. 334–35.

part one

Darrell Figgis

(1882–1925)

hen *The Return of the Hero* was first published in 1923, it appeared under the pseudonym "Michael Ireland." The book was well received; indeed, Andrew Malone claims that it "caused something of a sensation" when it was published.[1] Even James Joyce, resident in Paris at the time, owned a copy. The real identity of Michael Ireland was at first a mystery, but as the novel involved fantasy and the use of Irish mythological material, the author was initially widely believed to be James Stephens. The revelation that *The Return of the Hero* had been written by Darrell Figgis was met with general incredulity; for example, upon hearing the news, Yeats, who had at one point apparently referred to Figgis as "the most chuckled-headed, tongue-clotted of writers,"[2] is reported to have remarked, "I'm afraid we'll have to recognize Figgis as a literary man, after all."[3] James Stephens was equally perplexed. In his introduction to the book's American edition of 1930, he expressed the opinion that "*The Return of the Hero* does not exhibit any of the char-

---

1. Andrew E. Malone, "Darrell Figgis," *Dublin Magazine*, 1, 2 (1926): 25.

2. Quoted without source citation in Maryanne Wessel-Felter, "Darrell Figgis: An Overview of His Work," *Journal of Irish Literature*, 22, 2 (1993): 3. Brinsley MacNamara was of a similar opinion; in a letter to Frank J. Hugh O'Donnell dated 3 February 1920 he referred to Figgis as "an absurd buffoon of literature"; quoted in Robert Hogan and Richard Burnham, *The Art of the Amateur, 1916–1920* (Dublin: Dolmen Press, 1984), 251.

3. Padraic Colum, "Darrell Figgis: A Portrait," *Dublin Magazine*, 14, 2 (1939): 28.

acteristics of Mr. Figgis' ordinary writing," and that "temperamentally it differs from Mr. Figgis himself." He concluded that, "if Darrell Figgis wrote *The Return of the Hero,* then literary criticism stands baffled, and we must admit that occasions can arise in which the impossible becomes possible, and the unbelievable is to be credited."[4]

On the surface, Darrell Figgis seemed indeed an unlikely candidate for the authorship of a work of satirical fantasy based upon the legendary confrontation between Saint Patrick and the Old Irish hero Oisín, son of the great Finn mac Cumhal (Figgis's spelling; properly Fionn mac Cumhaill, or, Anglicized, Finn MacCool). Figgis was born to an Anglo-Irish, Protestant family in Rathmines, Dublin, in 1882, and spent his childhood in Ceylon. As a young man he worked for twelve years as a tea buyer and broker in London and Calcutta before leaving the business in 1910 to devote himself to literature. He worked for a time as literary adviser for Dent publishers and then as a freelance journalist. His first collection of poems, *A Vision of Life,* appeared in 1909. Like so many others of a similar background before him, he discovered his "Irish identity" around the year 1913 when he bought a cottage on Achill Island in County Mayo, and from then on until his death "all his work . . . was permeated with Irish history, politics and customs."[5] The transition from businessman to Irish enthusiast is reflected in his novels. Figgis's "detestation of trade and business is expounded in the chapters of *Jacob Elthorne* [1914], where the dull routine of an office almost drives Jacob to desperation."[6] By contrast, *Children of Earth* (1918) is set on an island off the West Coast of Ireland and deals with the life and character of the peasants there. Figgis was a prolific writer, if not a universally admired one. During his short life he produced several collections of poems and essays, a number of works of literary criticism (including studies of Shakespeare and George Russell [AE]), a book on the art of William Blake, a play (produced by F. R. Benson at the Gaiety), and four realistic novels, the most significant of which are the aforementioned *Children of Earth* and *The House of Success* (1921).

The fantastic subject matter of *The Return of the Hero* seemed doubt-

---

4. James Stephens, "Introduction," *The Return of the Hero,* by Darrell Figgis (New York: Albert and Charles Boni, 1930), xiv–xv.

5. Malone, "Figgis," 20.

6. Ibid., 16–17.

less unusual for a writer whose other novels had dealt so obviously with the real world, indeed, with his own experiences in the real world. There are, however, hints in Figgis's other work that anticipate the satirical fantasy of *The Return of the Hero*. Peter Costello has argued that Figgis first turned to satire with *The House of Success*.[7] That novel portrays, in dialogic form, the ideologically conflicting views of a father and son between the time of Parnell and the Easter Rising of 1916. There is a curious passage in the novel, spoken by Jeremiah Hare, which is significant because it is almost a description of the proliferation of texts Figgis was subsequently to use as the formal organizing principle of *The Return of the Hero*:

"Books, glory be. A man once saw something for himself, and he wrote a book about it. That book wasn't the thing he saw by a mighty long measure, you may be sure; just because he thought more of himself writing it than of the thing he saw. . . . Some other bright lad read that book, and he wrote another. Likely enough, a number of bright lads wrote books. And then the world was started on the business. Books came out on the top of books. Books were the children and the fathers of books. The leaf of one book became the whole of another book. Books were written to contradict books. Men wrote books because other men there wrote books. Men started to search out matter for the writing of books, and of course it was to other books they went. . . . Serpents growing out from the tails of serpents. Anything would do so long as a book got written on the head of it. . . . That's where books have brought us. That's the last old serpent that grew out of the tail of another. Books, books, books. The world is moidhered [murdered] with books. Books ever [over], books under, and books through-other, up and down, front and back. And in the meantime everyone forgot the poor old man that wrote the first book and the thing he saw for himself. . . . There aren't men and women. There are only books."[8]

The contention that there are only multiple texts reflecting each other rather than the external world, and that the truth is ultimately unknowable, is characteristic of the Menippean satirist, who typically makes it impossible to use his text to prove the truth of any statement about the world or about the author of the text. There are therefore profound

7. Peter Costello, *The Heart Grown Brutal: The Irish Revolution in Literature, from Parnell to the Death of Yeats, 1891–1939* (Dublin: Gill and Macmillan, 1977), 265.

8. Darrell Figgis, *The House of Success* (Dublin: Gael Co-Operative Publishing Society, 1921), 122–23.

ironies involved in a discussion of the intended significance of *The Return of the Hero* and the targets at which its satire is aimed.

It will be my contention here that the targets of *The Return of the Hero* are, at least on one level, political: for, apart from being a creative writer, Darrell Figgis had also been involved in the Irish nationalist movement since 1914, when he took part in organizing and carrying out the Howth gunrunning expedition with Erskine Childers. In addition to journalism, literature, and literary criticism, Figgis also wrote books on politics, economics, and history, including *The Gaelic State in the Past and Future* (1917). He was imprisoned several times for his political activities, once for eleven months, and wrote two prison chronicles. Although his relationship with other nationalists was always an uneasy one and he made many enemies, Figgis held a number of official positions in Sinn Féin between 1917 and 1922, including that of editor of the *Republic,* and chaired the committee that drafted the Irish Free State Constitution. His *Recollections of the Irish War* was published posthumously in 1927. It is not surprising that few people were able to connect this side of his personality with the satirical fantasy of *The Return of the Hero,* and to see that the book was in fact "Figgis with a difference, but very little difference."[9] A clue may be found in the fact that the book "was written in the period of guerilla warfare in Ireland, when a movement of young and very hopeful men had created in the country fighting bands that had some resemblance to the ancient Fianna—the more so through the fact that they were often led by poets."[10] The author's chosen pseudonym, Michael Ireland, also suggests that the book's subject matter was in some way "of . . . importance in the history of a nation."[11] Some of Figgis's own writings concerning the political developments around the time when the book was written help throw light on the book's mystery. On the basis of these writings, I read *The Return of the Hero* as a satirical depiction of the power struggle within the Sinn Féin leadership in the years after the Easter Rising.

9. Malone, "Figgis," 25.

10. Anon., "Introduction," *The Return of the Hero,* by Darrell Figgis (New York: Albert and Charles Boni, 1930), 5. This edition contains another introduction by James Stephens.

11. Darrell Figgis [Michael Ireland, pseud.], *The Return of the Hero* (London: Chapman and Dodd, 1923), 247. All page references in the text are to this edition. The book was issued simultaneously in Dublin by Mellifont Press.

chapter one

"Only What Is Unaccountable Is Significant"

The Return of the Hero

The dialogue between Saint Patrick and a member of the Fianna, either Oisín or Caoilte, survives in several different versions in the medieval literature that surrounds the figure of Finn mac Cumhal. In the *Acallam na Senórach* ("Colloquy with the Ancients") Oisín and Caoilte part company early on, and it is Caoilte who encounters the saint; in the *Duanaire Finn* ("Book of the Lays of Finn") and in *Laoithe Fiannuigheachta* ("Fenian Poems") it is Oisín who engages Saint Patrick in conversation. All these texts follow essentially the same pattern: after the battle of Gabhra, in which his son Oscar is killed, Finn mac Cumhal's son Oisín is invited to Tír na nÓg by the fairy woman Niamh. After spending several hundred years in the otherworld, he becomes homesick and wishes to return to Ireland. Niamh lends him her white horse, but warns Oisín that, should his feet ever touch the ground, he will turn into a withered old man. Upon his arrival in Ireland, where Christianity has meanwhile arrived in the person of Saint Patrick, Oisín finds the world changed and all his companions gone. When the hero comes to the aid of a group of men who are struggling under the weight of a large marble flagstone, the strain of his effort breaks his horse's girth, he falls onto the ground, and he turns into an old man. When Oisín (or, in the case of the *Acallam*, Caoilte) is brought before Saint Patrick, the latter engages him in conversation and asks him to tell him all about himself, his father, and his life with the Fianna. Oisín relates many tales, meanwhile lamenting at great length the loss of his comrades and his own present decrepit condition. In turn, Patrick endeavors to convert Oisín to Christianity, but this proves to be no easy task, and the two have many arguments as to who is more deserving of loyalty, the King of Heaven or the leader of the Fianna.

At the time when Figgis was writing *The Return of the Hero,* probably in 1919, a number of editions and translations of the Ossianic material would have been at his disposal. The best part of *Acallam na Senórach* had been published by Standish O'Grady in *Silva Gadelica* in 1892, and again by Whitley Stokes in 1900. The first part (of three) of *Duanaire Finn* was edited in 1908 for the Irish Texts Society by Eoin MacNeill (scholar and revolutionary—the same man, in fact, who had called the meeting that was to lead to Figgis's involvement in the Howth gunrunning escapade). While it is possible or even likely that Figgis was familiar with these texts, the material he used as a basis for the dialogue in *The Return of the Hero* was taken from the Fenian Poems published by the Ossianic Society in 1859 and 1861 and edited by John O'Daly. These show Oisín at his most defiant and Patrick at his most inflexible, as the following exchange between them illustrates:

> P.   Misery attend thee, old man,
>   Who speakest the words of madness;
>   God is better for one hour,
>   Than all the Fians of Eire.

> O.   O Patrick of the crooked crozier,
>   Who makes me that impertinent answer;
>   Thy crozier would be in atoms,
>   Were Oscur present.
>   Were my son Oscur and God
>   Hand to hand on Cnoc-na-bh-Fiann,
>   If I saw my son down,
>   I would say that God was a strong man.[1]

The verses in the two volumes edited by O'Daly contain all the details of the debate between saint and hero as rendered by Figgis; the 1861 volume also includes the story about the capture of the Fenians by Draoigheantoir, while the volume for 1859 contains a separate edition by Bryan O'Looney of the tale of Oisín's fall from the otherworldly horse that brought him back to the world of mortals;[2] both these stories are told by Oisín in *The Return of the Hero.* To give his characters more substance, Figgis borrowed a great

---

1. John O'Daly, trans. and ed., *Laoithe Fiannuigheachta; or, Fenian Poems* (Dublin: Ossianic Society, 1859), 47.

2. Bryan O'Looney, trans. and ed., *The Land of Youth* (Dublin: Ossianic Society, 1859).

deal of additional material concerning Saint Patrick and his bishops from the *Tripartite Life of Patrick;* he probably used the 1887 translation by Whitley Stokes.[3]

In any version of the tale, the confrontation between Saint Patrick and the hero is, by its very nature, a highly "dialogic" text, but there are important differences between the *Acallam na Senórach* and the other renditions of the encounter. In the former text, both saint and hero are courteous, and Patrick enjoys the old man's stories and promises him heaven for himself and the Fianna. Finn mac Cumhal is even said to have foreseen, and welcomed, the coming of Christianity to Ireland. In the later ballad versions the attitudes of both saint and hero become much more extreme: Patrick is depicted as a dogmatic sermonizer who pronounces the doom of hell upon the Fenians, while Oisín stubbornly and defiantly defends his pagan views. While the *Acallam* serves the dual purpose of preserving the heroic tales of the pagan past while at the same time endorsing the Christianity that has superseded that past, the ballad versions are much more subversive and serve to question and even defy the authority claimed by the Church. This type of dialogue is saturated with a carnival sense of the world, which turns authority on its head and questions the nature of truth itself. The *Acallam na Senórach* is really a monologic text disguised as a dialogue, because its single aim is to justify Saint Patrick's position, and the pre-Christian heroes are used as mere foils in this process. The ballad versions are true dialogues, where the participants defend opposed ideological viewpoints, and it is these versions that in themselves display most characteristics of Menippean satire. The conflict serves to put philosophical positions to the test and to question fundamental norms and values, in particular the norms imposed by those in a position of authority—in this case, the Church represented by Patrick and his bishops.

In *The Return of the Hero* Figgis does not essentially alter the idea and the nature of the confrontation between Oisín and Patrick (or Padraic, as he is called here[4]) which he borrows from O'Daly's translation. On the ba-

---

3. *The Tripartite Life of Patrick, with Other Documents Relating to That Saint,* Part 1, trans. and ed. Whitley Stokes (London: HMSO, 1887).

4. The text of *The Return of the Hero* does not use *fadas.* For the sake of consistency, however, I will refer to the hero as Oisín throughout, except where I quote directly from Figgis's text.

sis of *The Tripartite Life of Patrick,* however, he creates a context for the debate and adds details that give color and depth to the character of Saint Patrick. The saint in Figgis's version is more understanding of Oisín's position than he is in the source text; in fact, he is uncomfortably caught between the extreme but straightforward views of the pagan hero on the one hand and the dogmatic reasoning of his own bishops on the other. These bishops are mentioned in the *Tripartite Life* as having been ordained in Rome at the same time as Ireland's patron saint, but Figgis turns them into vocal and belligerent characters: they are Auxilius, Padraic's sister's son and bishop at Cill Usaile; Iserninus (or Fith); Seachnall, the writer of a hymn for Padraic; and Mac Taill of Cill Culain, the only Irish bishop (all the others are Galls), and the one most sympathetic to Oisín's predicament. Additional minor figures are the head dispenser Soichell, the host Luachra mac Lonan, and the scribe Brogan. The more voices or carriers of their own truth there are in a text, the greater the possibility for satire. The heteroglossia created by Figgis adds emphasis to the impossibility of establishing the incontestable truth or unquestionable authority of any character's position.

The elements of satire are already present in the Ossianic texts used by Darrell Figgis as "found material" in his own, twentieth-century satire: the texts borrowed by Figgis as part of the satirical process of subverting authority themselves also challenge authority by means of the same methods. Since Menippean texts (in fact, all carnivalized texts) are characteristically "hostile to any sort of conclusive conclusion" because "all endings are merely new beginnings,"[5] the inclusion of one Menippean text within another creates a pattern that is wrought, like the embroidery on Oisín's faded tunic, "in sinuous whorls that flowed endlessly and gracefully and returned upon their beginning" (16). This type of textual regression is one of the principles of satire on which *The Return of the Hero* is founded. In a Bakhtinian view, a dialogic approach to the truth is "counterposed to *official* monologism, which pretends to *possess a ready-made truth,*" and also to people "who think that they possess certain truths."[6] In *The Return of the Hero,* Bishops Seachnall, Auxilius, and Iserninus are representative of such characters. They are incapable of engaging in true dialogue, because

5. Bakhtin, *Dostoevsky's Poetics,* 165.
6. Ibid., 110.

they are unable to listen and respond to other points of view: "while the others were thinking of the things they had heard, these were thinking of the things they were about to say" (58).

There are really two separate dialogues at work in *The Return of the Hero:* first, that between "old" and "new" characters who represent different and opposing values and ideologies, and second, the dialogue between the older texts and their modern renderings. The interaction between these two separate dialogues creates a characteristically Menippean paradox. On the one hand, the dialogue between characters serves to question and undermine the authority of prevalent ideologies: Oisín's stubborn, uncomprehending, and heretical behavior consistently questions and undermines the authority of the Church. The dialogue between texts, however, sabotages the criticism of any particular ideology or authority implicit in the characters' dialogue by questioning the authority of the foundation on which *all* judgments of "the truth" are based: text, language, and meaning itself.

The dialogue between texts in *The Return of the Hero* is part of a framework of references within the book to the existence of multiple manuscripts, fragments, and versions of stories and texts. The novel's narrative framework draws attention to the fact that the texts we are reading exist *only* as texts: as someone's (often incomplete) version of actual events. At frequent intervals in *The Return of the Hero* we hear Padraic reminding his scribe Brogan to write down all of Oisín's stories. The scribe likes the old hero, because his stories "will make a great book for me to leave to posterity" and because his replies "make very good dialogue" (156). The narrator of Figgis's satire makes it clear that we have access to the characters and the story only via Brogan's text, which he is interpreting for us; Brogan is, in fact, "the original authority for these debates" (131). This places a series of narrators between the reader and the events recorded in the tale: the narrator tells us what Brogan wrote about what Oisín told Padraic that Finn said or did.

An important characteristic of Menippean satire is, as Bakhtin puts it, "its concern with current and topical issues." Menippean satires "are full of overt and hidden polemics with various philosophical, religious, ideological and scientific schools, and with tendencies and currents" of their own time.[7] Earlier commentators on *The Return of the Hero* never doubted that

7. Ibid., 118.

the dialogue between Saint Patrick and Oisín was meant to have implications for their own era. A. Norman Jeffares reflects the general attitude by stating that Figgis's book "is still worth reading (but did not endear him to an Irish public with its criticism of Ireland)."[8] The question remains what that "criticism of Ireland" exactly consists in. It will be clear that any interpretation of *The Return of the Hero* will read meanings into the text that Figgis himself implies are not there, and, because of the nature of the satire, no single interpretation can have an absolute claim on *the* truth. Several readings of the book have taken the religious nature of the debate between Oisín and the Church as the most important clue, and simply regard Oisín's onslaught against the medieval bishops as Figgis's attack on the twentieth-century Church. Thus, the book "implies a genial criticism of contemporary established religion and its inability, even at its best intentioned, to deal with the unfamiliar."[9] John Wilson Foster is aware of the pitfalls Figgis creates for his interpreters, but nevertheless argues that "*The Return of the Hero* re-expresses the Anglo-Irish fascination with the old literature, especially that of heroic Ireland before Christianity (that is, Catholicism) redefined Irishness too narrowly for Protestant nationalists like Figgis."[10] Costello, however, calls Figgis an atheist, and it is certainly the case that, while Figgis complains about many things in his political writings, he seldom if ever mentions the role of the Catholic Church. Foster does indicate that the satire's significance may extend beyond the merely religious: "At the end of the novel, Patrick and his bishops are not just the medieval church or even just an anti-Fenian church, but an occupying military power whose opponents will not admit defeat. In one sense an impressive retelling of an old tale, in another *The Return of the Hero* is one more attempt to recolonize real Ireland with the heroic spirit of a fictitious, pre-Catholic, pre-Colonial past."[11] The satire can therefore be read as being directed against the Catholic Church, against Great Britain, or indeed against any force or institution that oppresses personal or national freedom.

It is my belief that another specific reading can be added to the above—

8. A. Norman Jeffares, *Anglo-Irish Literature* (Dublin: Gill and Macmillan, 1982), 226.

9. *The Macmillan Dictionary of Irish Literature,* ed. Robert Hogan (London: Macmillan, 1980), 240.

10. John Wilson Foster, *Fictions of the Irish Literary Revival: A Changeling Art* (Syracuse, N.Y.: Syracuse University Press, 1987), 287.

11. Ibid., 287–88.

which would, of course, by no means invalidate these other interpreta-tions—one in which Figgis's barbs are pointed in the direction of internal Irish politics as much as religion. The attitude of the Catholic Church to-ward the modern Fenians was as condemnatory as Saint Patrick's had been toward their mythical ancestors. The contemporary political potential of the story of Oisín had already been apparent to W. B. Yeats when he wrote *The Wanderings of Oisin* (1889): in an 1867 sermon, "the Catholic Bishop of Kerry had denounced O'Leary and the modern Fenians with the words that 'eternity is not long enough nor hell hot enough' to punish them; the asso-nance with Oisin's conclusion [to rejoin the Fenians, whether they are in hell or not] would have been clear to Irish readers."[12] *The Return of the Hero* opens with a scene in which Oisín has just assisted in the placing of the heavy granite cornerstone for a new church: "It stood exactly in the corner of a great clearing where the sod had been cut away to its bed of gravel at the base of the mountain-side. It lay grey and comely in the soft evening light, shining against the orange gravel clearing that stretched like an inhu-man wound by the pale green of the verdure into which it had been cut" (9). It is possible to read the colors of the landscape as those of the repub-lican tricolor, and to see the foundations for the new church as the founda-tions for the new state that was to arise out of the ruin, the sacrifice, and the moral victory of the Easter Rising. Oisín, the Fenian, has placed the cor-nerstone; but who, then, are the bishops who make his life so difficult, and who ultimately decide that the church has to be built on a different site?

The answer is provided by Darrell Figgis himself in his *Recollections of the Irish War*, published after his death but probably written in 1921–1922. It contains the following illuminating explanation of the organization of Sinn Féin, which was officially adopted for it during the October Convention of 1917, of which Figgis was secretary:

For the scheme of local government adopted by England for Ireland has never ex-pressed in any real—economic or social—sense the life of the Irish people. It was taken over from England, where it was the result of historical origins, and put down in Ireland like a Procrustean bed into which the people's life had to be crushed. . . . For until the seventeenth century Ireland had had her own form of political gover-nance, strong in its local life till the end, but at one time with that local life gathered

12. R. F. Foster, *The Apprentice Mage, 1865–1914,* vol. 1 of *W. B. Yeats: A Life* (Oxford, U.K.: Oxford University Press, 1997), 84.

and comprised in a national system; and it was this form that the policy of Plantations had succeeded in uprooting and destroying in that century of violence.

Not completely, however. It had been preserved in the form of organization of the Catholic church. For St. Patrick, as great a statesman as a churchman, had modelled his church organization on the political—the social and economic—organization of the country, so that one fitted precisely with the other, each expressing different parts of the people's life in an identical pattern. Therefore, though the form of political governance was destroyed, its pattern was preserved—in spite of all changes and vicissitudes very remarkably preserved—in the organization of the Church by half-parishes, parishes, and bishoprics.

It was by this pattern that Sinn Fein was now organized.[13]

On the basis of this excerpt it can be argued that Saint Patrick and the bishops in *The Return of the Hero* represent the Sinn Féin leadership at the time of the book's composition. According to John Wilson Foster, the satire was written in 1918–1919;[14] however, by his own account Figgis was in jail from May 1918 until late February 1919, and while he claims to have spent most of his time there "making up arrears of reading" to the extent that he "had a considerable library to bring away with [him] in the end," he does not say that he did any writing in prison.[15] He mentions that he was back upon his literary work soon after his release, and it can therefore be assumed that the book was written after March 1919, even though the idea for the satire may have taken shape during his detention in Durham Gaol.

The developments within Sinn Féin during the period 1918–1919, and Figgis's reactions to them, deserve closer scrutiny. From his recruitment into the Volunteers in 1914 onward, Figgis was acutely aware of, and disturbed by, disagreements within the nationalist movement. When John Redmond and his nominees were ejected by the Executive from the

---

13. Darrell Figgis, *Recollections of the Irish War* (Garden City, N.Y.: Doubleday/Doran and Co., [1927]), 173. Figgis also merged religion and politics in his *Sinn Féin Catechism* (Dublin: Kiersey, [1918?]) by combining the format of the Catholic catechism with political content:

Q. What is your nationality?

A. *I am Irish.*

Q. What does it mean to be Irish?

A. *It means that I am part of the Irish Nation, to which I must give my true and best service, and to which I must always be loyal.* (3)

14. J. W. Foster, *Fictions*, 287.

15. Figgis, *Recollections*, 216.

Provisional Committee in the autumn of 1914, in a move that led to a split in the Volunteers, Figgis, having just been made inspecting officer of the Irish Volunteers in Mayo, attempted to remain impartial by suggesting to both sides that he not commit himself publicly to either side and take up his command on that understanding. Needless to say, this did not work. Soon he saw not only division, but "division within division,"[16] and his *Recollections* express an increasing disappointment with the leaders of the nationalist movement. It is this disillusionment with the authority figures in Sinn Féin that found expression in *The Return of the Hero*, with Figgis himself cast in the role of Oisín.

The purpose of Menippean satire is the testing of ideological truths and the questioning of authority. In *The Return of the Hero* the notion of authority indeed lies at the very core of the debate between Oisín and the bishops. The bishops' role in the narrative is to explain official Church doctrine to Oísin; Oisín's part is to question the logic and the purpose of this doctrine. On being told by Padraic that Finn is in heaven, Oisín immediately wishes to be instructed in the faith and baptized so that he can die and join his father. The bishops, however, first of all question whether it would be wise for them to use the authority invested in them by God to baptize Oisín: the baptism, once performed, cannot be undone, and they fear that Oisín, once in heaven, might not like it there and would create trouble for the Almighty. This might be especially the case once he found out that Finn was not in heaven; for the majority of the bishops disagree with Padraic and decide that Finn must, after all, be in hell.

When he is informed of the bishops' position, Oisín reacts with indignation: who does God think he is, that he should make so great and generous a hero as Finn mac Cumhal suffer the torments of hell? If Finn did not know God, surely he could not be blamed and punished for his innocence? Oisín's bafflement is touching and his arguments are logical and make common sense. Indeed, he has trouble understanding "the new trick of speech that men have adopted" (126); he is, in fact, a literalist incapable of understanding metaphor, ill-prepared by his heroic training for the subtleties of Christian theology. This first appears most poignantly when he decides to receive religious instruction to be saved and so go to heaven in order to be with Finn. Being possessed of a traditional memory, Oisín soon masters his

16. Ibid., 97.

catechism so that "no matter how ambiguous the questions, or how myste-rious the replies he was expected to make, he had them fitted each to each in all their possible variations. Word-perfect he was, and ready, utterly ready" (181). The dialogic question-and-answer form of the catechism is, of course, deceptive: as a dialogue it no longer has any connection with a car-nival sense of the world but has degenerated into "a simple form for ex-pounding already found, ready-made irrefutable truth."[17] Of what it all means, therefore, Oisín has not the least notion, and the biblical imagery remains a puzzle to him: "Time would accustom him to the Great Whore of Babylon, and he would not mind her at all. So also it would be, no doubt, with the unicorns and the many-headed beasts and birds. The crowds marching one way singing Woe, Woe, Woe, and the crowds marching the other way singing Holy, Holy, Holy, still troubled him a little. . . . What made Finn mac Cumhal choose such a country at all, he could not think" (209–10). Being averse to verbal contortions, Oisín prefers simple state-ments: "It means what it means," he tells Auxilius when the latter questions something he says (124). The bishops' incomprehension suggests, however, that meaning is a more complicated issue than Oisín suggests.

Rather than use words, Oisín prefers to express his opinions through physical force. Oisín's first act of violence in *The Return of the Hero* is the direct result of a misunderstanding, or misinterpretation, of another's ac-tions. At the heart of the incident lies the semiotic notion that meaning is not inherent in words or actions but is instead determined by culture, con-text, and point of view. Oisín's first meeting with Padraic is related entirely from the former's point of view and has the effect of "making strange" the familiar appearance of the holy man:

In his right hand he carried a strange weapon, the like of which Oisin had never seen. For the greater part of its length it was shaped like a spear, except that it was too weighty for the man, who bore it with difficulty. Besides, it was curved into a pattern at the top, and whoever saw a spear curved into a pattern where it should have been barbed and sharp? It might have been a shepherd's crook, to which it bore a distant resemblance. But whoever saw a shepherd's crook wrought in costly gold, and of so unwieldy a size?

It was the helmet this man wore that caused Oisin to omit [*sic*] an acrid token of his disgust. For it was shaped like a shovel—it was shaped like two shovels laid

17. Bakhtin, *Dostoevsky's Poetics*, 110.

base to base, with a space between their points open to any skipping swordsman. Besides, whoever heard of a helmet woven of cloth and tricked out with gold lace? (22–23)

The folded hands of those kneeling around this strange but imposing figure strike Oisín as a gesture intended to insult "this decent druid" (27), and his indignation is aggravated by the fact that "some of their thumbs appeared to be pressed against the orifice of their nostrils" (24). When the offenders persist in their insults, Oisín focuses on the man nearest to him and "noted that his eyes were closed and that his lips were moving, clearly in some malediction, for who that had anything good to say feared to say it aloud? So he lifted his hand and struck Conan with such force that he was stretched senseless on his back fully ten feet away" (27). In a heroic context, Oisín's judgments and actions make perfect sense, but, from a Christian perspective, he behaves like a madman. "We speak," says Padraic perceptively, "of different things" (26).

Oisín has cause to be wary of language in his present company. The bishops' authority, indeed, appears to be less a matter of common sense than, as the title of chapter 3 of the fifth book has it, "A Matter of Words." The bishops are masters of verbal acrobatics and casuistry, and even Padraic is said to use argument and persuasion with "wary skill" and "craftily" (130). The Church operates by its own rules whose only aim it is to uphold the authority of those in power. In the words of Auxilius:

"Ours is the Apostolic Succession. Whom we bind is bound. Whom we loose is loosed. How wise, then, were the words of our Blessed Master that on this rock would be built His Church, for without an absolute authority of this kind, lasting in its extent, and beyond the power of any to evade, it would be quite impossible to think of erecting any organisation so complicated as the Church. . . . All whom we send to heaven must remain there. All whom we send to hell cannot escape. And this, my brethren, is done by the sacrament of baptism, which is the act by which we accomplish the mystery, for if it once got abroad that the act was not sufficient, there would be an end of all authority." (168–69)

Auxilius upbraids his colleague Mac Taill for objecting that it is the spirit, not the form, of the sacrament that binds:

"That," he said, "I regard as a cardinal heresy. For what is heresy but the unloosening of authority? . . . Heresy is the teaching of the wrong doctrine at the wrong time, when that doctrine is not permitted to be taught; and so it is not heresy in respect of doctrine, but heresy in respect of authority, being a disregard of the authority at that time available. Anything that weakens the power of the Church is a heresy. . . . For where would the power of the Church be but for her authority?" (169–70)

Iserninus counters Oisín's common sense and honest logic with regard to Finn's innocence with another kind of logic and another kind of truth, suggesting that Oisín's reasoning is a threat to the very existence of the Church:

"Our strongest argument would be turned against us. Salvation would become a menace. We have already seen the effect of such an idea on this preposterous old hero. He said he would die in innocence. Naturally. Everyone would determine to die in innocence, and then what hope would there be of organising the Church? My dear brethren, I urge you to consider this. We cannot be too firm. It is even essential for the future of the Church that Finn Mac Cumhal be bound in hell." (176)

Iserninus had earlier explained that "sound doctrine was not a matter of sound sense, but of heavenly sense, which to human ears might sound nonsense" (165). Seachnall endorses this position: "It is one thing to say that what we teach is such manifest common-sense that it should claim the adherence of all men, but it is quite another, it seems to me, to say that because a proposition appears to be manifest common-sense it should therefore be incumbent on us to accept it, much less to preach it." Auxilius neatly brings the argument around to its beginning by adding that common sense, moreover, "appeals to private judgment, and so displaces authority" (178).

The unbridgeable gap between Oisín's faith in private judgment and the Church's insistence on authority is analogous to the conflict that formed the basis of Darrell Figgis's disillusionment with the nationalist movement. In his *Recollections,* Figgis describes how on various occasions a strong internal rivalry had threatened to tear Sinn Féin apart, but that the most important disruptive force had been "the struggle of the Irish Republican Brotherhood, generally known as the IRB, a pledge-sworn secret society, for political power and control."[18] Figgis himself had twice declined to take the IRB oath (perhaps analogous to Oisín's baptism in the satire) on the grounds that it was an insult to be bound by an oath rather than by a conviction. He describes how the IRB seized control after the October

18. Figgis, *Recollections,* 217.

Convention under the leadership of Michael Collins, whom he characterizes as "a man of ruthless purpose and furious energy, knowing clearly what he wanted and prepared to trample down everybody to get it."[19] Collins reputedly did not like Figgis either. The other force to be reckoned with, Cathal Brugha, was, in Figgis's terms, "stubborn, unbreakable, intractable," a man living for the dream of the Republic without dealing concretely with the details of policy or constitution.[20] Effectively, Figgis accuses the IRB leaders in his *Recollections* of having undemocratically taken over the government: Arthur Griffith, the original founder of Sinn Féin, had defeated Brugha in a vote and had, moreover, laid down the principle that the Constitution "was a question the people themselves must finally answer in the exercise of their freedom. And now had come the moment when the harvest of these victories should have been reaped. Instead of which, by the action of the British Government in arresting those whom the people had appointed, those who had been defeated were in power at the head of a triumphant organization at a time of General Election to carry out their purposes."[21] The new leaders had taken advantage of the fact that Griffith was in Gloucester Gaol, and all those who supported Griffith, including Figgis, were eliminated. Collins and Brugha are the counterparts of the bishops in *The Return of the Hero* who ignore Padraic's leadership and decide that Finn mac Cumhal is in hell, not because he is bad, but because that scenario accords best with their own political and ideological agenda.

Padraic's predicament in mediating between the pagan hero and his bishops is most poignantly expressed in the episode concerning Oisín's story about Draoigheantoir. The episode highlights the inextricable connection between meaning and context, a problem that lies at the heart of Menippean satire. Context plays a crucial part in the interpretation of words and actions and, as Bakhtin observes, "this context can refract, add to, or, in some cases, even subtract from the amount and kind of meaning the utterance may be said to have when it is conceived only as a systematic manifestation independent of context."[22] Unable to determine conclusively whether Finn is in heaven or hell and whether or not Oisín should be bap-

---

19. Ibid., 218.   20. Ibid., 220.

21. Ibid., 222.

22. Introduction to M. M. Bakhtin, *The Dialogic Imagination: Four Essays*, trans. Caryl Emerson and Michael Holquist, ed. Michael Holquist (Austin: University of Texas Press, 1981), xx.

tized, Padraic suggests to the bishops that they ask the hero for a story, and that they use the tale as a guide in their debate as to which decision is the right one. Mac Taill requests a tale of witchery and magic, and so Oisín decides to tell the gathering the Tale of the Mysterious Cup.

Before Oisín does so, and in preparation for their decision, the members of the household retire to pray for guidance. In doing so they all use the same form of words, "but each man of them all had a vision distinct and separate from the vision of any other" (111), because what each man sees is not an objective "truth" but a reflection of his own inclination. Luachra mac Lonan has a vision of a splendid warrior, "the Luachra mac Lonan of his dreams" (108). Iserninus prays by mechanically repeating "the words he had learned by rote" (109), and his vision is of an austere "Great White Figure on a Great White Throne," whose whiteness "excluded every other colour" (109). The episcopal figure with "cold, contemptuous eyes" condemns the insignificant figure of Oisín to be hurled into a burning lake of fire (110). What Iserninus sees is not, as he believes, a vision of God but "the Bishop Iserninus of his own dreams" (110). The insecure Seachnall is too confused to know what he should see. Auxilius's dream represents the Church as a powerful organization rooted in earthly riches by whose might Oisín is stifled, so that he is forced to submit "his will and soul" into its keeping (114). Soichell's patronizing vision is of an excessively spiritual Being who "lifted a hand over Oisín and gladly forgave him all his sins, though they were many" (114).

The visions of Mac Taill and Padraic are more complex than those of the other bishops. Mac Taill is distressed because during his meditation he keeps "repeating poems that he distinctly knew to be pagan of origin, even while he thought that he was saying Christian prayers" (115). His dialogic vision reveals a meeting between Christ and Oisín, and has the two powerful men going out to fight giants and monsters, "and to be such heroes as heroes never were before in all the world" (116). Mac Taill is tormented at having "confused Ireland with Palestine" (117), but the fact that he is capable of "seeing double" in this way, and that of all the bishops he is the least certain of his vision, implies that he is closest to the nature of truth and "praying for Oisin in the best of possible ways" (117). Padraic, on the other hand, has no such doubts because "he was his vision, and his vision was he, both having been well matured together" (118). In his vision, Oisín brings a smile of joy to the face of an experienced and wise Being who "loved heroes" (118).

Padraic's atavistic vision in *The Return of the Hero* owes not a little to William Blake, via James Stephens's *The Crock of Gold;* in fact, one might argue that the eventual outcome of *The Return of the Hero* shows to what extent Stephens's optimistic vision for Ireland had turned sour in the eleven intervening years. In *The Crock of Gold,* the character called the Philosopher is to tell a boy named MacCushin (Mac Oisín) that the Sleepers of Erinn have turned in their slumbers. The boy replies:

"I know," said he, "why Angus Óg sent me that message. He wants me to make a poem to the people of Erinn, so that when the Sleepers arise they will meet with friends."

"The Sleepers have arisen," said the Philosopher. "They are about us on every side. They are walking now, but they have forgotten their names and the meanings of their names. You are to tell them their names and their lineage, for I am an old man, and my work is done."

"I will make a poem some day," said the boy, "and every man will shout when he hears it."[23]

In Padraic's dream in *The Return of the Hero,* Oisín has awakened, but other heroes are still sleeping around Oisín and the wise Being, and it was "the purpose of the Being to waken those heroes, for . . . it could not tolerate the thought of anyone sleeping once the sun had burst the clouds" (118). Padraic confidently and optimistically sees it as his task to revive the Fenian heroism represented by Oisín in a benignly Christian Ireland, and the text notes that "it was impossible for him to think of any task in which he would not succeed" (119). Meanwhile, at the time when the bishops are experiencing their visions, Oisín sleeps soundly and obliviously through the night, in preparation for the telling of the tale.

The Tale of the Mysterious Cup told by Oisín is rendered exactly as it appears in John O'Daly's *Laoithe Fiannuigheachta,* where it is called "The Chase of Sliabh Fuaid." While the Fianna are hunting on this mountain, Finn and the musician Dáire get lost in a druidic magical mist. A gentle maid named Glannluadh tries to help the heroes, but they are all overcome by a fairy sleep. When they recover they find themselves imprisoned in the

23. James Stephens, *The Crock of Gold* (1912; reprint, London: Macmillan, 1928), 192.

fortress of Draoigheantoir, who accuses Finn of having gained victory at the battle of Cnoc-an-Air by treacherous means, and of having maliciously killed Meargach, the husband of his sister Ailne. Ailne soon afterward releases Glannluadh and persuades Dáire to make some music. The other Fianna are lured by its sound toward the dungeon and are likewise captured. Draoigheantoir begins to put the warriors to death, but when he comes to Conan the Bald—a man "big of speech and little of heart" (186)— the latter leaps from his magical thongs, leaving part of his posterior behind on the seat. He requests that he not be killed until his wounds are healed. Glannluadh had told the heroes that Draoigheantoir possesses a cup of powerful spells. Draoigheantoir places the magical cup in Conan's hands while Ailne "examined the back parts of Conan, and applied to them a large skin full of feathers, which adhered to that place for ever. To his rump it adhered, and he was never without his bye-name from that time out. Bald he was in head, but he was not bald behind" (186). In his haste to get back to slaughtering the Fianna, Draoigheantoir forgets that he has given Conan the Cup of Power; Oisín's newly feathered friend hides the object in his clothes and, when the enemy has momentarily turned his back, applies the virtue of the cup to his comrades and frees them all.

Padraic mac Alphurn had intended Oisín's story to be a sign to guide the bishops in their decision as to the fate of the souls of Finn mac Cumhal and his son, and the saint himself therefore loses no time in reading the story's significance: "And what was the sign that was given to us? We were told a story of how, when he was captive and sore to death, he was liberated by the virtue and sacred potency of a mysterious Cup. Could there have been a connecting link more clear? For I need not remind you, my brethren, what the uplifting of the Cup signifies for us. . . . There is no need for me to say more, my brethren, for the sign is clear, and only the dark of sight could fail to see it" (191–92). Padraic also perceives an analogy between Conan's bald head and the monastic tonsure. Auxilius is not so easily persuaded, however; although he, too, was impressed when he imagined the bald man uplifting the cup, he was aware of other signs, too: "I completed the picture, and in my mind I saw the skin of feathers hanging from that part of his body which cannot be mentioned. The symbol was destroyed utterly, for can such a disgraceful thing be imagined, as a sign of salvation to take so obnoxious a form? Therefore, I say that the story must be rejected as an invention, as an indignity, and indeed as a mere temptation of the Evil One to bring our sacred office into ridicule" (193).

Padraic's eagerness to convince the others of the truth of his own interpretation leads him into ever deeper waters of textual interpretation and arbitrariness. He argues that the part of the story dealing with the skin "is not essential to the tale. It is clearly a later accretion. It is easy to distinguish between the original tale in its purity and the additions of a later scribe moved by the Devil. It is the original tale that has been sent to us for a sign. The skin and feathers are a bawdy addition of the Devil to deceive and mislead us" (194). His reasoning fails to convince the other bishops, who remain suspicious of the "lewd" feathers and who also express concern about the role of Glannluadh, whose immodesty led her to accost Finn on the mountain side; the fact that her name means "Pure Conversation" means nothing, for "the foulest sins mask in the fairest disguises" (195). The bishops therefore conclude that the cup "must have been a mere pagan goblet or bowl" (196); they unanimously vote to reject the story and condemn Finn's soul to hell.

It is clear that all of the above interpretations of Oisín's story are the result of the context in which the story is perceived, and that each bishop reads into the tale the meanings he wishes to find. Earlier, Oisín had shrewdly observed to Seachnall that "men do not see other men but through their own eyes" (184), and Mac Taill, the Irish bishop, is the only one to discern the truth of this remark. A good story, he says, is memorable but not meaningful, and it has nothing to do with Finn's soul:

"There are many parts of this story that are memorable. The figure of Conan Maol uplifting this cup with the skin of feathers hanging from his back parts is especially memorable. But the story is also memorable as a whole; and therefore, as a story, it is a good story, and I like it. But in so far as it may be a sign, I am not concerned with it. Directly I suspect a story to have a secret meaning, I desert the teller of that story at once. It is the only thing to do. The other things one could do, all leave a bitter reflection." (197–98)

The other bishops, however, always have trouble understanding what Mac Taill is talking about, and they reject his speech on the grounds that it "does not savour . . . of pure doctrine" (200).

This is one of many episodes in *The Return of the Hero* to draw attention to the fact that there is no objective truth or meaning: that every perception of meaning is dependent on context and on an act of interpretation by the reader of the sign. In fact, the more meaningless the sign is in itself, the more one has to rely on interpretation—that is, the imposition of meaning. To Padraic, less meaning is more, for interpretation equals divine inspiration: "The more obscure a dream, the greater the divine gift in finding a meaning for it, and we must not wonder if the ungodly are astonished both by the dream and the meaning given to it" (189). His own calling had come to him in a dream in Gaelic, a language with which he was not very familiar, but "the sign was most clear then" (191). It is precisely in such meaninglessness and displacement, therefore, that Padraic discovers his calling and his identity. Padraic's faith makes him less consciously aware than Oisín that if the sign is meaningless, it can be interpreted to mean anything. When the pagan hero Oisín wakes up in alien surroundings (that is, out of his own context) on the first morning after his return from Tír-na-nÓg, he feels robbed of his identity: "'In the grey of morning a man would believe anything, and a man would disbelieve anything,' Oisín said" (34), and Brogan has to confirm that he is indeed Oisín the hero. Yet because Oisín is liberated from the context of his own place and time, he is also most truly himself: "This much is, if not true, at least undeniable, that men are what they are and that they cannot be anything else. It is the great fact established for all time by Oisin in his first conversation with Padraic. When they are liberated from the custom that perverts them, and when they are loosened from the framework that shuts them in, they simply with gladsome hearts become stupendously themselves—they simply are, and that is a stupendous thing" (106–7).

If, as the above discussion implies, anything can be believed in the interpretation of texts and signs because absolute truth and inherent meaning independent of context do not exist, this means that the ambiguous nature of meaning is the only truth we can take for granted. The paradoxical implication of this is that the only true significance is to be found in mystery and the absence of meaning. In *The Return of the Hero*, this is most clearly demonstrated by one mysterious word that is always vehemently uttered by Padraic in moments of crisis, and which has the effect of immediately silencing even his most heated opponents: "Mudebroth!" The expletive referred to in *The Return of the Hero* is uttered by the saint more than a dozen times in *The Tripartite Life of Patrick,* where Darrell Figgis must have come across it. In Stokes's edition the Irish word is spelled variously as "modebrodh," "modebrod," or "modebroth," and Stokes translates it as "my God's doom." There was, apparently, some controversy as to the meaning of the phrase, for the *Lebar Brecc Homily on S. Patrick* contained in the same volume translates the curse as "by my God of Judgment,"[24] while Cormac explains in *Extracts from Cormac's Glossary* that "*Mo-de-broth . . .* should be pronounced thus: *muin Duiu braut.* The *muin,* then, is 'my,' the *duiu* is 'God,' the *braut* is 'judge.'"[25] In *The Book of Irish Curses* Patrick Power translates "Mo débrod" as "My sorrow."[26]

Whereas in the *Tripartite Life* the meaning of "Modebroth" is not explicitly addressed, Figgis makes the significance of the word a central issue in the dialogue between Oisín and his antagonists and a measure of the distance between them. Questioned by Oisín as to the meaning of Padraic's expletive, Brogan replies that it is a great mystery: "It is plain that he means something, for he is a man of plain meaning. But he is a Gall, and stumbles in our speech. There are some who say he means 'Mo De broth,' 'my God's doomsday,' that is to say. It could be, but it is not rightly known" (70). Oisín, however, who believes that "only what is unaccountable is significant" (96), comes to a different conclusion: "That is not so. It is an incantation, and therefore means nothing. It is not possible for an incantation to have any power when it is known what it means. The value of all incantations is in the ignorance of the hearer, and it is because no one knows what it means that Mudebroth is a mighty spell" (70). The meaning of the word lies in the absence of meaning; its truth lies in its mystery, for "Truth is itself the greatest mystery of all. Men have been searching for truth ever since they invaded the earth, and though each generation of them has flung its cap in the air, and held the hidden treasure proudly in the hollow of its hand, each succeeding generation has mocked at it and done the same with some other discovery. So much for discoveries, and so great a mystery is truth" (106). In his debate with Oisín, Padraic more and more finds himself abandoning casuistry, logic, and rhetoric in favor of this one remaining truth. His initial confidence that he will be able to get through to Oisín because "different

24. Stokes, ed., *Tripartite Life,* 461.
25. Ibid., 571.
26. Patrick C. Power, *The Book of Irish Curses* (Dublin and Cork: Mercier Press, 1974), 40.

people in different times say different things, but they all mean the same" (128) gives way to despair when he begins to realize that "his wit could not span the infinity of time that lay coiled in the little space that separated their bodies. Their words were the same; but the meanings in them, how different!" (220). Finding it impossible to explain logically to Oisín why God should have put Finn mac Cumhal in hell, Padraic finds himself repeatedly telling the hero that "it is a mystery. We are not required to understand it, but to receive it" (223), until he realizes that "he had said that before. He was simply walking in a circle" (226).

In the political allegory of Figgis's satire, the figure of Padraic appears in part to be modeled on Arthur Griffith. The saint is depicted as a generous and understanding man who has been put in an unenviable position: he feels great sympathy for Oisín's point of view, but at the same time he cannot be disloyal to the Church he represents. All he can do is mediate between the two positions, but in the end he is forced to give in to the bishops, especially since their arguments are "enforced by a clear majority" (256). In *Recollections of the Irish War* Figgis expresses a great deal of admiration for Griffith's loyalty to the principles of democracy and fairness, qualities similarly highlighted by Terence de Vere White: "Arthur Griffith left behind him an unmatched record of selfless devotion to his country. His qualities were not of the kind that excite the imagination; he made no appeal to the passions: he was not less great for that."[27] De Valera saw him as "a man who, at the supreme crisis, put peace before everything."[28] The General Election of December 1918, fought on the basis of a carefully selected list of candidates, produced a Dáil whose members were mostly members of the IRB and the Volunteers: "[T]his meant the very result that Arthur Griffith had sought to avert. It meant a contest less for liberty than for a name; it meant rigidity; and it meant the shock of violence where violence might conceivably have been avoided."[29] On his release from prison Griffith became acting president of the fledgling Republic, and spared no effort to bring the divided parties together; he accomplished the impossible and managed to turn the divided Dáil into a united assembly while re-

27. Quoted in the Earl of Longford and Thomas P. O'Neill, *Éamon de Valera* (Boston: Houghton Mifflin, 1971), 198.

28. Ibid., 198.

29. Figgis, *Recollections*, 229.

maining loyal to his own principles. However, Griffith was aware that his colleagues were preparing for war, a course in which he did not believe, "and he knew that he was powerless to prevent it; and he accepted it as his simple duty to rally all sections together to face it."[30]

In *The Return of the Hero* Padraic likewise forces himself to side with his authoritarian bishops and abandon his principles by giving Oisín a choice: join Finn in hell, or forsake the Fianna and walk with the God of heaven. At this precise point, however, Oisín undergoes a strange transformation that leaves his audience speechless and in awe, while at the same time the narrative voice of *The Return of the Hero*, having demonstrated that authority is based on language and language is based on quicksand, begins to deconstruct itself. The authority of the book's narrator is, by his own proud admission, based on textual research, as he explains in a footnote. The note is attached to a description of Padraic from the point of view of Oisín when he first sets eyes on the saint; from the hero's perspective, Padraic is "the tallest man Oisín had yet seen, and he bore his body with the authority of a noble mind.[1] A grey, pointed beard flowed down to the arch of the solar plexus" (23). In the footnote the narrator explains that, "based as this book is on the finest historical research, it is to be hoped that this will bring to peace the unworthy suggestion that the Blessed St. Patrick was a short man and that he wore no beard" (23, note 1). The note implies that everything the book tells us is based on textual research and therefore true—including, paradoxically, the contention that truth is a mystery.

If one takes the textual authorities on which the narrator's "finest historical research" is based to be the works from which the narrator, and by extension, Figgis, derived his material for *The Return of the Hero,* these are, as noted above, the *Laoithe Fiannuigheachta* or Fenian Poems purportedly recorded by Padraic's scribe Brogan, and *The Tripartite Life of Patrick.* The former text has already been described as a highly Menippean dialogue whose characteristics are inconclusiveness and the subversion of authority, including its own, yet the narrator of *The Return of the Hero* takes its truth for granted when he says: "This saying of his [Oisín] is known for certain, because Brogan, the original *authority* for these debates, instantly recorded it as a model of classical reproof. It is to be found in his book" (131; italics added). The life of Saint Patrick poses its own textual problems. Patrick

30. Ibid., 260.

Power points out that it is remarkable "how radically different his personality is in the short autobiographical *Confessio* from that found in the *Tripartite Life of Saint Patrick*, written nearly four centuries later. In the intervening time, the humble harassed missionary has become a wonderworker and a hurler of maledictions on anyone who impeded his triumphal journey through Ireland."[31] While there may have been sound ideological reasons for these ninth-century alterations to the saint's personality ("The biographer attempts to show the saint as equal to or even greater than the pagan heroes whose fame was in the mouths of the storytellers"[32]), the discrepancies undermine the historical reliability of the text. The narrator of *The Return of the Hero*, however, accepts the anecdotes as truth. Padraic, he says, "could, with a word, have turned Oisin into a porpoise or a pelican"; in fact, he could have performed "any of the miracles that are recorded to his skill in the *unblemished annals* of his works, or have enriched his fame with some new and fantastic miracle, to mark the singular mood of his mind" (137; italics added). It will be clear that the narrator's confident reliance on the authority of his written sources is seriously compromised by the very nature and content of the material his narrative seeks to convey.

Toward the end of *The Return of the Hero* it is not only Padraic who finds his arguments going round in circles; the narrative itself as a whole, in spite of the narrator's confidence, displays a distinct lack of closure. Toward the end of his inconclusive but increasingly antagonistic argument with the bishops, Oisín changes miraculously, in an intangible manner: "[T]here were nothing but hints, though hints more persuasive than the resemblance of open day" (230). Oisín addresses his father, Finn, in a speech, but whether he is at this point speaking as a young man, an old man, or both, is not clear because, according to the narrator, "it is most unfortunate that at this point the texts vary considerably" (230). Not only does the story at this point break up into multiple versions, but meaning is to be found especially in those versions that seem most unreadable: "[T]he value of the texts at this critical moment seem[s] to increase with the degree of their inaccessibility" (231).

There are, we are told, three extant manuscripts describing Oisín's transformation. The text in the library at "Leipsic" is clearly written, well pre-

31. Power, *Irish Curses*, 38–39.
32. Ibid., 41.

served, and accessible to all without restriction, but it finishes at a loose end and reveals little of value. The text in the British Museum is fuller but is kept locked up in a strongbox, and is only shown to those of unimpeachable faith. It is in wretched condition, written in a crabbed hand and difficult to read, but it is priceless "for it continues from this vital moment. It gives the speech of an old man" (232). The fact that the third text, at Trinity College, Dublin, is virtually inaccessible probably says a great deal about Figgis's perception of the direction in which freedom of speech and of access to information were moving in Ireland at the time (the Censorship of Publications Act did not became law until 1929, but Figgis's journal the *Republic* was banned in September 1919[33]):

It is kept in a strong room, underground, at the end of a long, damp, dark passage. A posse of ripe and spruce Fellows, attended by suitable Proctors, mounts guard over it, night and day. . . .

It was only by bribing the most indulgent of the Fellows, and drugging the rest of the posse, that access was got to this precious text. Its binding is damp, and has nearly parted from its pages. It is written in a still crabbeder hand, unbeautiful to see, and is studded with abbreviations. It is, in fact, a hive where the abbreviations of antiquity have swarmed. There is hardly a word in it that is not abbreviated. It is, therefore, difficult to make out, and a joy to the modern bibliophile. But the text is most valuable, and is now used for the first time. It is an accomplishment to have been able to examine it at all. It gives what appears to be the speech of a young man. (232–33)

Not only are the most meaningful texts the most inaccessible and unreadable texts, but Oisín's speech, in which he expresses his undying faithfulness to Finn, appears "in both texts in difficult poetic structure" (242). The meaning of both texts, then, can only be the result—or the product—of much interpretation.

The two versions (both apparently written by Brogan) are given in the text in full. The gist of Oisín's speech is the same in both versions, with only minor variations in words and phrases. The account of the context of his speech, however, differs greatly, as a comparison reveals:

In the first of these two texts, as in the second, it is recorded that Oisin rose in his standing, vast and terrific; and that, as he arose, he was transformed internally by

---

33. See Hogan and Burnham, *Art of the Amateur*, 185.

the rage that was in him. It is said, too, that he stood thus for an incredible length of time—a length of time so incredible that it seemed that time slowed down in long, heavy throbs and finally at last stood absolutely still, while the company wondered what was next to happen. It is said that, as he stood thus, within his grey eyes red lights shone like camp-fires at a distance within a grey dusk. And that at last, when to the assembly it seemed that the roof of day would buckle inward and fall upon them, these words rushed impetuously towards them from the hero's lips: . . . (234)

In the second of these texts, as in the first, it is recorded that Oisin rose in his standing, shining and wondrous; and that, as he arose, he was inwardly transfigured by the splendour of his love for Finn. It is said, too, that he stood thus for so great a length of time that the company was raised to an incredible excitement—for it seemed that slow time was quickening its flight so swiftly that it became a reeling flutter of hours and years until time had ceased to be, its cycle full completed. It is said that, as he stood thus, within his eyes a gathering brightness shone like the rising of the sun beyond the grey dusk of dawn. And that at last, when to the assembly it seemed that, dizzy and fearful, they must fall from the unattainable heights to which they had been carried, these words poured melodiously forth from the transfigured hero's lips: . . . (238)

The events were filtered through the imagination of Padraic's scribe, so that Oisín's "fierce and splendid moment can only be perceived by us through Brogan's recollection in tranquillity" (242). Common sense dictates that Brogan's two conflicting accounts cannot both be true, and that their existence undermines the authority claimed for him by the narrator of *The Return of the Hero*. But if one accepts that all meaning is arbitrary and truth a mystery, then both versions written by Brogan can be true, even though the accounts are highly conflicting: Oisín must then have been *both* an old man *and* a young man, and he must have spoken *both* in angry *and* in loving passion, and time must *both* have slowed down *and* speeded up. The "double Oisín" of these accounts can be seen as a form of split personality, which is a common device in Menippean satire. Like the story in which he appears, the character "loses his finalized quality and ceases to mean only one thing; he ceases to coincide with himself" and comes to stand, as it were, in a dialogic relationship to his own self.[34]

Neither manuscript relates what happened to Oisín after he finished his

---

34. Bakhtin, *Dostoevsky's Poetics*, 116–17.

speech, for nobody saw him go and the only possible witness, Luachra mac Lonan, died on the spot before he could reveal anything. The narrator insists on examining every available scrap of written evidence that might throw light on the question of the story's ending, appointing himself as the interpreter of the material in such a way that "mere rumours are barred at the very frontiers of the enquiry" (247). The textual evidence proliferates at this point, for "in addition to the sources that have already been mentioned, four rooms at the Royal Irish Academy are piled thick, from floor to floor, with manuscripts dealing only with this point" (247). Half of the texts contain "rude remarks" and "obscene jests, in difficult Irish or still more obscure Latin. Others are filled with drawings that are perplexing to understand. Some of these drawings are of plumed and mysterious presences, but more of no kind of presences at all" (248). The narrator rejects all these because, "no matter how carefully they are examined to find an inner meaning," they make no sense (248). His outright dismissal of these perplexing and mysterious texts in his search for the truth completely ignores his earlier statement that "Truth is itself the greatest mystery of all" (106). The narrator, too, begins to speak with a forked tongue.

The narrator asserts that, after a careful examination of the remaining two roomsful, "and a careful collation of each with each, crossing out *all rumours that cancel one another,* the following few incidents drop through the finely meshed sieve of criticism, and may therefore *with authority* be dropped on this page" (248; italics added). The first text reports that an old man had seen "a strange and wonderful being" coming down the hill near Rathfarnham, and that both he and his wife agreed that "good times must be coming again to the country now that the gods were flying on the effluence of the sunset and revealing themselves to men" (249). The second recorded incident concerns a young man who suddenly entered his house with a pale and frightened face and told his mother "that he had seen a terrible demon stalking the road towards the ford," wildly gesticulating and possessed by an unearthly fury (250). Reportedly a third man, a Dane, told his wife that "he had seen a strange being, who was either one of the gods of the land, or one of the old sort of Irishman of whom he had heard; but that it was indifferent to him which it was, for, either of them, it boded no good for Danish establishments by the sea" (250–51).

One final text closes the series: an old and almost overlooked hagiology that, according to the narrator, contains "the one *priceless truth* in the century of credulous fables that encumber its pages" (251; italics added). It reports that a young herd had witnessed "a wonderful being" leaping across the beach and into the sea, whose appearance made him "proud to be young, and glad to be in life" (252). He heard the being call out, "Mannanán mac Lir!" whereupon, when he looked again, there was no longer anything to be seen. The young man confessed these things to a hermit who told him that he had seen a demon; the herd then "asked him if this was an omen that he would die by drowning; and the saint told him that he would not die by drowning if he never went near water" (253).

The narrator's references to the "authority" and "truth" of these accounts provoke some obvious questions, for how can they all be true at the same time, or any more true than the accounts he has rejected? In logical terms, the narrator's "truth" is nonsense, in which case we reject his claims to authority. In terms of the satire's statements about sense and meaning, however, which imply that there is no objective truth or meaning independent of context and perception, all the accounts are true, and the narrator does make sense. The paradox created by Menippean satire is that the "truth" asserted by the narrator is both nonsense and fact, and that the narrator's claim to authority can only be vindicated if it is accepted that authority is a myth. *The Return of the Hero* consists of a narrative framework of incomplete and fragmentary texts, and this means that the narrative itself cannot be anything but inconclusive. It *must be* inconclusive in order to prove its own internal argument about the inaccessibility of truth, the arbitrariness of meaning, and the random nature of authority. But at the same time, paradoxically, *because* the text is inconclusive and dismissive of authority, including its own, it proves nothing at all.

The reality of the events related in *The Return of the Hero* is further called into question by the suggestion that everything may have taken place in a dream. The twelve men who are the first to encounter the ancient hero Oisín are described as having "the look of men in a dream, snared by some inner mystery that had left them astonished" (10). Oisín himself feels compelled to compare the fairy Niamh, with whom he lived in Tír-na-nÓg, to "a dream which men cannot recover when they wake," even though "she was more real than a valley full of flowers" (49). In his final speech, Oisín says: "The world is a dream, O Finn. The world is a dream of our hearts. We can make it and mould it, O captain, according to the shape of our will" (235). The Ireland of Darrell Figgis's day was, in John Eglinton's words, "no longer a country in which it is permitted to dream dreams," but a place where "a fell disillusionment has seized upon many Irishmen with respect to the realization of long-cherished ideals."[35] Mac Taill compares a good story to a good dream: "It is pleasant to be remembered, and whether it is a sign of anything or not is of no consequence" (197). Since *The Return of the Hero* argues that stories, like dreams, simply "mean what they mean," the book implies that stories (including the one written by Darrell Figgis) mean nothing beyond their surface, whatever we may choose to read into them about the real world.

The portrait Darrell Figgis paints of himself in *Recollections of the Irish War* shows him as a defender of personal liberty and individual opinion whose voice is stifled by authority, traits that he has in common with Mac Taill, and with the Oisín of his satire. The time Figgis spent in prison had made him even more acutely aware of the importance of freedom: "Life is meaningless unless it exist for the production and perfection of personality, and personality is meaningless unless it mean the utmost differentiation of mind, the utmost liberty of thought and action, the utmost stretch of desire and will, without regard for interdictions and frustrations, as the only conceivable basis for fearless exchanges in the commerce of mortality. But the system into which I was introduced had engaged itself to blot all these things, and to treat human revolt as a crime."[36] Suicide, he claims, is the logical perfection of the system; when personality has been so far repressed, one might as well be dead—surely an interesting statement from a man who was to take his own life in 1925. The IRB leadership did not appreciate Figgis's independent mind, and the new Sinn Féin Executive took advantage of his imprisonment to strip him of his official responsibilities. Figgis claims he felt "as a soldier might feel in the front trenches of his army when he finds himself sniped from his own supports."[37] Toward the end of his prison term he began to feel the stress of being a lone voice in the wilderness:

35. John Eglinton, "Dublin Letter," *Dial*, August 1923, p. 182.
36. Figgis, *Recollections*, 164.
37. Ibid., 227.

I was troubled personally as well as nationally; for I had so often taken a different line from my colleagues that I feared to do so again, especially on so grave an issue [the Irish Petition to the Peace Congress], and especially when I had so summarily been dismissed from position and responsibility. Any action of that sort would leave them even more deeply angered with me, and leave me even more desolate, a pariah among politicals and an outcast among friends. More profoundly than ever I regretted that I had left my books, where at least a man's integrity could remain inviolate.[38]

It is not difficult to see in the above developments and in Darrell Figgis's increasing bitterness toward the national leadership the seeds for the satire of *The Return of the Hero*.

In *The Return of the Hero* Darrell Figgis makes Oisín say that the Ireland to which he has returned is a doleful place: "The mountains of Ireland were the same, and the valleys the same, but they were inhabited by pigmies instead of heroes. . . . It was a land under a curse to which I had come—a land blistered by a satire from the gods" (63). It is a country where the leaders refuse to build on the foundations whose cornerstone was put in place by a Fenian hero—even if the stone, in Mac Taill's words, "will not be easily removed" and "will remain for a memory of Oisin for ever" (256). That Figgis should cast himself in the role of his hero is perhaps a mark of his enormous egocentrism. Both Andrew Malone and Padraic Colum depict him as an astonishingly self-centered man, but Ernie O'Malley's is perhaps the most telling description of Figgis's demeanor and its effect on others: "Figgis was not popular; it was thought that he was too vain. Stories were told about his Christlike beard. His manner, his insistent focus of attention for his words, was of the porcupine quill effect of an artist amongst those who thought of nationality alone. He was egotistical; it could be seen in his face and mannerisms; his image was reflected in the half suppressed smiles of his listeners."[39] That Figgis should choose to express his criticism from behind the Janus-faced mask of a Menippean satire seems, on the one hand, something of a paradox, for it appears to compromise the very principle of individual integrity and freedom of opinion represented by his hero. On the other hand, the inconclusiveness and ambiguity of satire express most

38. Ibid., 236.

39. Ernie O'Malley, *Army without Banners* (1937; reprint, London: Four Square Books, 1961), 66.

adequately the frustration of a man who has consistently spoken his mind, and whose voice has equally consistently been ignored.

The final words of *The Return of the Hero* reflect this inconclusiveness. They are in Irish and read: "NI BEAG SAN" (256), that is, "not a little saint." The shift to a different language and the need for translation force an awareness on the part of the reader of the need for, and inescapableness of, mediation and interpretation in the use of all language. The message itself, in which Oisín is defined in negative terms, leaves room for such interpretation. If Oisín is not a little saint, what is he? How is he to be defined positively? The "true" interpretation remains a matter of choice. The bishops would take the view that Oisín is not a saint at all, not even a little one. The Fenian interpretation would argue that Oisín is not a little saint (like Padraic), but instead a great hero. A third, dialogic view (Mac Taill's, for example) would see no contradiction between heroism and saintliness and would view Oisín as indeed not a little saint, but a great one. The dialogic view is clearly favored by the narrative, but the opinion of the bishops prevails in the land. The tone of the book therefore reflects "regret for the glory that Ireland has allowed to slip away."[40]

After writing *The Return of the Hero* Darrell Figgis went on to chair the committee that drafted the Irish Free State Constitution, "now regarded in the light of the 1937 constitution as a model of liberalism," as Peter Costello remarks.[41] He represented South Dublin as an Independent candidate in the Dáil in 1922; during his campaign he adopted an antagonistic stance, telling the electorate that "if you support the Free State, then vote for me, the Free State candidate. A vote for me is a vote for the Free State. A vote against me is a vote against the Free State."[42] This apparently did not sit well with everybody: one night three men broke into Figgis's home and cut off part of his "Christlike" beard. After his wife committed suicide in 1924—the combined result, it seems, of her husband's unfaithfulness to her and of the hostility of his political opponents—Figgis gave up politics and moved to London. The event apparently left him greatly depressed. In London, he

---

40. Paul Deane, "The Death of Greatness: Darrell Figgis's *The Return of the Hero,*" *Notes on Modern Irish Literature,* 3 (1991): 35.

41. Costello, *Heart Grown Brutal,* 265.

42. Advertisement in the *Irish Independent,* 12 June 1922; quoted in *Irish Political Documents, 1916–1949,* ed. Arthur Mitchell and Pádraig Ó Snodaigh (Dublin: Irish Academic Press, 1985), 136.

lived with a young woman named Rita North; she died on 19 October 1925 of complications following an abortion. At the end of *The Return of the Hero,* when Oisín finds that the whole world has abandoned him, he walks into the sea and disappears from the earth. Eight days after his girlfriend's death, Darrell Figgis turned on the gas in his apartment in Bloomsbury and he, too, stepped out of this life.

part two

Eimar O'Duffy

(1893–1935)

*E*imar O'Duffy's career is an interesting one, both in its own right and because it resembles that of Darrell Figgis in a number of respects: both were involved in Irish revolutionary politics, both were disillusioned by the events of 1916 and their aftermath, both turned to Menippean satire after writing a variety of works of nonfiction and fiction (including, in O'Duffy's case, several plays, two of which were produced), and both died young. While some of these similarities are coincidental, the connection between their political disappointment and the shift toward satire in their writing is not. All the writers under discussion in this volume were, to a greater or lesser degree, affected by the period of change and upheaval in Ireland in the decades after the declaration of the Free State, but the direct involvement of Figgis and O'Duffy in those dramatic events makes the link between life and literature all the more poignant.

Eimar O'Duffy's pro-British father was dentist-in-ordinary to the viceregal household. At the outbreak of World War I he forced his sons to choose between enlisting in the British army or being expelled from home; Kevin chose the army (and was killed at Suvla Bay in 1915), but Eimar (who had also qualified in dentistry at the National University) took the second option and promptly joined the Irish Republican Brotherhood. Since he had received some military training while a cadet at Stonyhurst public school in England, O'Duffy was made an executive officer in the Dublin Brigade of the Volunteers; he also wrote articles for the *Irish Volunteer*. Although he was responsible for training soldiers, he believed that the Volunteers should be a defensive force against British aggression, and he rejected Pearse's belief in the need for a blood sacrifice. At the time of the Easter Rising he took the side of MacNeill, who sent him to Belfast to order Volunteers there not to resort to violence. Some of O'Duffy's bitterness about the events of 1916 is expressed in his novel *The Wasted Island* (1919), in which he included thinly disguised portraits of several of his relatives and acquaintances: Darrell Figgis appeared as Ompleby.[1] In *King Goshawk and the Birds*, O'Duffy's satirical use of Old Irish material was "impelled by deep disillusionment: his novel is the first exploitation of the old literature in the wake of the Irish Civil War and partition, and after such knowledge there is little forgiveness."[2] After he lost his job in the Irish Department of External Affairs in 1925, O'Duffy moved his family to England, where he eked out a living by writing books and journalism while his health deteriorated.

Eimar O'Duffy died young, and for a variety of reasons never achieved an established reputation as either a novelist or a dramatist. As is frequently the case with satire, the nature of his work was often misunderstood by critics looking for a continuation of his novelistic approach to literature: a contemporary American reviewer, for example, found *King Goshawk and the Birds* "decidedly inferior to 'The Wasted Island.'"[3] Likewise, Donnchadh Meehan was of the opinion that "the artistic, or if you like the fantastic unity of *King Goshawk and the Birds* is seriously impaired."[4] Only John Eglinton hailed O'Duffy as having emerged from his Gaelic studies "with a spirit emancipated by mockery and mischief. The gaiety and gusto of King Goshawk and the Birds quite carry you off your feet."[5] O'Duffy's obituary in the *Dublin Magazine* sums up some of the reservations most commonly expressed in relation to his work: "His trilo-

1. More information on O'Duffy's involvement in the Volunteers can be found in W. J. Feeney's "Eimar O'Duffy's 'A Military Causerie,'" *Journal of Irish Literature*, 10, 3 (1981): 91–108.

2. J. W. Foster, *Fictions*, 288.

3. Ernest Boyd, review of *King Goshawk and the Birds*, by Eimar O'Duffy, in *New York Herald Tribune*, 31 October 1926, p. 5.

4. Donnchadh A. Meehan, "Of Four Fantasies," *Irish Bookman*, 3, 1 (1948): 22.

5. John Eglinton, "Irish Letter," *Dial*, May 1927, p. 410.

gy *King Goshawk and the Birds* and its sequel made his name known to a wider public, though it did not quite come off." The piece goes on to say that "had he had the chance of writing leisurely and unworriedly, he would have become a very considerable satirical dramatist."[6] Ten years after his death, O'Duffy's work was virtually forgotten. In an article in the *Bell* designed to bring his undeservedly neglected writings back into the public eye, Vivian Mercier wrote that even during his lifetime O'Duffy "was simply ignored," and that "since his premature death in 1935 of duodenal ulcers—a satirist's occupational disease—what reputation he had has dwindled away to almost nothing."[7]

Before writing his satirical trilogy, Eimar O'Duffy had already made use of Irish legend to satirize contemporary society in his early play *Bricriu's Feast* (1919?). As a satirist, O'Duffy may have wanted to model himself on Bricriu "of the poison tongue," a mythological trickster notorious for stirring up argument and controversy; if he failed to become, like Bricriu, "the conscience of his race, the reason was not that he did not try, but that he was defeated by circumstances which he could hardly control."[8] Eimar O'Duffy's three satirical narratives, *King Goshawk and the Birds* (1926), *The Spacious Adventures of the Man in the Street* (1928), and *Asses in Clover* (1933), are usually referred to as the "Cuanduine trilogy," after their main protagonist. The immediate targets of the satire are twofold: rampant capitalism and narrow-minded sexual ethics. In the years leading up to the Great Depression, examples of the former were paramount all over Europe and the United States, and O'Duffy makes his prime capitalist monster a Manhattan wheat "king," Goshawk, who declares it his business to own the entire earth with everything on it, including its wild birds and flowers. The kind of puritanical thinking attacked in the trilogy, however, was much more specifically representative of growing repressive attitudes in the Irish Free State. After the signing of the Treaty, O'Duffy had become increasingly disgruntled with Irish politics. Although the broad satirical targets of the trilogy are the political, economic, and moral values of the Western world in general and Ireland in

6. P. S. O'H[egarty], obituary for Eimar O'Duffy, in *Dublin Magazine*, new ser. 10, 3 (1935): 92.

7. Vivian Mercier, "The Satires of Eimar O'Duffy," *Bell*, 12, 4 (1946): 325.

8. Robert Hogan, *Eimar O'Duffy* (Lewisburg, Penn.: Bucknell University Press, 1972), 25.

particular, in the manner of most Menippean satirists O'Duffy despairs of ever being able to change the world, due to the folly and pretensions of the human race. Ultimately the satire questions all ideological positions.

To prevent the satire from endorsing any one doctrine, the volumes of the trilogy are arranged in a polemical relationship to each other, creating, in Bakhtin's terms, a heteroglossia of actual and implied dialogical voices within and across the three books, but in such a way that each satirizing voice both undercuts and is undercut by other voices, a process that effectively undermines *all* expressions of authority. The perspectives of the first and the second volume of the Cuanduine trilogy are dialogically opposed to each other. In *King Goshawk and the Birds,* an insignificant Dublin philosopher named Murphy, worried about the excesses of capitalism, persuades the spirit of Cuchulain (properly Cú Chulainn, or the "Hound of Culann") to leave the Land of Heart's Desire and return to Earth. For this purpose, Cuchulain temporarily borrows the body of the grocer's clerk Aloysius O'Kennedy, but he gets himself into so much trouble that he gives up in disgust. His son Cuanduine (Cú an Duine, or the "Hound of Man") takes his place and, like his father, engages in discussions on politics and morality with the population of Dublin. Cuanduine is more persistent than his father but ultimately no more successful. Both Cuchulain and his son are critical of established norms and customs, but they are at the same time completely incapable of understanding the principles on which the status quo is founded. Thus both heroes, while acting as vehicles for the satire, are themselves also satirized for their limited perspective. A "hero" is defined in *King Goshawk* as "a person of superabundant vitality and predominant will, with no sense of responsibility or humour, which makes him a nuisance on earth" (34).[9] Heroes, therefore, are not necessarily to be regarded as alternative role models.

The second volume, *The Spacious Adventures of the Man in the Street,* inverts this perspective. While Cuchulain is in temporary possession of O'Kennedy's body, the latter's spirit arrives in the city of Bulnid on the planet Rathé where he temporarily adopts the body of Ydenneko. These names are simple anagrams or inversions of Dublin, Earth, and O'Kennedy, and the planet, too, is a semi-inverted, semiutopian version of

9. Eimar O'Duffy, *King Goshawk and the Birds* (London: Macmillan, 1926); all page references in the text are to this edition.

Earth. O'Kennedy is a staunch defender of Earth's values, and his attitude therefore stands in dialogical opposition to that of both Cuchulain and Cuanduine. At the same time he also enters into discussions with the Ratheans on aspects of their society from art to politics and morality, which—in an obvious analogy with Cuchulain and Cuanduine in the first book—he fails entirely to understand; as with the heroes, O'Kennedy's inability to pick up even the most obvious parallels between practices on Earth and on Rathé undermines his authority as a commentator.

The juxtaposition of one satire whose narrative perspective is critical of the status quo and supportive of change, and a second whose narrator supports the status quo and criticizes deviations from it, creates a dialogue between books as well as within each book. Cuchulain and Cuanduine, prototypical heroes, argue with the citizens of Dublin; O'Kennedy, the prototypical man-in-the-street, argues with the citizens of Bulnid, whose values are the opposite of those of Dublin. A dialogue between the values of the heroes and those of O'Kennedy is therefore implied. This chiasmic structure is further reinforced by the fact that many of the issues addressed in the first volume are also discussed in the second, but from an opposite perspective. The double-edged, oxymoronic nature of the mirroring technique makes it a perfect vehicle for satire. Since that which is satirized is itself always implied in the satirical inversion, the mirror image serves both as an inversion and an analogy. When the Rathean mirror image is understood as a utopian inversion, it shows up the foolishness of practices on Earth; but when the mirror image is perceived as an analogy, it implicitly satirizes Rathean beliefs as well. The chiasmic structure prevents the satire from endorsing a single point of view.

chapter two

"These Were the Days of Paternal Government"

King Goshawk and the Birds

One of the main purposes of Menippean satire is to address ultimate philosophical questions. While the rather flimsy plot of *King Goshawk and the Birds* revolves around the appropriation of the world's songbirds and wildflowers by the capitalist Goshawk, the book is really a series of Menippean digressions aimed at questioning the social and economic policies prevalent in the modern world. The satire's overall conclusion exposes the wickedness and folly of the human race, and deplores man's inability to change for the better. The timelessness and universality of this human flaw are emphasized by the satire's narrative point of view: while the book's social and political satire is clearly aimed at the customs and practices of the first decades of the twentieth century, the events are made to take place in the not-too-distant future (sometime in the 1950s), but they are narrated retrospectively by an unidentified first-person narrator from the perspective of an even more distant future. At the same time, O'Duffy introduces characters into this future who belong to the remote past of Old Irish epic literature, specifically the *Táin Bó Cúailnge*. The resulting misalliance between ancient and modern characters both emphasizes and dissolves the boundaries between past, present, and future and renders the quest for solutions to humanity's problems both timely and timeless.

A theme typical of carnivalized Menippean satire is "the relativity and ambivalence of reason and madness, intelligence and stupidity."[1] In the Cuanduine trilogy, the quest for the truth about the human race is initiated by a philosopher called Murphy "who lived in a little room in a tumbledown house in a back lane off Stoneybatter" (7). John Cronin has argued

---

1. Bakhtin, *Dostoevsky's Poetics*, 138.

that, stylistically, O'Duffy "bridges the period between the whimsical fantasy of James Stephens and the strenuously learned mockery of Flann O'Brien," and that O'Duffy's Philosopher "steps straight out of the pages of *The Crock of Gold*."[2] The Philosopher may be wise, but his potential for success is hampered by a lack of practical insight. The window of his room is caked with dirt, and "though the Philosopher had frequently rubbed it off the inside, it never occurred to him to clean the outside, his mind being so occupied with other matters that he overlooked that solution to the difficulty" (9). In other words, philosophers are passive creatures, and clear inner vision does little to remove whatever is wrong in the outside world. The wise man's marginal existence is an indication that he fulfills the role of the wise fool, the typical position of the wise man in Menippean satire in that he alone is aware of the truth, but is nonetheless ridiculed by everyone else. This becomes apparent when the Philosopher attempts to address the question of the songbirds in public: he is attacked by an angry mob and barely escapes with his life. Later he protests publicly against Goshawk's appropriation of the wildflowers, and this time he is derided as a crank and a madman. In spite of this proof that "mankind in a hundred [years] does not change at all" (19), the Philosopher can never reach an ultimate conclusion, for "the wise man knows there is finality in nothing" (11). The quest for the truth is more important than the answer; therefore, as soon as the reflection enters his mind that mankind, even when confronted with ridicule and criticism, will not change for the better, "he began to examine it, to question it, as was his nature" (19). The Philosopher, by virtue of being a wise man, is fated to go on questioning, while he is at the same time doomed to go on being, at best, ignored.

The Philosopher decides that the answer to the question of how man might be redeemed from "the course of wickedness and folly by which he was travelling to destruction" (23) is to be found in the life beyond, and for this reason invokes a thinker mightier than himself, the spirit of Socrates, now residing in the twentieth heaven. The satirist's choice of Socrates is not accidental: the carnivalistic base of the Socratic dialogue is addressed by Bakhtin in *Problems of Dostoevsky's Poetics,* as is the "Socratic notion of the dialogic nature of truth" in which truth "is born *between people* collectively searching for truth, in the process of their dialogic interaction. Socrates

2. John Cronin, *Irish Fiction, 1900–1940* (Belfast: Appletree, 1992), 102.

. . . brought people together and made them collide in a quarrel, and as a result truth was born. . . . But Socrates never called himself the exclusive possessor of a ready-made truth."[3] In *King Goshawk and the Birds* Socrates has still not found the truth, not even in heaven: "'Only this truth,' said the spirit of Socrates; 'that it is not to be found. . . . For in seeking there is life; but in finding there is stagnation, and stagnation is death'" (25). Although even Socrates is angered by Goshawk's actions, he decides that the world's needs are better met by a hero than by a philosopher. This is consistent with the tendency of carnivalized literature to transfer ultimate questions "from the abstractly philosophical sphere . . . to the concretely sensuous plane of images and events which are . . . dynamic, diverse and vivid."[4]

The Philosopher finds Cuchulain dallying with his otherworldly lover, Fand, in Tír na nÓg, the third heaven, where "the heroes take themselves and one another at their own valuation, regarding their weaknesses as strength, their defects as merits" (34). The hero is at first unmoved by reports of man's general wickedness, but upon hearing of the fate of the birds his outrage is such that he agrees to follow the Philosopher back to Earth at once, where he adopts the body of the grocer's clerk Aloysius O'Kennedy, which the latter's spirit has temporarily vacated at the behest of the Philosopher (O'Kennedy's separate adventures are related in the second part of the Cuanduine trilogy, *The Spacious Adventures of the Man in the Street*). Not surprisingly, the grocer's body and the hero's spirit find themselves at odds with each other. Satire typically includes such instances of separation and dissociation from the self, for the loss of self, or the observation of the self-as-other, creates unusual perspectives and "makes strange" what is normally taken for granted.

The view from the Philosopher's window, which shows a wall plastered with "flamboyant posters" and "mean little hand-bills" (15), reminds him why a hero is needed in Ireland and why "the song-birds could hope for little succour at the hands of his countrymen" (17). The rival political parties of the day in Ireland are the "Yallogreens" and the "Greenyallos," represented respectively by Blithero and Blathero. The difference between them is one of class rather than of substance: the Greenyallos defend their principles and ideals "for which our fathers faced the rack, the gallows, the gib-

---

3. Bakhtin, *Dostoevsky's Poetics*, 110.
4. Ibid., 134.

bet, and the gaol" (179), while the Yallogreens stand up for their "ideels an' principles, which is the same our fathers was executed and went to gaol for" (181). They are, however, united in rejecting Cuanduine's appeals for action regarding Goshawk's appropriation of the natural world.

Eimar O'Duffy's disillusionment with Irish politics is clearly expressed in the squabbles of the Greenyallos and Yallogreens who, as long as the Philosopher can remember, "had been thus abusing one another" (15). The Treaty Debate of 1921–1922 in the Dáil is satirized in *King Goshawk and the Birds* by means of simple inversion. Declan Kiberd's summary of the historical events provides a basis for comparison:

[Arthur Griffith] persuaded a majority of the Dáil to ratify the Treaty by 14 votes to 57. Éamon de Valera, the sole surviving commander from the Rising, argued that the Dáil had no right to do wrong. He and his followers opposed the oath of loyalty to the British Crown. . . .

A bitter election was fought on the issue in June 1922, with 58 pro-Treatyites returned, 36 against, 17 for labour, and 17 representing other groups including farmers. A civil war of unparalleled bitterness then ensued. . . .[5]

When the Treaty was put to the Dáil for ratification, all six women deputies (including Countess Markievicz, who is portrayed by O'Duffy as "Madame Przemysl") "spoke trenchantly against it. During the long and heartrending debate, Cumann na mBan attempted to hoist a Union Jack over the building, as a mordant commentary on what was being proposed." Mary MacSwiney, widow of the hunger-striking lord mayor of Cork, said she would "have neither hand, act nor part in helping the Irish Free State to carry this nation of ours, this glorious nation that has been betrayed here tonight, into the British Empire." Indeed, "if England exterminates the men, the women will take their places . . . and if she exterminates the men, women and children of this generation, the blades of grass, dyed with their blood, will rise, like the dragons' teeth of old, into armed men and the fight will begin in the next generation."[6]

In *King Goshawk and the Birds* the Philosopher recalls the "great civil war that had been waged" between the Yallogreens and the Greenyallos "over the question of rejoining the British Empire, from which the Irish people had seceded some years earlier" (15). The reunion was proposed in the Dáil

5. Kiberd, *Inventing Ireland,* 194.
6. Ibid., 402.

by "Seumas Vanderbags, leader of the Yallogreen party" (15), but the motion was lost by seven votes. The Philosopher "could still see in imagination the pale thin face of Vanderbags as he rose to his feet to announce that he would not abide by the verdict, and to utter his famous pronouncement that the people had no right to do wrong. Never could the Philosopher forget the horrors of the subsequent fighting. . . . Half the city of Dublin was laid in ashes, and most of the country devastated" (15–16). The English government rejected the Irish application for incorporation in the Empire, but the Yallogreens were not daunted:

Vanderbags declared that the right of Ireland to belong to the British Empire was inalienable and indefeasible; and Miss O'Grady said that the Irish People were citizens of the British Empire whether they or the British liked it or not: such was their love for the Empire that they would lay all its cities in ashes and slaughter every man, woman, and child within its borders sooner than be thrust out of their inalienable inheritance. The sequel of all this was burnt deep into the Philosopher's recollection: the mad declaration of war against the British Empire; the destruction of the Irish navy; the invasion of Ireland by the British; and the forcible re-establishment of the Republic. (16–17)

Simple inversion of this kind serves a dual purpose, since it typically ridicules both poles of the equation. Taken as a satirical reversal, the passage criticizes contemporary republicanism, which O'Duffy perceived as being extreme and wrongheaded. Taken literally, the notion of Ireland forcibly trying to rejoin Britain is clearly ridiculous. The satire is, however, more subtle than it seems. The Treaty had been signed by Cathal Brugha and Austin Stack without the president's consent, in a form that was unpalatable to him; according to de Valera's biographers,

[T]he Treaty was examined clause by clause. The President pointed out where, and how far, it departed from cabinet policy. The first four clauses in particular *brought Ireland firmly back into the British Empire* [italics added]. The oath would mean that they would have to swear "to be faithful to H. M. King George V, his heirs and successors." The King would be part of the constitution to which they would have to swear allegiance; they would be compelled to take an oath which precluded them from advancing any further along the road of independence. The delegates insisted that the alternative was war.[7]

---

7. Longford and O'Neill, *Éamon de Valera*, 169.

When O'Duffy inverts the issues of the Treaty Debate, and pretends that it was about Ireland's rejoining the British Empire, he simultaneously tells a subtle form of truth: the version of the Treaty that was signed was indeed perceived as such by de Valera and his followers.

The poignancy of these passages notwithstanding, Irish nationalism is not at the top of O'Duffy's satirical agenda. His main interest lies in economic theories, and he relentlessly satirizes the evils of capitalism and materialism by means of exaggeration, literalism, and inversion. In *King Goshawk and the Birds* Dublin is a city literally ruined by war and by corrupt and incompetent politicians. Most of its buildings are in a state of collapse: "To what shall I compare it? A festering corpse, maggot-crawling, under a carrion-kissing sun? A loathly figure, yet insufficient: for your maggot thrives on corruption, and grows sleeker with the progression of putridity (O happy maggot, whom the dross of the world trammels not, had you but an immortal soul how surely would it aspire heavenward!). But your lord of creation rots with his environment; so the true symbol of our city is a carrion so pestilent that it corrupts its own maggots" (52). When the Philosopher takes Cuanduine on an educational tour of the world he points out all the evils in it, especially those that are the result of poverty and excessive wealth. All its inhabitants, however, are equally degenerate, for while the rich are unhealthy because of decadence and overindulgence, the poor are diseased because of destitution and bad habits (which, the Philosopher points out, are the result of "civilization"): "What stink of breath and body assailed his nostrils; what debased accents, raucous voices, and evil language offended his hearing; what grime, what running sores, what raw-rimmed eye-sockets, what gum-suppuration and tooth-rot, what cavernous cheeks, what leering lips and hopeless eyes, what pain-twisted faces, what sagging spines, what streeling steps, what filthy ragged raiment covering what ghastly-imagined hideousness of body sickened his beauty-nurtured sight" (53–54). Such grotesque and ugly passages are a common way in satire of creating *dis-ease*, of overturning "the bourgeoisie's own world of sanitary and sanctimonious normalcy and diurnal mediocrity."[8] O'Duffy was a believer in the benefits of socialism, and in *King Goshawk and the Birds* he makes a point of depicting the evils of capitalism as graphically as

---

8. John R. Clark, *The Modern Satiric Grotesque and Its Traditions* (Lexington: University of Kentucky Press, 1991), 25.

he can. The dehumanizing "signs of progress and private enterprise" (54) are evident throughout.

Apart from the distribution of wealth, another concern that became particularly pressing for writers and intellectuals in the 1920s, especially in Ireland, was that politics and the law increasingly began to extend themselves into all areas of public and private morality. During the 1920s a series of laws was adopted in Ireland to protect moral values, the overly puritanical interpretation of which is satirized at length in *King Goshawk and the Birds*. The Censorship of Films Act was adopted in 1923, the Intoxicating Liquor Acts of 1924 and 1927 reduced the number of public houses and restricted their opening hours, and the Censorship of Publications Act of 1929 prohibited the distribution of "indecent or obscene" literature and banned all literature advocating birth control. O'Duffy's narrator explains to his future-based audience that "you must understand that in those days every action, word, and thought of which man is capable was most thoroughly regulated by law" (80)—so thoroughly, in fact, that forty thousand Dubliners one day "found themselves lodged in gaol for blowing their noses in public, being unaware that this action had just been incorporated as Schedule 678 of the Public Modesty Act" (81). Although *King Goshawk and the Birds* predates the Censorship of Publications Act by several years, it accurately foretells the consequences of its passage into law.

O'Duffy ridicules censorship by starting with a realistic premise that he then takes to its logical and literal extreme. It must be understood, he argues, that "these were the days of paternal government. All over the world the governments had decided to abolish temptation, it being generally conceded . . . that man's character was now so weak that at the mere appearance of temptation he must instantly succumb. The manufacture of wine, beer, spirits and tobacco had long since been entirely suppressed. . . . Substitutes for the banned commodities were, however, illicitly manufactured in great abundance" (81–82). Temptations of the flesh are subject to even more stringent legislation, and the arts suffer accordingly:

The nude was a forbidden subject, and there had been a great holocaust of existing works in this genre many years ago. Fully two-fifths of the world's literature had suffered the same fate, and another fifth had been so mutilated by the expurgators as to have been rendered unrecognisable to its authors. The Old Testament had been reduced to a collection of scraps, somewhat resembling the Greek Anthology; and even the New Testament had been purged of the plainer-spoken words of Christ which were offensive to modern taste. All new works had to undergo a prolonged inspection by a board of Censors, whose jurisdiction, however, did not extend to musical comedies or Sunday papers. (83–84)

This would be funny had not the subsequent reality—the banning of virtually every author of merit, the removal of all nudes from Dublin's Municipal Gallery, and so on—managed to upstage the satire. However, O'Duffy takes the abolition of temptation to even greater extremes that reveal both the absurdity of the notion itself and its tendency to lead not to more protection of the public, but to greater injustice and corruption. In O'Duffy's hypothetical future it is a crime for a person to entice another person into murdering him, thus turning the victims of crime into criminals, while the practice of calling witnesses in legal proceedings has been abolished to save people from being tempted to bear false witness. The narrator observes that, in spite of these draconian measures to eradicate temptation, there is still no improvement in the human race: "So much for the measures taken for the elimination of moral temptation from the ways of the world" (85).

Compared to the puritanical attitude toward sexuality in O'Duffy's Ireland, Cuchulain's direct, not to say blunt, approach to matters of the flesh represents the other extreme. Still in the guise of O'Kennedy, he outrages the object of his first courtship, a girl from Drumcondra, when he woos her as he had courted his wife Emer: "My desire is for two snowy mountains, rose-crowned, that are fenced about with thorns and barriers of ice" (77). The girl calls him a dirty fellow and has him arrested by a police force especially created for such eventualities: "Their clothing was all white, though somewhat soiled. . . . On their collars were these words in letters of ivory: CENSOR MORUM" (77). The officers barely have time to threaten Cuchulain with incarceration in the Lothario Asylum for making love without matrimonial intent before the hero ties them into "a truelove knot" (79).

Tired of O'Kennedy's body and of the "dunghill of meanness and silliness" that is the Earth (95), Cuchulain announces his departure for Tír na nÓg, but when the Philosopher pleads with him he finally agrees to father a child who will be more suitable for the task of dealing with modern man: "As man he will be able to endure their ways: as hero he will see to it that they shall not continue them" (96–97). To carry out this plan, the Philosopher advises Cuchulain to woo discreetly with a view to marriage, and in order to find a suitable bride he puts the hero up as a member of the Bon Ton Suburban Tennis Club. The hero is unsuccessful but fails to see why his straightforward marriage proposals—"then straight to our nuptial couch and forge us goodly offspring" (99)—are perceived as rudeness. Although O'Duffy uses Cuchulain's behavior as a tool to satirize excessive puritanism, the absurd extremity of that behavior, coupled with the hero's total lack of human warmth, at the same time precludes it from being authorized as an acceptable alternative. The narrator himself expresses doubt as to the origin of the hero's emotions: "For myself, I cannot tell whether this love impulse of Cuchulain's came from God or from the Devil" (87). Eventually, however, his ardor is returned by Thalia Boodleguts, a girl reluctantly facing marriage to the son of a wealthy "onion king," arranged by her capitalist father (who made his fortune in tripe). Cuchulain solves her problem by eloping with her to the Land of Heart's Desire. In doing so, he leaves O'Kennedy's body behind on a refuse heap, where it is found by the Philosopher, who eventually returns it to its rightful owner.

The offspring of the otherworldly union of Thalia and Cuchulain is Cuanduine, the "Hound of Man." Despite his heroic faults (he is very disobedient, addicted to lying, and infernally curious about women), the boy is "a fine little lad" (130). His father teaches him all the heroic virtues and feats, and also sends him to the Heaven of Realities to make him more human and to equip him with "the gift of self-distrust, the gift of incredulity, the gift of incertitude, the gift of clear-sightedness, the gift of hardness, the gift of kindness, the gift of unscrupulousness, the gift of shamelessness, the gift of humour" (133). Cuanduine vows never to rest "until the birds and the flowers are freed, and Goshawk chastened in his insolence" (135); afterward, he is resolved to teach mankind "the wisdom of Charity" (136). His father and the Philosopher are skeptical: "'Too soon for that,' said the Philosopher. 'First teach us the folly of killing.' 'Too soon for that,' said Cuchulain. 'First teach them to fight decently'" (136). In spite of his lofty ideals, Cuanduine is aware, like Socrates, that he does not know the "Truth," only "some of the Truth" (170), which he is willing to share with mankind.

Carnivalized literature typically stresses the reproductive power of the earth and of the body, because the reigning ideology rejects the healthy, "natural" functions of the body; hence O'Duffy's ridiculing of Irish puritanism and its fear of sexuality. As Frank Palmeri points out, the "pretense of cutting one's body off from the processes of the physical world and denying its products provides an inexhaustible series of objects for satire."[9] These bodily products are often conceived of as scatological, but in O'Duffy's case they are the products of sexual intercourse. As much as O'Duffy ridicules Irish puritans for their fear of sex, he is even more scathing about sexual reformers who wish to indulge freely in sensuality while denying the natural fruits of their bodies.

The two main satirical targets of the Cuanduine trilogy, capitalism and matters of sexual morality, appear at first sight to have little if anything in common, and to have been chosen by O'Duffy largely because his own life had been adversely affected, first by his quarrel with the Irish sociopolitical climate and then, after his move to England, by the worldwide economic depression. On closer consideration, however, O'Duffy's discussion of both economics and sexuality hinges in many instances on the common denominator of birth control. The connection between fertility and economics is most graphically demonstrated by the story of Saint Progressa, O'Duffy's lengthy, vitriolic, and at times misogynistic satirical attack on reproductive "Procrusteanism," the system of economic thought that requires people to adapt their personal circumstances to their economic conditions, rather than vice versa. This attack shows O'Duffy's growing obsession with what he regarded as wrongheaded economic measures, a fixation that led him eventually to put forward his own solution to the world's economic crisis in a serious work called *Life and Money,* published in 1932[10]—namely, monetary reform and the introduction of a social credit scheme.

"Saint Progressa" is a satirical reference to Dr. Marie Stopes, whose book *Wise Parenthood* was among the first to be banned in Ireland under the 1929 Censorship Act. In 1921 she had started the United Kingdom's first family planning clinic, and in 1922 she founded the Society for Constructive Birth Control and Racial Progress.

Marie Stopes emphasized that the Society was in no way to be regarded as advocating unnecessary restriction of babies: "We are profoundly and fundamentally a pro-

9. Palmeri, *Satire*, 11.

10. I have taken my information about this work from Robert Hogan's *Eimar O'Duffy,* 68–73.

baby organization, in favour of producing the largest number of healthy, happy children without detriment to the mother, and with the minimum wastage of infants by premature death. We, therefore, as a Society regret the relatively small families of those best fitted to care for children. In this connection our motto has been 'Babies in the right place,' and it is just as much the aim of Constructive Birth Control to secure conception to those married people who are healthy, childless and desire children, as it is to furnish security from conception to those who are radically diseased, already overburdened with children or in any specific way unfitted for parenthood."[11]

In O'Duffy's version, the Lord appeared to Progressa in a vision and told her: "Tell mankind . . . that I did not really mean what I said when I bade them increase and multiply. I was young and unpractised in those days, and had not made a study of political economy. This is the new Gospel: 'Dwindle and Diminish'" (231). Progressa calls the new gospel "Babylove" and makes it her mission to rid the world of its greatest plague, babies, declaring reproduction an inconvenience intervening with the Higher Development of Woman, especially in the areas of dancing, hunting, and voting in elections. The religious overtones of O'Duffy's satire have their origin in the address Stopes delivered to the Conference of Anglican bishops during its session at Lambeth in 1920. The text of the speech was published in 1922 under the title *A New Gospel to All Peoples: A Revelation of God Uniting Physiology and the Religions of Man*. In this address, she spoke to the bishops "in the name of God. You are His Priests. I am His Prophet,"[12] and raised the issue of married couples "who use the means which God now sends through Science to raise the race. These shall lead the peoples of all the world to a higher potentiality for His service than ever has been known."[13] O'Duffy quotes from the gospel of "Saint Progressa" directly, in

11. Keith Briant, *Passionate Paradox: The Life of Marie Stopes* (New York: W. W. Norton, 1962), 151.

12. Marie Carmichael Stopes, *A New Gospel to All Peoples: A Revelation of God Uniting Physiology and the Religions of Man* (London: Mothers Clinic/Arthur L. Humphreys, 1922), 9.

13. Ibid., 26–27. In *Studies in the Psychology of Sex,* vol. 2 (1910), Havelock Ellis had expressed similar ideas in comparable terms, claiming that "humanity has spawned itself . . . in thousands of millions of creatures . . . a large proportion of whom . . . ought never to have been born [and] the voice of Jehovah is now making itself heard through the leaders of mankind in a very different sense. . . . [T]he question of the procreation of the race [has gained] a new significance [and has even taken on] the character of a new religious movement. . . . [T]he claim of the race is the claim of religion." Quoted in Mary Lowe-Evans, *Crimes*

order to show "the beautiful and logical mind of its prophet" (231). His careful selection of quotations reveals inconsistencies in Progressa's arguments: while she contends in one passage that "the natural desire of the sexes, formerly regarded as a survival of the animal in man, is now known to be a purely spiritual attraction" (231), she contradicts this in another statement by claiming that "the most elementary knowledge of Nature makes it clear that the male's powers of self-restraint are limited. A superficial observation of the habits of cats, dogs, and barn-door fowl will make that plain to the most ignorant" (232).

O'Duffy's satirical method in the instance of Saint Progressa is to select, edit, and exaggerate Stopes's ideas—and he does not need to exaggerate very much, as the following examples illustrate. In *King Goshawk* Progressa's followers are dismayed at their initial lack of success among the poor, since their "depraved taste for offspring" must lead to "the multiplication of the least desirable elements of the community—of the idle, the thriftless, the vicious, and the unfit—at the expense of the hard-working, provident, and virtuous rich. What a prospect was this for the future of the race" (233). They promote several acts of Parliament to enforce family planning for the poor. Their ideas and methods may be compared with what was proposed by Stopes: "The other obstacle presents a deeper and more difficult task. It must deal with the terrible debasing power of the inferior, the depraved, and feeble-minded, to whom reason means nothing and can mean nothing, who are thriftless and unmanageable yet appallingly prolific. Yet if the good in our race is not to be swamped and destroyed by the debased as the fine tree by the parasite, this prolific depravity must be curbed. How shall this be done? A very few quite simple Acts of Parliament could deal with it."[14] Stopes has in mind compulsory sterilization for those totally unfit for parenthood, possibly using "the direct action of X-rays" as a painless alternative to surgery.[15]

---

against Fecundity: Joyce and Population Control (Syracuse, N.Y.: Syracuse University Press, 1989), 71.

14. Marie Stopes, *Radiant Motherhood: A Book for Those Who Are Creating the Future* (New York and London: G. P. Putnam's Sons/Knickerbocker Press, 1921), 247.

15. Ibid., 249. Eugenics as a "scientific" creed was widespread in Europe and the United States in the 1920s and 1930s. The Scandinavian countries, for example, all passed eugenics laws between 1929 and 1935 that allowed for the forcible sterilization of people deemed unfit for parenthood for social, mental, or physiological reasons.

Economic factors were also taken into consideration: while she emphasizes the need for "a consideration of the essential medical and physiological factors of contraception apart from a controversial cult of economics
and party politics,"[16] Stopes also argues that in homes "where permanent
poverty or inferior wage-earning exists and where there are already as many
children as the parents can bring up decently, contraception is obviously indicated rather than the saddling of the community with children of a very
doubtful racial value."[17] The rigidity of the economic argument is what
most infuriates O'Duffy. The followers of Progressa, he states with outright
sarcasm, "were no puling sentimentalists nor wicked subversives to think
that the race could be saved by tampering with the laws of economics,
which are as old as the laws of the Medes and Persians, and like them do not
change" (233). The saint's solution is therefore not to increase people's in-
comes but to cut down their families, since the rights of property are more
sacrosanct than those of unborn babies. Ultimately she succeeds: anticon-
traceptive literature is banned, and priests who object to the practice are
imprisoned. Contraception is defined as a dogma by the "Sacred Congregation of Advanced Thinkers, which is infallible" (237), and ten years later Progressa is declared a saint by the "General Consensus of Modern
Thought, which is more infallible still" (237).

In spite of its vehemence and the directness of its attack on the likes of
Marie Stopes, the satire of the passage concerning Saint Progressa is characteristically double-edged and inconclusive. In terms of the attack on economic Procrusteanism, not to mention women's liberation, the practice of
birth control is ridiculed and condemned as a means of putting the cart before the horse. As a direct, parodic inversion of Roman Catholic dogma,
however, the passage, by borrowing the language of religion, appears to
ridicule the Church's extreme position on contraception as well, and therefore to reinforce the satirical invective against repressive attitudes toward
sexuality in Ireland. Generally speaking, O'Duffy criticizes those who deny
the body's reproductive functions in the name of idealism or material
progress. In the absence of a hell, Cuanduine assigns such souls to the low-
est heaven, that of Material Delights: "There dwell all sinners against life,

---

16. Marie Stopes, *Contraception (Birth Control): Its Theory, History, and Practice. A Manual
for the Medical and Legal Professions* (London: John Bale, Sons/Danielsson, 1924), 318.

17. Ibid., 37.

the Devil's own children, with Mammon for their God, and Procrustes his prophet: that is to say, all hunters after wealth; all puritans, and teetotallers by conviction; all devotees of art and beauty; all enemies of the light; all who wrest the living to the service of the inanimate" (297). A woman named Ambrosine falls in love with Cuanduine and tells him that love and beauty are the only things that matter in life. The hero blames her for wanting to poison him with a "barren love" and lectures her on the truth of life:

"Life survives only by sheer prodigality: prodigality in seed, prodigality in sowing. Like the sower, he scatters his seed broadcast on the wind: it is Death, the reaper, that conserves. And now the Devil has whispered [to] the noblest of God's creatures that he must be provident: he has wrapped the red story of life in a pale romance of love and beauty, as the flaming stars are veiled by the light of the moon; and man stands listening, bewitched, while Mammon and Death and the Devil await his abdication. The first of living creatures, shall he be the first to fail in the fight?" (299)

Cuanduine's campaign in favor of natural life in the form of the wild-flowers and songbirds meets with little success in Ireland. The first crowd he addresses goes berserk with rage; on a second occasion, he is greeted with great roars of laughter. The English press subsequently reports that "renewed political and sectarian strife appears to be breaking out in Ireland as a result of the speeches of a man named Cooney, evidently a Bolshevik" (201). Having failed with his countrymen, Cuanduine moves to England at the invitation of Lord Cumbersome, a newspaper magnate. His lectures are well received by large audiences, and the newspapers praise the "sheer brilliance" of his "whimsical satire," "trenchant criticism," and "deliberately topsy-turvy viewpoint" (260). The self-reflexive nature of these comments places O'Duffy, along with Cuanduine, in distinguished company, for "what Cuanduine said of mankind and his works that evening was not very different in substance or intent from what has been set down in their books by the great satirists of the world: by Lucian, by Juvenal, by Martial, by Rabelais, by Swift, by Voltaire, by Samuel Butler, by Bernard Shaw" (260). Cuanduine initially thinks he is making more progress with the English: "How ready they are to acknowledge their own wickedness and laugh at their own folly; how eager to admit themselves in the wrong" (261). Before the satire turns into a moral tract, however, the text begins to cast doubt on its own effectiveness and to question whether satire can ever be successful in changing the status quo. Encouraged by his success, Cuanduine urges "the immediate liberation of the song-birds and wild flowers from Goshawk's control" (264), only to be greeted with coldness and silence. Now that Cuanduine has ceased to be an entertainer and become a man with a mission, his audience dwindles. His friend Ambrosine tells him: "Like the great satirists of the past, you have moved the people to laugh at their follies, but not to renounce them" (300). Like them, Cuanduine is doomed to fail in his mission. Human nature does not change and neither, it seems, do the satirists, who never learn from previous failed attempts and who, generation after generation, persist in trying to change the world even while they are aware of the futility of this task. Satirists, after all, are human too.

The limitations of satire and of the satirist's authority to pronounce on weighty matters are also implicit in the narrator's use of references to other texts to back up his claims. Having appropriated the hero Cuchulain from the *Táin Bó Cúailnge*, O'Duffy inserts further references to the epic into his narrative: *King Goshawk and the Birds* begins with the "pillow talk" of Goshawk and his wife Guzzelinda concerning the ownership of the world's songbirds. In case the reader thinks that some of these events are too strange to be believed, O'Duffy issues an invitation to "poke your misbelieving nose into the pages of the Book of Leinster or the Book of the Dun Cow or the Yellow Book of Leccan, where all these things are faithfully recorded, with a good deal more that I spare you" (36). Elsewhere in *King Goshawk and the Birds* O'Duffy incorporates a ten-page parodic newspaper into his narrative, including news items, advertisements, society columns, and an editorial, which he uses in part to satirize contemporary attitudes toward such diverse issues as crime, entertainment, and divorce. The newspaper also reports incidents from the Ulster Cycle: there are, for example, accounts of the naming of Cuchulain, and of the events that took place at Bricriu's Feast, in "Mr. Brickyew's residence" (257). The truth of the accounts in the ancient epics and the modern newspapers is equally open to doubt, but the narrator comments: "For myself, I think the chroniclers are the more trustworthy, as they are certainly the more entertaining; for, if they lie, they lie for the fun of it, whereas the journalists lie for pay, or through sheer inability to observe or report correctly" (59). This argument is similar to Mac Taill's defense of Oisín in Darrell Figgis's *The Return of the*

Hero: the value of stories does not reside in their message, for that is open to interpretation, but in their capacity to entertain.

O'Duffy's description of the celebration of the Centenary of Bernard Shaw in the hypothetical future of *King Goshawk and the Birds* makes clear the extent to which the satirist's art is futile, even counterproductive. Shaw has become the hero of Dublin's millionaires, politicians, and archbishops, who attend a great dinner in praise of the "innocent gaiety" (252) of the plays of this "imperial asset": "in these days of polemical art it was refreshing to take up such a classic as *Mrs. Warren's Profession* or *Getting Married,* and give oneself to the pure enjoyment of Shaw's delightful human creations, untroubled by the cloven hoof of the propagandist, so commonly obtruded in the so-called plays of the present generation" (251). The millionaires' misinterpretation of the "intentions" behind Shaw's plays may be laughable, but it is also shrewd in that it renders Shaw's social criticism ineffective without the use of antagonism or hostility. At the same time, the very possibility of an "innocent" reading of Shaw's works—a literal reading that is oblivious to his use of irony—problematizes the objectives and the effectiveness of O'Duffy's own satire. In fact, O'Duffy invites such a nonsatirical reading of his own work by prefacing one particularly critical passage—in which the Philosopher demonstrates to Cuanduine the evils of capitalism by taking him on a tour of the world—with an authorial disclaimer deploring "the intrusion at this point of some regrettably grave and disturbing matter into the even flow of my hitherto frolicsome, adventurous, and, I hope, artistically constructed narrative. Believe me that I do so with no intention of harrowing your feelings or pricking your consciences: which is a liberty I should be the very last to venture on" (175). O'Duffy deliberately places himself along with Shaw and other socialists in a position similar to that of the Philosopher in *King Goshawk and the Birds:* social critics are either denounced, ignored, or willfully misinterpreted, but they do not change the world. Given this state of affairs, no single ideological position ultimately has the authority to make the world a better place. Where the question of the birds and the flowers is concerned, therefore, O'Duffy depicts all hues of the political spectrum as equally hostile and incapable of dealing with the question in other than meaningless social and economic terms. The right-wing papers condemn Cuanduine's "anarchical proposal" as "a violent attack upon the rights of property and the freedom of the individual" (265); the moderate newspapers warn that "we must not mistake a poet's dream for a practical possibility" (266); while two "wretched little sheets" representative of the extreme left propose that the only way to keep the birds and flowers out of private hands is to nationalize them, or to abolish them altogether (267).

The satirist, in this view, is little more than a clown or a comedian who makes people laugh. Counterproductive as it may seem, however, carnivalized laughter may in fact be the strongest weapon against the forces of darkness. After all, Cuanduine describes himself as "The Hound of Man: the messenger of life: the laughter of God" (298). Cuanduine realizes he has failed in all the tasks he had set himself: "I have not freed the song-birds nor the wild flowers; I have not taught men the wisdom of Charity; I have not taught them the folly of fighting" (308). The Philosopher advises him that he may yet teach people to fight decently; now that he has given up on the birds and flowers, he finally has time to settle the ongoing dispute between the Wolfians and the Lambians in the "Not-Very-Far-East," where the Wolfian leader, Nervolini, has persisted in defying the League of Nations. The reference is, of course, to Mussolini, whose dictatorial power was well established by January 1925, having been endorsed by the—doubtless fraudulent—1924 elections. In a final epic gesture, Cuanduine retrieves from the museum the sword his father Cuchulain "had lost on Baile's Strand the time the druids set him to fight the waves of the sea in atonement for killing his son Conlaoch" (312), and "shook great circles of light that dazzled even the sailors of the Wolfian fleet and filled them with forebodings of doom" (312–13). Nervolini demands Cuanduine's surrender, whereupon the hero challenges the dictator to a duel and humiliates him in single combat. Then "he advanced upon Nervolini, and, taking him by the scruff of the neck, he bent him across his knee and slippered him very soundly" (317). Afterward, Cuanduine appears with Nervolini on the balcony of the leader's palace:

There stood Cuanduine leaning over the marble balustrade, and balanced upon one hand was their revered and worshipped lord, Nervolini the Fifth, the Great, the Earth-shaker. There he dangled with his breeches down, as red as the setting sun of Wolfia's glory. For a moment the great people of Wolfia were silent in stupefaction; then they did what a great people could only do in the circumstances: they burst into a roar of laughter that shattered every pane of glass in the windows of

Wolfopolis, and reverberated from the encircling hills over the waters of the sea to the Lambian coasts beyond. (318)

The dictator's perspective is, literally, turned upside down, and the display of his bottom is "one of the most common uncrowning gestures throughout the world."[18] From then on there is peace between the Wolfians and the Lambians. Bakhtin stresses that laughter "overcomes fear, for it knows no inhibitions, no limitations. Its idiom is never used by violence and authority."[19] This type of carnival laughter is not purely negative: it is liberating laughter in reaction to a crisis, in which ridicule of the authority figure, dangling upside down with his trousers around his knees, is fused with rejoicing at the renewal of life.

Laughter is as paradoxical and ambiguous as anything in *King Goshawk and the Birds:* it is used against Cuanduine when he attempts to preach the gospel of the birds and the flowers, but it also has the power to bring down dictators. Absolute authority demands absolute seriousness; laughter is therefore a subversive weapon. The satirist uses laughter to undermine reigning ideologies; but the moment the serious message underlying his own satire is revealed, it becomes itself an authoritative statement, and the satirist finds himself staring into the barrel of his own gun. The satirist is caught in a trap of his own making and can never make ultimate pronouncements; he can only adopt the attitude of the Philosopher in *King Goshawk and the Birds:* "Was he happy? Was he sad? Wisdom brings neither happiness nor sadness but a remarkable lack of both: for happiness is possible only where there is a sense of finality, and the wise man knows there is finality in nothing; by which knowledge he also escapes sadness" (11).

18. M. M. Bakhtin, *Rabelais and His World,* trans. Hélène Iswolsky (Bloomington: Indiana University Press, 1984), 373, note 2.

19. Ibid., 90.

chapter three

"Fantastically Utopian and Impossible"

The Spacious Adventures of the Man in the Street

The second volume of Eimar O'Duffy's Cuanduine trilogy, *The Spacious Adventures of the Man in the Street,* inverts the perspective of *King Goshawk and the Birds.* While Cuchulain is in temporary possession of the grocer's clerk O'Kennedy's body, the latter's spirit floats off into space and arrives in the city of Bulnid on the planet Rathé, "a great world just like our own, with hills and rivers, and green fields, and roaring oceans breaking on its beaches" (6).[1] He enters the world just in time to witness the execution of a man called Ydenneko. Before departing to his eternal sleep, the man's ghost reveals to a puzzled O'Kennedy that the death penalty had been his punishment for committing an act of carelessness (one of the worst crimes on Rathé), but that in fact he died of fear seconds before being shot, thus conveniently leaving an uninjured body for O'Kennedy to borrow. The story of *The Spacious Adventures of the Man in the Street* is narrated retrospectively by O'Kennedy himself: it is his lengthy explanation for his absence to his employer, Mr. Gallagher, and is followed by a humble plea to be taken back into his job as a grocer's assistant.

O'Kennedy is a staunch defender of the capitalist values prevalent on Earth, and his attitude is therefore the opposite of that of both Cuchulain and Cuanduine. In fact, his outlook is closer to that of their archenemy, Goshawk: "The Rentheans seem to have no sense of urban land values. Think of those vast acres, which might have brought in millions in rent, lying waste under grass and trees. Think of the priceless opportunities for the speculator in real estate, and not one solitary Renthean with the grip or en-

---

1. Eimar O'Duffy, *The Spacious Adventures of the Man in the Street* (London: Macmillan, 1928); all page references in the text are to this edition.

terprise to take advantage of them. Well, said I to myself, here's the chance for you, my son. Just give me time to find my feet and learn a little of their ways, and I'll be top dog in this planet. Damn me, I said, I'll be Goshawk to these birds" (109). From the moment O'Kennedy arrives on Rathé he enters into discussions with the Ratheans on aspects of their society from art to politics and morality, which—in an analogy with Cuchulain and Cuanduine in the first book—he fails entirely to understand. O'Kennedy's inability to pick up even the most obvious parallels between practices on Earth and on Rathé undermines his authority as a critic and a commentator, and it is this lack of insight that eventually contributes significantly to the failure of his ambitious plan to become the leader of Rathé. Vivian Mercier saw this quality of O'Kennedy's as a failing of the book: "It is a great pity that O'Duffy does not sustain the character of O'Kennedy throughout. . . . If O'Kennedy were more often 'in character,' *The Spacious Adventures* would be much more pointed in its satire."[2] However, if O'Kennedy's character were more consistent, the satire would not be Menippean: no single authoritarian voice is allowed to monopolize the discussion.

Where politics is concerned, O'Duffy's main interest lies in economic theories: he relentlessly satirizes the evils of capitalism and materialism by means of exaggeration, literalism, and especially utopian inversion. Mercier finds that he "plays the topsy-turvy game with a crazy logic."[3] Most of the names in *The Spacious Adventures* are simple anagrams or inversions (of Dublin, Earth, and O'Kennedy, for example)—a trick "obviously derived from Butler's *Erewhon*."[4] Life on the planet Rathé, too, is a semi-inverted, semiutopian version of life on Earth as it was so graphically depicted in the trilogy's first volume. In *King Goshawk and the Birds*, Dublin is depicted as a city literally ruined by corrupt and incompetent politicians. *The Spacious Adventures of the Man in the Street* presents the opposite picture. In contrast to Dublin, nobody lies or steals in Bulnid; the arts are held in high esteem, and the city is clean and its people well dressed. There is no mass production, and factories are models of cooperative effort. The economy uses no

2. Mercier, "The Satires of Eimar O'Duffy," 331–32.

3. Ibid., 330.

4. Alf Mac Lochlainn, "Eimar O'Duffy: A Bibliographical Biography," *Irish Book*, 1, 2 (1959–1960): 37.

money, working instead via a system of controlled exchange of goods; there is equal distribution of wealth, and no poverty, unemployment, or pollution, but there are restrictions on the availability of certain nonessential goods which the Ratheans accept because they are not materialistic by nature and upbringing. The only thing that is not pleasing to the eye is the natural landscape, which consists of ugly blue, red, and yellow hills (unlike the beautiful green hills surrounding dirty Dublin), in spite of incessant Bulnidian efforts to improve its appearance.

O'Kennedy is unappreciative of the clean, safe, and egalitarian society he encounters in Bulnid and denounces it as primitive. To improve conditions, he advocates the introduction of money, mass production, and remuneration on the basis of merit. Ironically, the Bulnidians are dubious that such an impossibly utopian system could function anywhere: "'What unpractical dreamers you must be' smiled her Ladyship. 'Idealists, of course, I admit, but how utterly unpractical! How can you possibly estimate with any sort of accuracy the comparative values of each and every trade? And after that, how are you to proportion the houses? Why, my dear boy'—with an impatient shrug of the shoulders—'the whole thing is fantastically Utopian and impossible. It could never work out in practice'" (166–67). O'Kennedy, staunch defender of private enterprise, objects that the system functions quite well on Earth, but everything he says to prove his point condemns it further in Rathean eyes. In his turn, O'Kennedy fails to understand how the Bulnidian system, operating as it does on the principles of common sense and individual responsibility, can survive at all without giving rise to massive and unbridled corruption.

O'Kennedy's ideological conflict with the Ratheans ends in a stalemate, because the Rathean model is eventually disqualified as an alternative option for the people of Earth by the fundamental wickedness of the human race. Yasint (the voice of "Sanity") tells O'Kennedy: "Every objection you have made to our institutions simply demonstrates the silliness and malignity of the race from which you spring. The only difficulties you have seen in their working are such as would not arise unless we were all as worthless as yourselves" (183). The argument between O'Kennedy and the Ratheans about the merits of their respective judicial systems is similarly aborted. There is very little crime on Rathé and no prisons, but when O'Kennedy inquires how they deal with the likes of cold-blooded murderers, he discovers that such crimes are unknown in Bulnid: "What a dreadful world yours must be," they exclaim (205). The view that Ratheans are simply better than Earthlings problematizes the conclusion that within the Cuanduine satire Rathean society serves as a viable alternative to the established situation on Earth; both perspectives represented in the conflict are, in one way or another, invalidated.

Menippean satire typically operates on three planes: heaven, earth, and the netherworld. The planet Rathé is divided into three parts analogous to these planes: a Sunny Zone; a Middle Zone, consisting of shady zones and twilight zones; and a Dark Zone. The sunnier the climate, the more civilized its inhabitants, as O'Kennedy is allowed to discover during his travels to these various lands. The superior creatures live in the Lands of the Sun. Their children are born very highly evolved, and they subsequently strive to increase the power of the mind and to dispense with the body as much as possible, preferably altogether; love is regarded as a shameful weakness, only to be tolerated in the very young. Mature Sunlanders discuss philosophy, think, and pray. Not surprisingly, O'Kennedy soon finds himself bored with them. In their extreme asceticism, aloofness, and virtuousness the Sunlanders suffer from the same drawbacks as Swift's Houyhnhnms: their moral superiority is undermined by their almost total lack of human warmth.

Given this parallel with *Gulliver's Travels*, one might expect the inhabitants of Rathé's Dark Hemisphere to resemble Swift's Yahoos, and to be morally crude and physically disgusting. O'Duffy, however, prefers to express gross materialism and lack of civilization in economic terms, embodied in *The Spacious Adventures* by the inhabitants of the capital of the Black Lands, the city of Harpaxe (from the Greek for "rapine"). The Harpaxeans are devoted servants of darkness, and renowned for their exploitation of other Ratheans. The Outlanders in particular have allowed themselves to be enslaved by the Harpaxean overlords, who are "paying in meagre doles of fungus for the labour of serfs who are seemingly as patient as tinkers' asses" (295). O'Kennedy, however, finds Bulnidian accounts of Harpaxean cruelty greatly exaggerated: "I learnt that the Harpaxeans are most considerate masters, supplying their serfs with medical attention, keeping their houses and drains in repair, and in general doing for their comfort all those things which they are too ignorant or busy to do for themselves. The only thing in the nature of cruelty that I could discover is their habit of sterilising every man who has had two children; but even this is done painlessly" (296). Admittedly, many Outlanders are eaten by "hordes of horrible carnivorous beasts called Showps" (296), but the Harpaxeans, while honestly regretting the carnage, "think that to be eaten by a showp is no great inconvenience to an Outlander,—or at any rate far less so than to one of themselves" (297).

In the Cuanduine trilogy O'Duffy's most persistent satirical attacks are reserved for what he calls "Procrusteanism." Whereas in *King Goshawk and the Birds* his prime target was reproductive Procrusteanism (represented by Saint Progressa), in *The Spacious Adventures* he satirizes the effects of economic Procrusteanism. The Harpaxean system of economic thought requires people to adapt their personal circumstances to their economic conditions, rather than vice versa—in the most literal sense of the word. Typically, satire transfers a philosophical issue into the material realm, and in this instance concrete physical mutilation graphically represents what O'Duffy would regard as crippling economic practices:

In obedience to the law of mass production all boots for adult Outlanders were made the same size and shape, and the feet of the people were trimmed to suit them. For the same reason the hips of the women were compressed so as to make them fit the standard breeches worn by both sexes. It was also customary to eradicate the hair and trim the nose and ears to minimise the danger of getting caught in the machinery. Altogether the Outlanders had shown a most reasonable spirit of compromise in grappling with the problems of a highly industrialised civilisation, and a praiseworthy readiness to adapt themselves to the conditions of the age which had produced them. (313)

Outlanders also have their legs shortened artificially in infancy to adapt themselves to the size of their houses, since there are not enough bricks to build bigger dwellings. During O'Kennedy's visit they initiate a campaign to demand the right to neck-shortening since "without a shorter neck further economic progress for the people is impossible" (316); without a neck, moreover, they "can no longer be compelled to bow the neck in servitude" (317). In addition, they argue that, since they do not have enough to eat, an obvious remedy to the problem is to reduce the size of their bodies. O'Kennedy ridicules these practices but at the same time fails to see their metaphorical correlation with the economic theories of Earth which, on another occasion, he himself enthusiastically defends against the criticism of the Bulnidians.

At the same time that Procrustean thinking is reducing the bodies, and the dignity, of the Outlanders in the Dark Hemisphere to a minimum, the status of their pets is being raised proportionately as a direct consequence of the country's economic principles. While domestic human slaves serving the Harpaxeans are surgically deprived of all their human feelings and emotions (by a process called "pithing"), dogs are implanted with "the excised tissue obtained in the process of pithing servants" (338). This process is described to O'Kennedy as "an excellent example of the economic exploitation of the by-products of industry, such as would only be possible in a highly competitive civilisation" (338). The absurdity of a society that encourages dogs to become human, while humans are reduced to something less than animals, all in the name of economic progress, hardly needs further comment. It is further put into perspective by one of the epigraphic "QUOTATIONS A PROPOS" on the flyleaf of *The Spacious Adventures of the Man in the Street,* a citation from Mr. Gordon Selfridge, Junior: *"There is not a single commodity this world uses that someone or other at some time or other hasn't made a fortune out of it."* O'Duffy labels the statement "GREAT THOUGHTS FROM THE CONCRETE AGE."

In addition to cities with thinly disguised familiar names such as Bulnid, Donlon, and Israp, Rathé's Middle Zone also includes Tigers' Island, referred to by O'Kennedy's friend Camino as "a sort of asylum for hopeless cases. People were sent there who made nuisances of themselves by persistently breaking the law, and yet were not dangerous enough to justify their execution" (201). Having been warned that the inhabitants of the island are utter savages, simpleminded, licentious, and totally uncivilized, O'Kennedy is astonished to discover that Tigers' Island is much like any large city on Earth: "There were buses and trams and lorries and taxis and delivery vans all rushing along in the homeliest manner. There were bustling people on the sidewalk dressed in proper breeches and skirts like ourselves. There were ten-storeyed houses, and smoking chimneys, and advertisement hoardings, and yelling newsboys, and policemen, and loud speakers and skysigns, and a millionaire in his car, and a group of unemployed at the corner, and all the other signs of a progressive community" (210). Delighted, O'Kennedy concludes that "these people weren't savages. They were almost as civilised as we are" (211). The satire carnivalizes the familiar, civilized world by placing it in an alien context: the "progressive community" of O'Kennedy's minority perspective is, according to the dominant, Rathean viewpoint, an isolated group of socially ill-adapted outcasts. O'Kennedy's identification with the islanders only serves to prove his lack of refinement in Rathean eyes.

In accordance with the principle that "Bulnid" represents a distorted mirror image of "Dublin," O'Duffy's method of depicting Rathean practices in the second part of the trilogy often consists of more or less straightforward inversion of common practices as they would be found in Ireland and the Western world at large. Bulnidians worship the Devil, as taught by the Great Book of the Ratheans—"In the beginning was Darkness; and Darkness was everywhere; and all was Darkness" (217)—but their beliefs are continually put to the test by the conflict between science and religion.

"At one time our scientists used to teach that the sky was a metal sphere revolving round Rathé at a distance of 4004 miles, and that the sun, moons and stars were fixed to it. Of course all this was exploded long ago by the imagination of poets and religious thinkers, and only the most lowly-evolved people continued to believe in it. But lately the scientists have been trying to regain their influence by pretending they never taught that the old theory was *literally* true, and claiming that it is true in a figurative sense and therefore doesn't really clash with modern religious discoveries. They've regained some ground in consequence—that's what they call the scientific revival—but their real grip is gone for good, and your coming will finish it. . . . (63–64)

On Rathé, mathematicians are the equivalent of Earth's theologians, and Rathean lives are guided by the laws of mathematics. Priests called "diabologians" lead services in gloomy churches where darkness is worshiped, and where hatred, selfishness, and materialism are preached. The Devil's prophet is Procrustes, and his main message, that children are an abomination, is similar to that of Saint Progressa. O'Kennedy serves as devil's advocate among the Ratheans, for to his grocer's ears the values propounded in the diabologian's sermon sound eminently sensible; he is, however, disappointed in the response of the Bulnidians, who lead their lives in direct violation of the precepts of Procrustes. They "prayed on their knees to Darkness, and his name was ever on their lips. But they obeyed not the commands of Darkness, but increased and multiplied and loved one another, and recreated the beauty of Rathé" (219). O'Kennedy finds the attitude of the Ratheans toward their religion incomprehensible: "A more complete system of hypocrisy and superstition I cannot imagine" (230).

When O'Kennedy questions the Rathean wisdom of relying on "a dubiously worded book written thousands of years ago" (251), instead of relying upon scientific discovery, he fails to see that religion is observed in much the same way on Earth—but then, as Frank Palmeri has pointed out, characters in narrative satire are typically literalists incapable of reading metaphors: "Recognitions, like metaphors, depend on seeing resemblances between previously unrelated persons or objects; consistent with its omitting of significant recognitions, narrative satire also avoids metaphoric transferences, emphasizing literal meaning instead. Satire's depiction of reversals without recognitions helps determine its unresolved, problematic conclusions."[5] If Rathean society is a utopian alternative to our own, this is only because, like most Earthlings, Ratheans do not follow their beliefs to the letter. The point is, however, that even if the Ratheans are as irrational and inconsistent in the observance of their beliefs as the people of Earth, their inverted world is nevertheless a much happier place.

Other inversions in the book are less utopian and, while reflecting less positively on the Bulnidians, serve rather to point directly to questionable practices on Earth. In Rathean schools there are no lessons, and there is no punishment and no compulsion. The boys have complete authority over their masters, who are there merely to help and encourage them, and whom they are allowed to flog. The Ratheans admit that teachers are often beaten for the wrong reasons, but by and large fail to agree with O'Kennedy that "the infliction of the punishment on a particular part of the body was an unnecessary degradation" (114). O'Kennedy himself, at the same time, believes that "discipline" is necessary in schools in order to make boys do their work, although he is forced to admit that this discipline has not so far managed to eradicate ignorance from his world. By arguing against the other's practices and defending their own, without realizing that they are each other's mirror images, the characters unwittingly make a convincing case against corporal punishment in any form or context.

O'Duffy uses a similar technique to deal with issues of love, sex, and marriage, which are of even more central concern in *The Spacious*

5. Palmeri, *Satire*, 4.

Adventures of the Man in the Street than they were in *King Goshawk and the Birds:* the issue, in the form of an elaborate analogy, takes up at least half the book. The Bulnidians on Rathé regard eating in exactly the same way that Dubliners regard sex, whereas the former feel about sex the way Dubliners feel about eating. Bulnidians have liberal views on sex and marriage, but any mention of food or hunger fills them with outrage, or makes them cringe with embarrassment, even though they are secretly obsessed with the subject. Rathean novelists can apparently write about little else: take, for example, a work entitled "The New Politician" by "Mr. Slew" concerning "a man of brilliant talents but insatiable appetite, who, after a youth misspent in pursuit of the fruits of the field, at last settles down with a dainty cherry tree" (131). O'Duffy's reference here is to H. G. Wells's *The New Machiavelli* (1911). Or take the book called "A Picture of My Youth" which "gave a horribly detailed description of the effect on a clever and imaginative boy of all this suppression, and thwarting, and confusion with guilt of a perfectly healthy appetite" (132–33). The allusion is, of course, to James Joyce's *A Portrait of the Artist as a Young Man* (1916).

O'Kennedy's attitude toward food is much like Cuchulain's attitude toward sex in *King Goshawk and the Birds:* he does not understand what all the fuss is about. Just as Cuchulain commits one faux pas after another by talking openly about sex, O'Kennedy's repeated requests for something to eat drive his hosts nearly to distraction. The implication of the satirical analogy between both types of appetite seems obvious: since both are natural, physical phenomena, it makes no sense to make a moral distinction between them, and since eating is not a controversial issue in the world as we know it, sex should not be either. This conclusion, however, becomes problematic if we heed the Philosopher in *King Goshawk and the Birds* when he explains to Cuchulain that the painful feeling experienced by O'Kennedy's body "is called hunger, and it is the prick of the goad with which King Flesh reminds us that we are his slaves, forcing us to cram ourselves with bread and meat, which we metabolise into energy, which we must use to procure more bread and meat, thus remaining in a vicious circle of uselessness, eating to live and living to eat, instead of turning our minds to the pursuit of wisdom" (49–50). Eating is not necessarily the innocent business we think it is; for each voice in the trilogy there is a countervoice, and no conclusion is allowed to stand as the final word.

The equation between food and sex is worked out by O'Duffy in great detail: he even invents a kind of "food brothels" where Ratheans go in secret to indulge in meals which, though invariably highly praised by the keeper of the house, are of dubious quality and not infrequently lead to a bad case of indigestion.[6] He also sets out the various philosophies held by Ratheans as to why people eat in the first place: the orthodox view states that nothing should be eaten without the express intention of manufacturing it into tissue and energy; the advanced and opposite view is that eating is a pleasurable process unrelated to any purpose whatsoever (146).

Ratheans, and especially Bulnidians, are "monophagous" as prescribed by the laws of mathematics, and O'Kennedy is told that in order to eat he needs a license. In a manner reminiscent of Cuchulain's infelicitous proposal to the girl in the Bon Ton Tennis Club, O'Kennedy immediately demands a license for the first fruit that comes to mind, "one of those big yellow things" (119), before it is explained to him that once he has chosen he will never thereafter be able to change his mind, and that a "decree of tmesis" (from the Greek for "division") or license for a change of diet is very hard to obtain. O'Kennedy holds forth at length on the unreasonableness of this arrangement, explaining the eating situation on Earth. Mr Juicewit ("Jesuit"), the Rathean Professor of Mathematics, is particularly horrified by his description of such "'hideous debauchery'" (123), and refuses to believe O'Kennedy when he maintains that this freedom actually leads to very little overindulgence. O'Kennedy's arguments (in favor of greater freedom of choice but against overindulging) fall on deaf ears, since the final and unanswerable Bulnidian argument is always that, like it or not, "you can't get away from mathematics" (137). O'Kennedy's subsequent political campaign to change the dietary habits of the Bulnidians is unsuccessful, and even those who can see his point of view (Yasint, for example, who represents the voice of sanity) argue that the law is better than any of the alternatives, given the weakness and irresponsibility of the human race.

Up to this point in the debate O'Kennedy has adopted what appears to

---

6. Kurt Vonnegut uses a similar analogy in *Breakfast of Champions* (New York: Dell, 1974). Science fiction writer Kilgore Trout makes up a novel in which an astronaut lands on a distant planet where eating is considered a pornographic act. Prostitutes "offered them eggs and oranges and milk and butter and peanuts and so on. The whores couldn't actually deliver these goodies, of course" (61).

be a logical and reasonable stance; however, his credibility is impaired when his Rathean girlfriend rejects his marriage proposal but offers to go on a honeymoon with him instead. Ratheans, it turns out, have no formal marriage ceremony, and a union can be broken off at any time by either party. They do get married, however, because "marriage is a healthy and very agreeable habit which had gradually grown up and been found generally suitable to human needs" (156). Shocked beyond belief at this immorality, O'Kennedy starts a long discussion on sex, marriage, and divorce that repeats almost verbatim all the arguments of the debate on Rathean food laws, but now with the positions reversed. Neither party is capable of recognizing that both arguments are exactly identical. After his attempt, and failure, to alter the monophagous eating habits of the Bulnidians, O'Kennedy paradoxically starts a campaign to introduce and enforce the idea of monogamous marriage-till-death-us-do-part, with an equal lack of success. If, metaphorically speaking, the two arguments are essentially identical, it must be concluded that O'Kennedy argues both in favor of and against the same notion, as do the Ratheans. This makes a mockery of the polemic between the two opposed ideologies, and undermines both positions.

O'Duffy elaborated on the issue of birth control at some length in *King Goshawk and the Birds,* and indirectly returns to the problem in the second volume of the trilogy in the context of the discussion on Rathean food laws. Here, however, the polarized, oxymoronic dialogue typical of satire is surprisingly absent, for even O'Kennedy, who advocates such radical food law reforms, draws the line at the practice of "food control," or taking emetics after a meal:

"Now it was an article of faith with all advanced people that this pretty practice was not only justifiable but necessary, and not only necessary but highly meritorious. . . . Indeed, Food Control, as they called it, had become for them an essential part of the scheme of things. It was simply taken for granted. Well, I couldn't stand for nonsense of that sort, but told them flat that the thing was disgusting and indecent, to say nothing of the danger to their health. . . . It shocked the advanced folk even worse than my attack on the food-law had shocked the respectable." (146)

Just as O'Kennedy balks at food control—although he does end the debate by saying that "if you think vomiting a pretty operation, go on vomiting"

(148)—the Ratheans, who are so sexually liberated, do not practice birth control by means of artificial methods. In each of these instances, O'Kennedy and the Ratheans present the laws of nature as a third alternative to extreme and ideologically opposed positions. O'Kennedy advises Ratheans that eating is neither shameful (the orthodox view) nor beautiful (the advanced view), but only natural, and therefore should not have to be regulated by law in the first place: "Why can't you just take the thing easy and natural? Most of you are best suited by a monophagous diet, and I think the lot of you are healthier when you stick to one fruit at a time. Well, why not recognise that and stop worrying about the subject? You know all this advanced humbug about free eats and the rest of it is only possible if you go in for this food-control business, and that you must know, if you've any sense of delicacy at all, to be a very nasty practice—" (147–48). Ratheans, on the other hand, have found that nature regulates and protects decency and traditional family values better than any form of moral or restrictive legislation, which is often counterproductive:

At first sight you would imagine that they [Rathean women] had an inferior status. They don't attend the Assembly, for instance; but that is only because their right to do so has never been disputed, and they have found by experience that they aren't much use there. Neither do they enter men's professions, for the same reason. But in their own sphere they are accorded a supremacy like nothing on our earth. Motherhood is recognised not only as the greatest profession for women, but the most important of all professions, and the whole Rathean social and economic code is arranged accordingly. . . . Their families are of moderate size, not limited to two children like the English and French, nor going to the length of a dozen of whom ten die in infancy, like in holy Ireland, but averaging from five to eight. This they manage without any artificial methods because, in spite of all their immorality, they are rather austere in their habits. (190–91)

The tenor of such passages further invalidates the kind of irresponsibly liberal behavior Cuchulain displays in *King Goshawk and the Birds* and modifies that novel's seemingly radical criticism of puritanism and restrictive legislation in Ireland.

Nature in this context takes up the middle ground between two ideological extremes, an uncommon device in narrative satire, which usually excludes a middle. The implication of this is that every form of dogmatism or extremism is a crime against nature, a conclusion that underlines the sig-

nificance of the trilogy's seemingly flimsy frame story, Goshawk's transgression of the laws of nature when he imprisons all the songbirds and buys
up all the wildflowers, and Cuanduine's subsequent mission to restore the
natural order. Yet the satire does not allow the middle ground to prevail.
Greed and corruption have turned the human race against nature, and
therefore against its own survival. Cuanduine's crusade in *King Goshawk
and the Birds* was doomed to failure, and the book ended with the hero's alternative mission to end the war between the Wolfians and the Lambians,
and to put a stop to the authoritarian rule of the dictator Nervolini. At the
end of *The Spacious Adventures of the Man in the Street*, by contrast,
O'Kennedy attempts, Goshawk-like and by means of a military coup, to impose a capitalist economic system on the citizens of Rathé. Although
Cuanduine and O'Kennedy represent opposite ends of the ideological spectrum, they are both misfits among alien people in alien worlds, and equally unsuccessful in changing their ways.

In order to carry out his plan of leading the Procrusteans into battle
against the Middle Zone and of taking over the leadership of Rathé by revolutionary force, O'Kennedy—now referred to by his followers as the "Man
from the Stars"—teams up with two dubious characters who are as dissat-
isfied as he is with the placid and utopian character of Rathé. One is the
would-be capitalist entrepreneur Bhos Kwashog (an anagram of Goshawk),
who is about to be banished to Tigers' Island when O'Kennedy enlists his
services; the second is the thoroughly unsavory and unreliable Ensulas
("Sensual"), who initially served as O'Kennedy's guide to the dubious eater-
ies of Bulnid's seamy side, and who is particularly fascinated by his friend's
tales about the unlimited types and quantities of food freely available on
Earth. O'Kennedy convinces himself that black is white and describes
him as

really a thoroughly sensible and decent fellow, and without exception the finest man
in the whole of Rathé. . . . To a superficial observer his pimply complexion and corpulent figure were decidedly unattractive; and he had a queer sidling sort of walk,
which, coupled with his furtive way of looking at you, and his hesitating, almost
whispering voice, was hardly calculated to inspire immediate confidence. . . . He
had moreover a weak, somewhat irritating giggle, and a whole heap of nervous
mannerisms (among which I remember chiefly a trick of starting guiltily when one
came on him unawares) so that altogether one would have had to look very deep in-

deed for any sign of those magnificent characteristics which raised him far above all other Ratheans and were eventually to make us close friends and partners in the most colossal enterprise that ever shook the universe. (102–3)

In spite of the fact that he lacks any form of expertise in matters of combat, O'Kennedy is appointed as the military strategist of the campaign to take over the government of Rathé. It is not long before his armies are hopelessly confused and in a state of total chaos. Kwashog's organizing skills are needed to return a semblance of order to the disorganized troops, but in spite of this fiasco the general consensus remains that "the Man from the Stars must lead us into battle" (370). O'Kennedy's renewed confidence soon borders on hubris: "To think that I, with no advantages of birth or education, a mere nobody in my own land, should have come to this! By jove, it was stupendous" (372). However, as the general leads his armies into the epic Battle of the Plains of Yllab (a nearby town, or "bally"), his moment of glory is undercut by several instances of carnival slapstick. In contrast with Cuanduine, who at the end of *King Goshawk and the Birds* had gone into battle brandishing the flaming sword of his illustrious father Cuchulain, before dangling Nervolini over the edge of his balcony with his trousers down, O'Kennedy in his haste catches up his umbrella instead of a weapon as he rushes out of the palace, to discover the unfortunate mistake only as he is about to order the army's advance into battle. Several moments later his attempt to strike a heroic pose causes him to slip "as if [he] had trod on a banana peel" (375), and to fall, topsy-turvy, on his behind in the mud. The leader is decrowned: "The shock of that sit-down drove all the military spirit out of me, but of course I had to march on all the same, and beastly uncomfortable I felt too, with the twice-muddied umbrella gripped in my fist, and the soaked seat of my breeches clinging cold and clammy to my nether parts" (376). O'Kennedy's literal fall precedes his military collapse. The Ratheans suppress his violent revolution entirely by nonviolent means, "armed only with a soporific gas" (379).

In the deliberations that follow O'Kennedy's arrest, the Ratheans find his behavior so anomalous that they begin to have serious doubts whether he is a human being at all, and fit to be put on trial, or whether he should be destroyed as a dangerous animal. Eventually, however, given the "rudimentary reasoning powers," "primitive artistic instincts," and "elementary religious ideas" of his race, and in spite of a long list of "markedly simian indications" (381), the prisoner is given the benefit of the doubt, and the trial begins. Trials are common in Menippean satire as a means of testing the truth. Since what is at stake is "the testing of an *idea*, of a *truth*, and not the testing of a particular human character, whether an individual or a social type,"[7] such trials are really tests of the character's philosophical position in the world, and what is on trial is the philosophy rather than the individual. In this respect it is significant that there are no judges or solicitors on Rathé, but that the court consists of "a sort of committee of experts . . . who are called Gogaleths, or . . . Truth-Finders" (198); the judicial system is "designed specially to elicit the truth" (199). O'Kennedy is on trial as a representative of the human race and for defending Earth's economic ideas, which are themselves subjected to careful scrutiny by the court, rather than for his personal transgressions.

It is the nature of Earth's economic philosophy, then, rather than any crime committed by O'Kennedy, that receives the greatest attention of the Rathean Truth-Finder:

In the course of a prolonged and tedious cross-examination you utterly failed to produce any facts which disprove the *a priori* arguments which have prevented us from adopting a system of economics based on money and the principle of exchange. On the contrary, the conditions which you have described as obtaining in your world have perfectly confirmed all the conclusions to which abstract reasoning had already led us. For you must not imagine that this idea is a novelty in Rathé. Indeed it has always been a favourite theme with those cranks, Utopians, and other feeble-minded dreamers, who imagine that the admitted disadvantages of our existing system of fellowship and co-operation would vanish under a system of competition and exchange. But, as our economists have pointed out, a system of exchange, though excellent in theory, cannot work out in practice. (382–83)

The problem, he argues, is that money would cease to be a symbol and would become a commodity, after which the money would inevitably accumulate in the hands of a few, and one part of the community would become the hired servants of the other part. Such a "perverted science" of finance "could prove scarcity to be better than abundance, or a stone or a dog of more value than a man. It could prove birth a calamity and fertility a disease" (384). The result of its adoption would be that "vast masses of people

---

7. Bakhtin, *Dostoevsky's Poetics*, 114–15.

would lead dreary, narrow, purposeless lives, working at dull monotonous meaningless tasks in other people's service, dwelling in small, ugly houses in cheerless neighbourhoods, with moderate animal comforts, but starved of beauty, art, and joy, and drugged to all thinking" (385). "In short," the Truth-Finder concludes, "the consequences of our adopting a monetary system would, say our philosophers, be exactly what you have described as the accepted conditions in the world which you have come from" (385–86). Finding that O'Kennedy's extenuating plea, namely, the "honest desire to assist the progress of this world by imposing upon it the social-economic system which has conferred such benefits" on Earth (382), is in fact an aggravating factor, the court sentences O'Kennedy to death, reminding him that it was not the Ratheans, but O'Kennedy himself who pronounced the condemnation of his race.

At this point the second part of the Cuanduine trilogy comes full circle: O'Kennedy is taken to the great cemetery where his spirit first entered the planet of Rathé, and "there was enacted a scene which reproduced exactly that which [he] had observed as a spirit not so long before" (388). This time, Ydenneko's body is genuinely killed, and O'Kennedy's spirit drifts off beyond the stars, into outer blackness, asking the same kind of fundamental questions that were voiced by the spirit of Ydenneko at the beginning of the book: "Is there reward and vengeance? Is there eternal rest? Is there life everlasting? Does the Devil rule, or God? or does Chance solve all riddles?" (12). At the point of separation of body and spirit, caught between worlds, a dissociation from and questioning of the self takes place:

All that remained of Aloysius O'Kennedy, the Me that was in him and made him, was going out like the last red point on the wick of a blown-out candle. And it was just then that I realised somehow that Aloysius O'Kennedy was not such an important person as I had always imagined him. I looked at him in a queer detached sort of way as if he was somebody else, and asked myself what on earth he had ever been up to. . . . He had never thought anything worth thinking, or known anything worth knowing. What was he up to? What was he for? (390)

As soon as he has expressed it, O'Kennedy's urgent desire to find a purpose for himself-as-other brings his spirit face to face with a series of five different gods, all of whom engage him in conversation. These can be regarded as "threshold conversations," as Bakhtin calls them: encounters taking place on the boundary between worlds, and between one's own and someone else's consciousness.

The five gods who offer O'Kennedy's spirit their credentials are not independent authorities or representatives of a higher truth: they merely represent different ideologies existing on Earth. The first god, Moloch, is a monstrous, destructive being: "Thou shalt worship me with blood and thy wailing shall be as music in my ear. Bow down and adore me" (391). The second, Zeus, tells his disciples to "eat, drink, and be merry, for to-morrow you die. But keep thy fingers from my cup, and thine eyes from the woman of my desiring" (391). These two gods are easily dismissed when O'Kennedy tells them he does not believe in them and does not worship them.

The third god, however, represents something much closer to his own way of thinking. This is the capricious Omnipotent-Benevolent god, who tells O'Kennedy:

"I am the All Just; who chose one people, and left the rest to wallow in idolatry and abomination. I would have all men know the truth: therefore I spoke only to the West, and left the East in darkness; and to the West I spoke in so uncertain a voice that my words were interpreted in seventy senses, and men thought to please me by burning one another over the difference. I am he who damned mankind for one crime, and demanded a worse crime in reparation for it; and all this without imperilling my immutability. I am the Omnipotent-Benevolent; and if my deeds seem to belie my character, remember also that I am inscrutable. Believe in me, and you shall dwell in eternal bliss: reject me, and you shall be delivered to eternal torment." (392)

When O'Kennedy expresses his belief in this god—because he had always been told "not to question your ways, and that thinking would destroy my faith" (392–93)—the god, being unpredictable and capricious, begins to question the wisdom of this unquestioning faith: "You think me a perfectly credible figure? . . . Think again, Aloysius" (392). O'Kennedy is sorely disappointed when he learns from the god that no deed of his, however good, could ever merit eternal happiness. When he complains that this is unfair, the god leaves him to his own devices with the words, "if I were omnipotent, would I have made a mistake like you?" (396).

O'Kennedy's next encounter is with the god of science and reason, a woman who has "a steel triangle in one hand, a hypodermic syringe in the other, and a flayed dog writhing beneath her feet" (396), and claims to be "the god that man found it necessary to invent" (396). He dismisses her when she tells him that "the sum of your pleasures is less than the sum of your pains. Therefore your life is not worth living. Therefore you were better dead" (397).

She is followed by a strange figure: "It had the head and bust of a woman, but the rest of it was more or less masculine. . . . 'I am Beauty and Love' he said, smiling lusciously. 'I am the great god Moderntwaddlums. Am I not adorable?'" (398). This god combines what O'Duffy regarded as the worst excesses of modern thinking, including reproductive and economic Procrusteanism. Claiming that "love justifies all things" (399), the god urges his followers to enjoy themselves:

"Don't take on responsibility too early, or you'll be old before your time. Young people must be free to have a good-time, and how can they keep a car if they're tied down by children? Live your own life: Life isn't your concern anyway. Live your own life, even if you spend it hopping from one bedroom scene to another. Live your own life, even if that means playing and kissing away the earnings of other men. You aren't responsible for the way things are managed, so you may take the world as you find it. Other people would have a good time if you were down and out: why shouldn't you have a good time if—" (400)

This religion, however, is not for grocer's clerks like O'Kennedy: "The full free life can only be sustained by a system of privilege, which must be based upon the labour of the unintelligent and undistinguished" (401). Exit, therefore, Moderntwaddlums.

Eventually O'Kennedy comes face to face with the Devil, who informs him that the gods of his earlier encounters were not real, but created by O'Kennedy himself in his own image and likeness: a common technique of Menippean satire is to externalize the internal, and to concretize what is philosophical and psychological. The Devil, on the other hand, is no figment of the imagination: "I am the unimaginable and the undeniable. I am Darkness. I am the enemy of the gods. I am he that has marred all the gods of your making. I stand between you and the god that is to be" (402). In a topsy-turvy satirical universe, the Devil's voice is frequently the most truthful of all.

The ending of *The Spacious Adventures of the Man in the Street* establishes a direct link with the events described in the first volume of the Cuanduine trilogy and brings the story back to where it began. Just when O'Kennedy's spirit is about to fade away, it is returned to its original body by the hypnotic powers of the Philosopher Murphy. That body is at that moment lying in the ashpit of the kitchen garden of Castle Boodleguts, where Cuchulain had abandoned it in *King Goshawk and the Birds,* and it is in such a state that its original occupant hardly recognizes it when he puts it back on: "The feel of it was loose and unfamiliar—like as if it was a suit of clothes that had been worn by somebody three sizes too big for it: which indeed was exactly what had happened" (406). O'Kennedy is himself again; Cuchulain is back in Tír na nÓg; and Goshawk is still in possession of the birds and the flowers. Only the existence of a third volume, *Asses in Clover,* raises the possibility that the stalemate of the first two books of the Cuanduine trilogy may yet be broken.

chapter four

"This Isn't Utopia, You Know"

Asses in Clover

The dialectical structure of the Cuanduine trilogy leads one to expect a reconciliation of the opposite perspectives of the first two books in the third volume. In Menippean satire, which resists closure, this cannot, of course, be the case. *Asses in Clover* has often been criticized for being, in Robert Hogan's words, "much more rambling and ineffectual" than the first two satires. One of the reasons for this may well have been, as Hogan suggests, that O'Duffy was suffering acute physical pain during much of the writing.[1] Digressiveness and inconclusiveness are, however, integral elements of Menippean satire and by no means necessarily signs of authorial weakness. Menippean satire typically resists a conclusive conclusion; a common manifestation of this in all such texts is that, toward the end of the narrative, things fall apart, not because the center cannot hold, but because the satire has convincingly demonstrated that there is no center.

Asses in Clover takes place some time after Cuanduine has settled the dispute between the Wolfians and the Lambians described at the end of *King Goshawk and the Birds,* and shortly after O'Kennedy, the hero of *The Spacious Adventures of the Man in the Street,* has returned from his expedition to Rathé. By now, Goshawk has become lord and master of the whole earth, and all the songbirds are in the possession of his wife, Guzzelinda. Bankers and business tycoons rule the world, which is in the throes of a worldwide depression. In this capitalist realm, God and Mammon metaphorically and literally go hand in hand: the Temple of the Reverend Doc. Bargold, "Bishop of Broadway" and head of all the churches except "that obstinate out-of-date church that sitteth upon seven hills"

---

1. Hogan, *Eimar O'Duffy,* 74.

(7),[2] is a huge skyscraper on Broadway, and on either side of its door are colossal figures representing Christ and a stockbroker clasping hands above the lintel. The more strictly religious parts of the great cathedral are dedicated to Saints Sisyphus and Procrustes—"the patrons of toil and scarcity" (10)—and Saint Progressa, but the edifice is in reality a business empire including a 666-room hotel, "speakeasies and dope dens," telephone booths, and general stores (8). Capitalism, in other words, is dogma, rigorous and monologic in nature, whose strict observance is overseen by the "Sacred Congregation of Sound Economics and of the Financial Inquisition" (9). This institution was founded by Slawmy Cander—Goshawk's secretary but in reality the power behind the throne as the director of all the banks in the world—and its task is to "suppress all false and unorthodox teaching by heretics and cranks" (10).

According to the leaders of the financial world, Cuanduine, the champion of the natural world, is one of the most dangerous and subversive heretics. The object of their wrath, meanwhile, is being offered a reward by a grateful crowd of Wolfians and Lambians for putting a "laughable end" to their war (3). When the hero unexpectedly and unheroically asks for money, however, they abandon him in disgust and accuse him of being selfish and materialistic. Offended by so much hypocrisy, Cuanduine walks away in the company of Mr. Robinson, a newspaper reporter, and vanishes from the public eye. His disappearance leads to the widespread belief that he was killed by Goshawk's men, and this allows him to travel around undisturbed to observe the state of the world. Given the monologic, authoritarian nature of the world's new capitalist dogma, O'Duffy's satire in *Asses in Clover* operates predominantly by presenting a multiplicity of voices, rather than by means of the overt dialogue and polemic central to the trilogy's first two volumes. The book is essentially a long series of encounters with different characters who speak in their own voice and who represent different aspects of the established ideology; these encounters are alternated, in carnivalistic fashion, with chapters containing songs and poems, mostly parodies of modern popular music and verse. This multivoicedness, however, is itself "dialogized" because each voice is a parody of a type of realistic dis-

2. Eimar O'Duffy, *Asses in Clover* (London: Putnam, 1933); all page references in the text are to this edition.

course and therefore, as Bakhtin puts it, "aimed sharply and polemically against the official languages of its given time."[3]

One of Cuanduine's first visits is to "a Modern Home" where the husband keeps house and the wife goes out to work. The couple tell the disapproving hero that they cannot afford children unless they *both* work. O'Duffy's satire here anticipates a phrase in de Valera's 1937 Constitution to the effect that the state should "endeavour to ensure that mothers shall not be obliged by economic necessity to engage in labour to the neglect of their duties in the home."[4] The man of the house speaks and behaves in a stereotypically feminine fashion, while the woman's words and actions are stereotypically masculine, and Cuanduine and Mr. Robinson eventually leave the house in some confusion as to which person is of which sex. Similar satirical methods of male-female role reversal had, of course, been used by Bernard Shaw in *Mrs. Warren's Profession,* and by Oscar Wilde in *The Importance of Being Earnest.* In Wilde's case, "[A]t the root of these devices is his profound scorn for the extreme Victorian division between male and female, which he saw as an unhealthy attempt to foster an excessive sense of difference between the sexes."[5] O'Duffy's satire is more ambiguous; its barbs are clearly aimed in the direction of modern trends within the family, of which O'Duffy appears to have disapproved, but the stereotypical behaviors in this case are so extreme that the reversal of genders operates as a distorting mirror of the status quo that points up the risibility not just of turning the world upside down, but of all extreme forms of behavior.

Cuanduine's most significant encounter, in terms of exposing the nature of the world's capitalist dogma and the essential incorrigibility of the human race, is with a man called Mac ui Rudai (Mr. "Thingie"), whose name implies that he represents the common as well as the "material" man. On the face of it, he appears to be ordinary but decent, and would "eat when he was hungry, drink when he was thirsty, and preferred wine to water when he could afford it; besides which he was of a mind to marry when he fell in love, and embrace his wife under the promptings of passion" (38). Mac ui Rudai tells Cuanduine that he is one of five brothers who all went their separate ways in the world. The other four had ambitions of wealth, power,

3. Bakhtin, *Dialogic Imagination,* 273.
4. Quoted by F. S. L. Lyons in *Ireland since the Famine* (London: Fontana, 1973), 546.
5. Kiberd, *Inventing Ireland,* 39.

fame, and success with women, and all were fabulously successful. His own goal in life is much more modest, but he has not yet achieved his ambition because "this isn't Utopia, you know" (42). Cuanduine expresses some skepticism whether Mac ui Rudai will actually be content once he attains his simple dream. The latter, however, is adamant: "Isn't bite and sup and the wee houseen and the bean a' tighe [woman of the house], with the bit of work for my two hands, good enough for the likes of me?" (43). Cuanduine promises him that "the whole universe shall be turned topsy-turvy to provide a cottage for Mac ui Rudai" (43).

Mac ui Rudai's ambition in life, expressed in stage-Irish terms, is strongly reminiscent of the vision for the new, independent Ireland as it was expressed by Éamon de Valera. In 1926, one of the aims of Fianna Fáil was "the distribution of the land of Ireland so as to get the greatest number possible of Irish families rooted in the soil of Ireland."[6] De Valera himself was a frugal man, whose economic policy was aimed at self-sufficiency and "modest comfort for all with no vast differences between rich and poor. Ireland was a small country and should not try to act as if it were the center of an empire."[7] In 1928 he stated his party's aims as follows: "We believe there ought to be available for every single man in the country employment which will bring him in enough recompense to enable him to maintain his family, and the whole organisation of the State ought to be to that end."[8] De Valera expressed his "unworldly vision," as John A. Murphy calls it, on numerous occasions, and always in similar terms: "The Ireland we dreamed of would be the home of a people who valued material wealth only as the basis of a right living, of a people who were satisfied with a frugal comfort and devoted their leisure to the things of the spirit."[9]

Mac ui Rudai's account of his activities between parting from his brothers and meeting with Cuanduine consists of a long summing up of people he encountered on the way—priests, economists, and industrialists—and of what each of these had to say about the financial and spiritual condition

6. Quoted by John A. Murphy, in *Ireland in the Twentieth Century* (Dublin: Gill and Macmillan, 1975), 68.

7. Longford and O'Neill, *Éamon de Valera*, 267.

8. Quoted in Longford and O'Neill, *Éamon de Valera*, 268.

9. Speech given on St. Patrick's Day, 1943; quoted by Murphy, in *Ireland in the Twentieth Century*, 84.

of the world. His function throughout is merely to listen passively to the voices. He is neither a rebel nor a hero, but instead a willing victim who has internalized his abusers' values and accepts their views without question. In fact, he himself holds highly dogmatic and, at times, paradoxical views. John Cronin finds that "O'Duffy rather undoes his own satirical effects by presenting Mac an [sic] Rudai not as an effective antagonist of the system which enslaves him but rather as the most conventional of believers in it, thus making him 'a not very inspiring person to fight for.'"[10] Such inconsistency, however, is the stuff Menippean satire is made of. The clothes Mac ui Rudai wears are ancient and disgusting, and the food he eats is unpalatable, but he refuses to wear or eat anything he is unfamiliar with, however much he might benefit from a change of habit. His attitude is summed up in these words: "Why should anyone want to be different from me?—me being all right, as you see" (81). His ambiguous status as the dogmatic victim of a dogmatic system is expressed linguistically in his relations with Cuanduine by means of a kind of "doublespeak," an ironic form of language that allows Cuanduine simultaneously to agree and to disagree with his views. For example, Mac ui Rudai disapproves of the scientific notion that he might be descended from a monkey, and invites Cuanduine likewise to express his disbelief in the Darwinian theory. The hero ostensibly concurs with his companion, but only because "it seemed to Cuanduine that the fellow could not be descended from anything better than some monstrous marriage between an earth-worm and a laughing jackass; so he said very truly that he did not believe Mac ui Rudai to be the offspring of a monkey" (83).

Together, Cuanduine, Mac ui Rudai, and Mr. Robinson visit the Kingdom of Assinaria, the epitome of asinine economic thought and behavior. In a setting reminiscent of Swift's Academy of Lagado in *Gulliver's Travels,* Assinarian scientists "were massaging earthworms with lanoline in the hope of making them grow wool; while some were rubbing young lambs with depilatories to prevent overproduction of wool" (89). When Assinaria goes to war in Faraway, both Cuanduine and Mac ui Rudai take part in the effort. Thankful for "the gift of unscrupulousness that had been bestowed on him in the Fourth Heaven" (125), Cuanduine is employed by

---

10. Cronin, *Irish Fiction,* 102.

the Propaganda Department to stir up hatred in the Assinarians against the Farawavians, and it moves him to "exquisite" if rather cynical laughter "to watch their goggling eyes and gaping mouths as they poisoned their souls with the stuff they paid him to write" (126). Mac ui Rudai, meanwhile, becomes rich by inventing and producing weapons. He no longer desires the little houseen and the bean a' tighe that had once seemed the quintessence of happiness. Instead, he marries a frivolous modern girl who does not love him. Having a baby soon becomes boring, and in an unguarded moment the child falls off a windowsill and dies. The wife has an affair with another man but returns to Mac ui Rudai, only to leave him again when she hears that he has gone bankrupt spending all his money on trivia. These traumatic experiences have no effect on Mac ui Rudai whatsoever; after all, in satire people do not learn from their mistakes. Penniless, but none the wiser for his pains, he rejoins Cuanduine and Mr. Robinson.

After seeing Mac ui Rudai try his hand at marriage, and fail, it is Cuanduine's turn to fall in love. The hero gets married to the vision of his heart's desire, and becomes the father of two sets of twins: boys, who are raised as heroes by the greatest in Tír na nÓg, and girls, who are beautiful and happy. As a father, he finds himself confronted with the modern problem of sex education. The episode serves as a vehicle for further heteroglossia, as Cuanduine is addressed in a mystical vision by a series of voices from different realms of myth (Saint Maceratus, Bricriu of the Bitter Tongue, Saint Progressa), which all express different but equally dogmatic views on the subject of sexuality. Cuanduine finds all these opinions a little extreme (a comment on the nature of O'Duffy's own satire as much as on the uncompromising nature of these dogmatic views), but a compromise position is not offered. Of all these voices, however, Progressa's turns out to be the most reasonable—a surprising development given the vehemence of O'Duffy's attack upon her in *King Goshawk and the Birds*. The argument returns to birth control, with Progressa making a case in favor based on the woman's health and appearance, and Cuanduine wondering rather crudely how sex can be a passionate spontaneous act if the lovers "go to it in a coward fear of fruition, first poking and fiddling with your damned apparatus like plumbers at a sinkhole?" (156). In spite of these differences, the two adversaries come perilously close to meeting in the middle and resolving their differences, and hence to undermining the satire: "'Unreasonable as your arguments are,' said Progressa, 'it is at least something that you are not influenced by the musty dogmas of the churches. I begin to think that your opposition to my ideas is due rather to misunderstanding than to religious and narrow-minded objections. Your love of life is up in arms against what you conceive to be a gospel of death. You must understand, therefore, that we do not propose to abolish mankind altogether—'" (157). At this point, the hero turns the tables on Progressa: "'What a pity,' said Cuanduine. 'I sometimes think that would be a very good idea'" (157). When Progressa accuses him of being inconsistent, he retorts: "Not a whit. For it is only natural to wish that this pitiable squinting race of self-complacent vermin, so riddled with superstition and disease, so stupid, so selfish, so covetous, so ferocious, so lecherous, so much addicted to hypocrisy and cant, so wasteful and destructive, so blind to reality, might be wiped out of existence and the earth left clean for some better breed. Nevertheless, as we are brethren, and as we know that the Gods had some higher purpose in starting the experiment, we put the wish away as unkind and unreasonable" (158). Cuanduine's contrary attitude seems self-contradictory, but is explained and perhaps even justified by the ambiguous nature of the cause he is championing. Mac ui Rudai demonstrates how a victim of authority can be dogmatic himself, and with mankind playing the parts of both victim and perpetrator, Cuanduine is alternately (or even simultaneously) the champion of man and a misanthrope. The apparent inconsistency of his attitude is a result of this paradox.

The action of book 2 of *Asses in Clover* is triggered by the escape of a blackbird from Queen Guzzelinda's aviary, and returns the focus to Cuanduine's original mission of liberating the songbirds from Goshawk's grasp. The bird finds sanctuary in Ireland, and when Slawmy Cander suggests "that a force of international Air Police . . . be raised to keep the small nations in order, these being the real menace to international peace" (173), the Irish begin to prepare for war. The situation soon reaches stalemate, however, because the conflicting policies to deal with the crisis developed by the two Irish parties, the Slashers and the Trimmers, almost lead the country into civil war: "the people of Eirinn have never failed to quarrel in face of a foe" (183). Meanwhile the blackbird is snared by a private speculator, and returned to Slawmy Cander.

Toward the end of both *King Goshawk and the Birds* and *The Spacious*

Adventures of the Man in the Street, a form of resolution was achieved, at least temporarily, by means of war, and *Asses in Clover* also follows this pattern. Cuanduine is summoned by Badb the War Goddess to go and do the work the gods have appointed. In a parody of mythical-heroic conventions, particularly those associated with Cuanduine's father, Cuchulain, the Badb lays three geasa upon him: "not to kill a lion and spare a jackal; not to answer the questions of White on the lips of Black; not to contend with the Headless Men of the Woods" (185). *Geasa* are magical prohibitions or obligations imposed upon a hero or king; breaking these magical and often incomprehensible prohibitions will inevitably lead to defeat or death. Ominously, in most mythological tales geasa are introduced only so that they can subsequently be broken. The death of Cuchulain, for example, is foreshadowed in his breaking of all his geasa shortly before he meets his end.

Cuanduine proceeds to build a war plane worthy of mythology:

It was one of the three great engines of destruction, the other two being the Wooden Horse of Troy and the Super-Dreadnaught. It was one of the three great helpers of man, the other two being the fire-bearing reed of Prometheus and the Kettle of Watt. It was one of the three perfect works of art, the other two being the Parthenon and the Ninth Symphony of Beethoven. It was one of the three great discomforters of fools, the other two being the Socratic Question and the works of Voltaire. Because it was to be a taker of cities, Cuanduine gave it the name of Poliorketes. (193)

Having defeated Slawmy Cander's International Army in the epic Battle of the Atlantic, Cuanduine decides to fly low over Dublin "to receive the plaudits of the people" (214). The plane's propeller raises a storm of dust, filth, and refuse over the city, and the blast also rips everybody's clothes off, turning the world upside down and exposing people for what they really are underneath their polished exteriors:

Stout pillars of society stripped of their importance; prominent public figures shown up for what they were; people of influence left without a rag of self-confidence; proud people cringing in dark corners; bankers without a shred of credit; materialists crying for the moon; bullies and oppressors shrieking to heaven for protection; politicians running away from their seats; journalists afflicted with shame; publicity mongers looking for a hiding place; fine ladies in reduced circumstances; hard riders to hounds skulking to earth like foxes; the whole mass of humanity blushing for itself for the first time in history. It would have made Mrs Grundy laugh to see them all—all that vast modest miserable mob scurrying like rats from the sight of each other's eyes, and locking and bolting themselves into their homes, and burying themselves in their beds, where they lay wondering how they were ever going to face the world again. (215–16)

The event becomes subsequently known as "The Scouring of Dublin," and O'Duffy gives it a place among other mythical "Feats of Scavenging, the other two being the cleansing of the Augean Stables and the purging of Pantagruel" (218). It does little to endear Cuanduine to the city's population, "for though people like to be saved from oppression and danger, they do not like to be shown up" (216).

Cuanduine's final target is Goshawk's Manhattan castle. Before he can attack his mortal enemy, however, all the city's hungry people storm the castle, and Goshawk dies of a heart attack. Queen Guzzelinda dies of suffocation, either because she has taken refuge in an ashpit, or because she chokes herself with her undershirt, being unable to undress herself without assistance. The narrator dismisses the details as unimportant: "You can believe which story you like, for all I care" (224). With these enemies disposed of, the Philosopher Murphy, having completed the task he had set himself, and having lived far beyond his allotted span, decides to die as well.

The deaths of Goshawk and Guzzelinda focus global attention once more on the fate of the birds, as a storm of voices addresses the issue without reaching any form of agreement or compromise. There are reactions from governments, political parties, the League of Nations, as well as the pope, who declares in his encyclical *Quae Cum Ita Sint* that "whereas the monopoly of all singing birds by one individual was a grave abuse, nevertheless human inequalities were decreed by divine law, and the doctrine that all private ownership of birds was itself wrong was contrary to the teaching of Holy Church" (229). This is probably a parodic reference to the 1931 encyclical of Pope Pius XI, *Quadragesimo Anno*, which addressed vocational organization and representation and was generally "devoted to mitigating, or removing, the evils alike of unregulated capitalism and of excessive state intervention."[11] The pope's words are followed by those of the

---

11. Lyons, *Ireland since the Famine*, 575.

newspapers, which pay lip service to the social class of their readership while keeping their noses clean. In a babble of conflicting voices, the world at large shows itself indifferent to the fate of the birds, and the narrator of *Asses in Clover* adds his own despairing voice when he exclaims, "Juvenal, Rabelais, Voltaire, Swift, do your spirits slumber in Elysium, that your laughter does not come rolling in thunder about our ears?" (237).

As before, laughter is the final weapon. When Professors Banger and Whipcord address the general public authoritatively on the subject of the "Utopian ideal" but economic impossibility of liberating the birds, Cuanduine finds their theories hysterically funny:

He rolled in his chair, holding his sides, and kicking the floor to pieces with his heels, while the thunder of his merriment shook heaven and earth. 'Twas such a laugh as had not been heard in the world since the mockery of Voltaire made oppressors turn pale in their council chambers, nor even before that if the truth were known. I think Master Rabelais must have laughed in the same fashion, all by himself, when he was writing his flim-flam stories: but the secret of such mirth is lost. His microphone was in the room with Cuanduine at the time, so that his jubilant bellowings were carried to every listening ear. But of the whole multitude there was not one to share the joke. They all sat there as solemn as gelded clerks. (248)

Although Cuanduine's hilarity fails to be infectious, carnivalized laughter is the hero's final and only weapon against dogmatic economic theories. If he can only make other people laugh in the face of the deadly seriousness of these authority figures, their grip on the world will be loosened. He spends the night "reading Bergson on Laughter" (256), and the next day begins to play tricks upon the economists during their public performances. One carnivalized authority falls flat on his face, splits and drops his trousers, and ends up stuck in a wastepaper basket, "which threw the world into such paroxysms of glee that you would have thought he had given them a solution of all their troubles, past, present, and to come" (257). Another professor appears on television dressed as a clown and recites a thirteen-stanza parody of Lewis Carroll's "The Walrus and the Carpenter":

The sun was shining brightly
Upon the fields below:
He did his very best to make
The corn and fruit to grow;

And that was wrong because it brings
The prices down, you know. (260)

But despite his initial success, Cuanduine's attempts to make people laugh are quickly thwarted; Slawmy Cander brings the professor to his senses, and after insulating the studio against the influence of Cuanduine's hypnotism the economists experience no further disturbances.

Cuanduine breaks the first of his geasa, not to kill a lion and spare a jackal, when he decides to spare Slawmy Cander's life during the attack on Goshawk's castle: for "though Goshawk was but a mangy lion, Mr Slawmy Cander was a jackal of parts" (223). When Cuanduine addresses the people in a futile attempt to arouse their interest in the fate of the birds, Slawmy Cander interrupts his speech; Cuanduine answers back that he has come to liberate the birds not for the sake of the people but for the birds themselves, and thereby breaks the second of his geasa, "namely, not to answer the questions of White upon the lips of Black: for wisdom appears as folly to darkened understandings" (241). The third geis, not to contend with the Headless Men of the Wood, is broken when Cuanduine delivers another angry speech against all economics professors: "for the Economists were headless men, wandering in a dark forest of dead ideas, and the only weapon that could avail against them was laughter" (268). Like so many other heroes of Menippean satire, Cuanduine has been defeated by the doublespeak of metaphor. From the moment the geasa are broken, every cause the hero has espoused turns against him. Mac ui Rudai, the man whose dream of owning a little cottage and a field Cuanduine once promised to fulfill, heckles him from the audience: being both common and materialistic, he now runs the highly successful "Ultra-Modern School of Selling" (270). The greatest betrayal comes from the songbirds: when Cuanduine finally makes it to their aviary, rips open the door with his sword, and begs them, "Away! Away! / Your wings spread wide. / On the winds of the world / In freedom ride" (270), the creatures "were so much accustomed to captivity that they would not stir, and pecked him viciously when he tried to shoo them forth" (271). The hero in Menippean satire is used to being ridiculed as a madman, alone as he typically is in the knowledge of the truth; but toward the end of *Asses in Clover*, Cuanduine discovers that the truth for which he has fought so long and hard no longer exists—if it ever existed at all. The rug has been pulled from under his feet, along with the solid ground beneath it.

With the question of the birds now a moot point, the economics professors turn their attention toward developing new export markets and decide to concentrate their efforts on the Moon, proposing to sell goods to the Selenites and buy raw materials from them. Their attitude is one of economic imperialism: "'They are an extremely primitive people, though by no means savages. That is to say, they live a very simple life, with few wants, and with no mechanical equipment of any kind; but so far as a hasty observation can judge, they are peaceable and inoffensive. I need hardly explain what ideal conditions of trading are possible with a people like that.' (Cheers)" (273–74). Aloysius O'Kennedy, the hero of *The Spacious Adventures of the Man in the Street,* is brought forward at this point as someone who has experience in traveling to other planets; he also offers to help Slawmy Cander and his consorts defeat Cuanduine. The latter, however, finds out about the plan and, with the aid of his plane and his sword, scares the villains into a different way of thinking.

O'Kennedy relates to Slawmy Cander how he was sacked from his job in the grocer's shop after his return from Rathé. On the advice of the Philosopher, he wrote down his adventures in a book, which he insists "is a true book. I mean, it isn't a novel" (277). Since Slawmy Cander is "the shrewdest man in the world," he realizes "that if the book was not true, it was the work of a very fertile imagination; and it was clearer still that Mr O'Kennedy was a man without a spark of imagination of any sort" (277). However, O'Kennedy also reveals that the publishers found the story too fantastic and suggested that he cut down on the serious material and add a love interest and plenty of excitement, whereupon the book sold over a hundred thousand copies. The effect of this revelation is to undermine and trivialize the significance of *The Spacious Adventures of the Man in the Street,* since that is the book purportedly written by O'Kennedy. *Asses in Clover* thus manages to show not only that the cause established in *King Goshawk and the Birds*—the liberation of the songbirds—was futile and pointless, because the birds do not wish to be rescued, but also that the second part of the trilogy, *The Spacious Adventures of the Man in the Street,* is fictitious, spurious, and inconsequential, since whatever "truth" it contained was subsequently tampered with in the interest of financial gain. Rather than meaningfully reconciling the opposites of the first two books of the trilogy, as a dialectical structure might lead one to expect, the third volume merely deconstructs the premises carefully set up in the first two volumes, thereby demonstrating that the entire three-story satirical edifice was built on quicksand.

No longer having a quest to pursue, Cuanduine returns home to the Golden Valley, which has changed ominously in his absence: "The guardian Gods had departed: no nymphs played in the river, no dryads in the forest; the pipes of Pan were silent" (295). At home he faces a final and personal ignominy. During his absence his own children have changed greatly: they have adopted every modern vice abhorred by their father, and they all have jobs in business and finance. In a supreme irony, therefore, Cuanduine himself has engendered precisely the kind of modern capitalist attitude that he was brought into the world to combat. With the battle lost on all fronts, Cuanduine and his wife fly away from the world in Poliorketes and are never seen again. Typically, the satire's narrator leaves the hero's fate unresolved: "Whether he found rest in Tir na nOg, or fresh fields for noble deeds in some corporeal world lit by some better sun, or whether he still rides through space in search of his heart's desire, nobody knows" (297).

The conclusion of *Asses in Clover* provides an account of the manners and customs of the Selenites, "written by a journalist who accompanied the expedition" to the Moon (305). The Selenite lifestyle is reminiscent of that of Rathé in *The Spacious Adventures of the Man in the Street,* and functions as a semiutopian alternative to the customs of Earth. Selenites enjoy themselves, live simply, and do without many things; everyone has enough money, from work or private income. They have no religion but worship themselves; marriage is a contract but divorce is rare. Selenites are also, it seems, better economists than Earthlings: in spite of their laziness, they grow richer all the time, while the Earth's economy is beginning to fail. Earth's solution to its economic woes is to declare war on the Moon, but the Selenites defend themselves effectively with an electric field, which destroys most of the attacking ships, after which the Earth sinks into a black trade depression and gradually turns into a wilderness.

The final episodes of *Asses in Clover* look at the Earth from a distant, future perspective, which illustrates the ultimate consequences of economic Procrusteanism. People stopped having children altogether due to the economic depression; eventually, the species died out, and human beings became museum pieces. Earth's last human being, Henri Coquin ("Henry

Rascal") is on display in a glass case in the Louvre, where he awakens from a trance after innumerable years to a Paris whose streets are overgrown with weeds and grass: "Not a hundred yards from where he stood was what looked like a pigmy town. The little houses, barely knee high, were built neatly of sods, and arranged in straight streets around a larger central building of the same material. The streets were crowded, and one glance revealed to him who were the inhabitants of this singular city. They were rabbits" (326). The human race has been superseded by rabbits: the most prolific of species has inherited the Earth. *Asses in Clover* ends with a discussion among the Gods in an even more distant future, millions of years after the Earth has fallen back into the Sun. The Gods question whether the universe "is of the homely old shape, straight and infinite, described by Newton, or curved and finite, after the bizarre pattern of Einstein" (329). The narrator's own theory is that "the Universe is hour-glass shaped, and held about the waist by the grip of Ἀνάγκη ["Necessity"]: hence the number of fools it contains. A straight, or even a moderately curved, universe would surely have room for a little more wisdom" (330).

O'Duffy's theory of the shape of the universe is a parody of Plato's description of the universe in "The Myth of Er" as "the spindle of Necessity, which causes all the orbits to revolve."[12] Plato describes not an hourglass shape, however, but a set of eight whorls, fitting one inside the other, resembling "a nest of bowls."[13] The myth (Plato's format for conveying religious or moral truths) also addresses life after death and the process of the transmigration of souls. The choice of souls after death depends to a large degree on the former existence of the deceased:

. . . the man with the first lot came forward and chose the greatest tyranny he could find. In his folly and greed he chose it without examining it fully, and so did not see that it was his fate to eat his children and suffer other horrors. . . . He was one of the souls who had come from heaven, having lived his previous life in a well-governed state . . . and indeed, broadly speaking, the majority of those who were caught in this way came from heaven without the discipline of suffering, while those who came from earth had suffered themselves and seen others suffer and were not so

---

12. Plato, *The Republic*, 2nd ed., trans. with introduction by Desmond Lee (Harmondsworth, U.K.: Penguin Books, 1974), 450.

13. Ibid., 450.

hasty in their choice. For this reason and because of the luck of the draw there was a general change of good for evil and evil for good.[14]

Plato's universe is inclusive, while his myth suggests that, even if evil exists, humans learn from their mistakes and turn evil into good according to a cyclical pattern.

The shape of O'Duffy's universe, an hourglass, is divisive, and mankind so incorrigible that it destroys itself. Man "achieved a mastery of natural forces that was marvellous in a race so stupid, but his wickedness and folly were such that it did him more harm than good" (330). The hourglass shape of O'Duffy's universe is suggestive of the structure of Menippean satire, in that it consists of two extremes without a center: where the center ought to be, there is instead the iron hand of necessity, keeping the two poles apart. Unlike Plato's, O'Duffy's universe is far from harmonious, and there is no place for the harmony of the spheres or the music of sirens. The only music in the universe is a faint, manmade reminder of what might have been: "The Gods were silent; and the ghost of the Ninth Symphony came stealing through the ether" (331). In most readers' minds, the ghost of Beethoven's music carries with it the echo of Schiller's poem "An die Freude" ("Ode to Joy"), but in *Asses in Clover,* man's wickedness has ensured that there are no humans left to hear the music, or the ode's utopian wish: "Freude, schöner Götterfunken / Tochter aus Elysium . . . Alle Menschen werden Brüder / Wo dein sanfter Flügel weilt."

The relationship between the three parts of the Cuanduine trilogy illustrates Frank Palmeri's contention that narrative satire presents an unresolved dialogue between opposed ideologies without authorizing either position, forming merely "a continuing process of unsettling hierarchies of value and systems of thought."[15] The Cuanduine trilogy satirizes specific contemporary Irish issues as well as matters of more general, global relevance. On the one hand, it contains one of the earliest public protests against the climate of censorship and repression introduced by the Irish Free State. On the other hand, O'Duffy appears to imply that he condemned such legislation less for what it was trying to achieve than for his belief that the effect of moral legislation is usually the opposite of what it

14. Ibid., 453.
15. Palmeri, *Satire,* 3.

desires to accomplish. Where the international focus of O'Duffy's satire is concerned, especially his obsession with economic theories, his voice on more than one occasion lapses into monologue: this is where the satire itself becomes dogmatic, and where it creates an "overriding impression of mere crankiness."[16] The ultimate purpose of *Asses in Clover*, however, is to destabilize and nullify any ideological points scored in the preceding two volumes. It seems that the successful satirist can—indeed, must—both have his cake and eat it, while at the same time implying that the cake is worth neither having nor eating. In that sense, the Cuanduine satire offers an open-ended, unresolved questioning of the irrational, or, as O'Duffy would have it, unnatural aspects of human behavior.

16. Cronin, *Irish Fiction*, 104.

part three

Austin Clarke

(1896–1974)

*T*he literary reputation of Austin Clarke is largely based on his satirical poetry, but he also wrote three prose narratives that he referred to as "prose romances," and which he set in the Middle Ages. Commentators have noted, however, that the narratives are not so much "charming historical romances about medieval Ireland" as they are "protests of a satirical nature against the complacency of the Irish of Clarke's own day."[1] While the first of these narratives, *The Bright Temptation* (1932), and the third, *The Sun Dances at Easter* (1952), are light-hearted in tone and optimistic in outcome, the second book, *The Singing-Men at Cashel* (1936), is much more dark and brooding in both respects. For all the differences between them, however, the three narratives reflect many of the same attitudes and contain similar ingredients; in fact, many of the images and themes of *The Bright Temptation* recur in the later narratives, but with a different emphasis.

As Northrop Frye points out in his invaluable discussion of genre, Menippean satire and prose romance are often confused with each other.[2] Both types of discourse frequently portray characters on a journey, and as a consequence the shape of the narrative is loose-jointed and rambling. One important difference between the two types of narrative is that,

---

1. Susan Halpern, *Austin Clarke: His Life and Works* (Dublin: Dolmen Press, 1974), 176.
2. Frye, *Anatomy*, 309.

whereas romance emphasizes positive values and idealizes heroism and purity, satire focuses on human evil and folly as expressions of diseased mental attitudes. Romance tends toward allegory, whereas satire represents its characters as mouthpieces of the ideas they represent. In addition, the structure of Menippean satire often produces "violent dislocations in the customary logic of narrative,"[3] whereas the "complete form of the romance is clearly the successful quest."[4] Although the objectives of satire and romance appear on the surface to be diametrically opposed to each other (one criticizes and leads toward disintegration, the other idealizes and leads toward wish fulfillment), the two formally overlap to a certain extent: both deal with stylized characters rather than "real people," and both contain an element of the fantastic. Both are essentially dialectical in structure, but whereas in romance the conflict between extreme forces (good and evil) takes place in "*our* world, which is in the middle, and which is characterized by the cyclical movement of nature,"[5] in Menippean satire the conflicting extremes are equally unacceptable, and the middle is excluded. Elements of romance are often found in satire, and vice versa; there is, for example, "a strong admixture of romance in Rabelais" even though he is to be regarded primarily as a Menippean satirist.[6] Whether one characterizes a text as a romance or a satire, therefore, depends to a large degree on the prevailing tone and emphasis of that text.

It could be argued that Austin Clarke's *The Bright Temptation* is essentially a romance with satirical overtones. His second narrative, *The Singing-Men at Cashel,* reshapes and rearranges elements similar to those of the first romance—complicates them, one might say—in such a way that the emphasis shifts away from romance and toward Menippean satire. Much of this complication has to do with structural dislocation and the breaking up of narrative logic and continuity. *The Sun Dances at Easter* restores narrative continuity to some degree, as it carnivalizes rather than satirizes the world it depicts.

There is no question in Austin Clarke's work as to the nature of the authority at which his satire is aimed: Clarke's name has become virtually synonymous with anticlericalism and protest against the dogmatic and

3. Ibid., 310.
5. Ibid., 187.
4. Ibid., 187.
6. Ibid., 309.

authoritarian teachings of the Catholic Church, particularly with regard to sexual morality. In part, the vehement and almost obsessional quality of Clarke's attitude had its origins in unfortunate personal experience: persistent questioning about masturbation during his first confession at the age of seven left him traumatized and "disturbed by a sense of evil."[7] Clarke's first marriage was a marriage in name only and ended after a matter of days; it also lost Clarke his teaching post at University College, Dublin, apparently because his wedding had taken place in a registry office rather than a church.[8] Clarke belonged to a relatively small group of Irish writers in the 1930s who stood up for intellectual and artistic free-dom when they witnessed the closing of the Irish mind and saw their own and other artists' works banned in the interest of public morality. They were isolated in their protest, for during this period there existed "so far as religious values are concerned, a remarkable consensus in Irish society. There was overwhelming agreement that traditional Catholic values should be maintained, if necessary by legislation. There is no evidence that pressure from the hierarchy was needed to bring this about: it ap-pears to have been spontaneous."[9] All three of Clarke's prose romances were banned in Ireland.

The world depicted in Austin Clarke's prose narratives is that of early medieval Ireland before the Norman Conquest of the twelfth century. Clarke's interest in what he called the "neglected Celtic-Romanesque cen-turies" stemmed from a conversation he had as a student with his friend, the poet F. R. Higgins, who explained to him the tradition and simple na-ture of the early Celtic Church.[10] The period appealed to Clarke for two reasons. First, it was more relevant to modern Ireland than the more dis-tant and mythological past that had appealed to the earlier revivalists of the "Celtic Twilight" period (although that mythological past is by no means absent from Clarke's work): in the Church of both the Celtic-Romanesque and the modern period Clarke perceived a strong emphasis

7. Austin Clarke, *Twice Round the Black Church: Early Memories of Ireland and England* (1962; reprint, Dublin: Moytura Press, 1990), 130.

8. Clarke relates these experiences in *Black Church,* 87–88.

9. J. H. Whyte, *Church and State in Modern Ireland, 1923–1979* (1971; 2nd ed., Dublin: Gill and Macmillan, 1980), 60.

10. Austin Clarke, *A Penny in the Clouds: More Memories of Ireland and England* (1968; reprint, Dublin: Moytura Press, 1990), 17.

on asceticism and mortification of the flesh, which offered greater scope for criticism and satire of contemporary Ireland. Second, however, the Irish Church of the Celtic-Romanesque period was different from the modern Church in that "it was in some respects independent of Roman control, had superb achievements in scholarship and art, . . . whereas the modern post-Tridentine Irish Church was controlled by the Papacy and neither the clergy nor the people were distinguished for their intellectual independence or their artistic achievements."[11] For Clarke, who was strongly concerned with the position of the arts and with freedom of artistic expression in a country dominated by a puritanical Catholic morality, the Celtic-Romanesque Church thus formed a dualistic image of praise and blame: an institution simultaneously to be denounced and commended.

There are a number of reasons why the subject matter of Clarke's prose narratives is in many ways more compatible with satire than with romance. Practically all of his work revolves around the issues of sexuality and religion and targets the Church's insistence on the repression of the body in favor of the spirit, and the sexual trauma and mental suffering this caused for many of his countrymen, including himself. His "romances" all present journeys away from physical repression toward sexual liberation. Clarke's concentration on the physical, sexual aspects of love would naturally put his work closer to Menippean satire (which emphasizes the material basis of all spiritual value systems) than to romance (which idealizes heroism and purity). Clarke, moreover, presents sexual love as an antiauthoritarian act of defiance; such "scandalous" acts aimed at breaching accepted moral norms are typical of Menippean satire. In his prose narratives the marriage between this subject matter and the romance form is therefore in many ways an uneasy one.

11. Maurice Harmon, *Austin Clarke, 1896–1974: A Critical Introduction* (Totowa, N.J.: Barnes and Noble, 1989), 32–33.

chapter five

"The Beginning Was the End"

The Bright Temptation

Austin Clarke's first prose romance, *The Bright Temptation*, recounts the love story of Aidan and Ethna. The plot takes the form of a journey in the course of which the lovers meet, are separated, and eventually refind each other in a happy ending. Aidan, a young scholar at the monastic settlement of Cluanmore (a fictitious place, but clearly based on Clonmacnoise), believes one night that he hears a voice calling him; the bright but indistinct vision he sees suggests to him that it is the voice of an angel, but subsequent clues suggest that the guiding force that brings the lovers together is none other than the Celtic god of love, Aongus of the Birds. Aidan wanders away from his cell in the dark; accidentally—and symbolically—experiences a fall; and is swept away by the River Shannon. Stripped naked by the strong current, he eventually comes ashore in a strange part of the country. His desperate search for clothes leads him to a house and to a confusing encounter with a young woman named Credë, whose sleeping quarters he enters by mistake. Dressed in her foster brother's clothes he leaves the house, only to be mistaken for the other boy, abducted by three soldiers, and taken to the house of a man named Moran. He is rescued by Ethna, Moran's daughter, who had fallen in love with him at first sight and who now spirits him away from his pursuers. The young people travel together for a while; however, Aidan's confusion stemming from his sexual awakening leads to their separation. On his way back to Cluanmore Aidan has to contend with hostile villagers, a grotesque giant, madmen in Glen Bolcan, a puritanical saint, and pillaging Danes, before the lovers are finally reunited and able to consummate their love. In its basic form the story therefore represents an allegorical journey from innocence to experience and from repression to liberation—a fairly typical romance development.

The contemplative, monastic world of Cluanmore depicted at the beginning and end of *The Bright Temptation* forms a sharp contrast with the
"bardic world of fear and violence" outside its walls where Aidan learns to
love Ethna (48).[1] Clarke complicates this simple contrast, however, by depicting Cluanmore in a state of chaos and the monks in a comical panic as
a result of the arrival of the Danes. The night of fear, ominous dreams, and
portents in the sky with which the narrative opens is responsible for Aidan's
fall into the river; and, when he eventually manages to return to Cluanmore
at the end of his journey, the Danes are in the process of literally and figu-
ratively turning the settlement upside down. In this way, the idealized world
of the romance of Aidan and Ethna is narratively embedded in the topsy-
turvy world of satire and carnival.

The inconclusive structure of Clarke's romance has a textual counterpart
in the manuscripts at Cluanmore. In the opening scene of the book, the
chief illuminator of manuscripts is interrupted while working on a diminutive illumination involving the intricate pattern of a dragon's tail, and loses
the place where he left off: "For hours he sought patiently and with increasing prayer among those multitudes of interwoven lines for the tip of
the dragon's tail, but such was the intricacy and minuteness of his own
work that he could not find it." Eventually, "he found that he was going
round and coming back like the bewildered Children of Solomon in the
pentagons and magical circles of their craft, so that at the end of his search
he was no farther than he had been at the beginning" (2–3). In a dream that
night, Torbach pursues his fruitless quest but finds himself in a strange, fantastic world where "the beginning was the end and the centre was its own
circumference" (3). On one level, the nightmare is emblematic of the self-
defeating quest of the Menippean satirist, who can never allow the questions he raises to be answered conclusively. The image of the artist engaged
in a convoluted and pointless artistic task that leads nowhere and becomes
hopelessly frustrating is a recurring one, not only in *The Bright Temptation*,
but in many other satires of the same period.

Torbach's dream is only the first of a number of perplexing events that
take place at Cluanmore that night. Suddenly, all the books in the scripto-

---

1. Austin Clarke, *The Bright Temptation: A Romance* (1932; reprint, Dublin: Dolmen Press,
1965); all page references in the text are to this edition.

ria, the libraries, and the copying cells fall down from their places on the racks and desks, resulting in the mixing up of wildly divergent texts, and ideological and stylistic confusion:

The Book of Rights had been overthrown by the Brehon Laws, and the Chronicle of Eusebius knocked down by the arguments of Augustine. The geographical works of Dicuil, who had known the darkness beyond the icy north and the burning canals of the south, were mixed among the early fathers and grammarians. Saint Jerome had fallen farther than the heretics he had refuted, Pomponius had been crushed by Orosius, the Calendar of Aongus hidden by the spurious Epistle to the Laodiceans. Adamnanus was flung beyond the Apocrypha, Prosper of Aquitaine had divided the Tripartite Life of Patric, Priscian still hung upon a rack, but Sedulius was outcast among pagan poets. (7–8)

The textual confusion leads to further linguistic Babel as the panic-stricken scholars revert to their own mother tongues: "Little wonder that the crowds babbled as though a pentecostal fire had divided among them, and that many strange tongues were heard. For in their excitement the tall fair-headed strangers who had received the grace of baptism and come to Cluanmore to learn Greek and Latin talked in rough gutturals, the Saxons grunted again, the Franks grew shrill, and the men of Ireland in their various dialects were troubled and confused" (8). Heteroglossia, which is always "aimed sharply and polemically against the official languages of its given time,"[2] thus invades and upsets the monologic and authoritarian world of the medieval Church, whose unitary "one language of truth . . . gives expression to forces working toward concrete verbal and ideological unification and centralization."[3] The students only come to their senses when, much to their amusement, they discover the corpulent backside of Colcanon, the bursar, protruding in an undignified manner from the narrow doorway of the round tower where he had become stuck while attempting to hide Cluanmore's treasures from the Danes. Bodily elements such as the bursar's backside, his girth, and the culinary overtones of his name, are forms of the contrary that carnivalize Church discipline and austerity, and turn such monastic values upside down.

Several commentators on Austin Clarke's oeuvre have noted the impor-

2. Bakhtin, *Dialogic Imagination*, 273.
3. Ibid., 271.

tance of linguistic ambiguity and multiple meanings, such as those created by puns and homonyms, for the satirical impact of his poetry. By means of such double discourse language itself becomes a subversive instrument, disallowing "what all authorities would wish—that words should have one meaning and one meaning alone. For it is always possible that at the edge of one meaning waits another subversive thought undermining the language as an instrument of control."[4] The strange events at Cluanmore are seen by the monks and scholars as signs which they, too, interpret in various ways, each individual producing a different meaning according to his own concerns. The bursar and others see the portents as evidence that the Danes are about to arrive, while Torbach interprets the falling of the books as a sign of the Devil. The abbot's first thought is of his pupils' disobedience: "This is not a mortal danger but an angered sign from heaven. Only by earnest prayer and enquiry can we discover the meaning of this portent. It may be that some among you are evil or have sinned against the holy purity of Ireland" (6). Old Father Cronaun believes that the books have fallen because they "grieved for one who would master them" (10): that is, they mourn the departure of his best pupil, Aidan, whom he believes to have been carried off by the Devil in the course of the confusing night. The falling of the books, the ensuing linguistic chaos, and the difficulty of interpreting the significance of these events reveal the limitations of what Bakhtin calls *"the forces that serve to unify and centralize the verbal-ideological world,"*[5] and highlight the precarious tasks of the artist who seeks to create a written text and the reader who attempts to find meaning in it.

Father Cronaun regards Aidan as a promising scholar whose learning might one day restore Cluanmore to its former intellectual glory. That scholastic reputation had been under a cloud since the wicked teaching of MacOnan the heretic. The thought of MacOnan's sins still makes the abbot flinch: "Many years before, this round-headed scholar had crossed to Europe that he might uphold Irish scholarship and dispute with the Burgundian bishops over the Paschal date. None could withstand his arguments, and swollen with spiritual pride he had written a book on the corporeal nature of angels, which had been condemned by an oecumenical

---

4. Terence Brown, "Austin Clarke: Satirist," in *Ireland's Literature: Selected Essays* (Mullingar, Ireland: Lilliput Press, 1988), 139–40.

5. Bakhtin, *Dialogic Imagination,* 270.

council. But MacOnan persevered in his heretical doctrines and defeated his opponents in argument, to such bad purpose had he put the logic which he had learned at Cluanmore" (9–10). As his name implies, MacOnan was guilty of masturbation. There are several other overt references to the subject in *The Bright Temptation:* it is the main cause of the madness of the unfortunate souls Aidan meets in Glen Bolcan, and the reason why sports are encouraged among the students at Cluanmore, "so that they might be wearied at night, and in this way the Devil was defeated" (98–99). MacOnan's overt sins include being an intellectual, moving to Europe, writing a book that is frowned upon by the Church, and showing an interest in bodily matters ("the corporeal nature of angels"); these vices, of course, also add up to an ironic portrait of James Joyce. Like Joyce, Clarke was educated by the Jesuits, "mainly at Belvedere College, where his schooling so closely resembled that of James Joyce that the account in *A Portrait* seemed like his own experience."[6] MacOnan's transgressions, of course, resemble Austin Clarke's own "sins" as an Irish writer as well as Joyce's, and when one bears in mind the traumatic experience of Clarke's first confession, the name "MacOnan" establishes a further connection between the author and the unmentionable heretic. In *A Penny in the Clouds*, Clarke recollects a visit to Joyce in Paris in the 1920s, and remembers wondering "if he had been addicted in youth to our national sin."[7] If Aidan is a potential successor to MacOnan, Clarke sets himself up as a potential successor to James Joyce.

The description of MacOnan can be read as a portrait of the Irish artist, in particular the Irish writer. It suggests the position of the intellectual who is perceived as being clever, even brilliant, but immoral, and dangerous because his irrefutable use of logic and argumentation constitutes a threat to the Church's authority. The Church's only weapon against such a threat is to silence the intellectual's voice and to deprive him of an audience. Austin Clarke's obsession with masturbation may have had personal origins, but it also reflects the lonely "sin" of the writer who persists in writing subversive books even without the benefit of an audience, of which he has been deprived by the moral censor. This image of the lonely writer is also reminiscent of Flann O'Brien's portrait of the isolated Irish artist in "A Bash in the

---

6. *The Oxford Companion to Irish Literature*, ed. Robert Welch (Oxford, U.K.: Clarendon Press, 1996), 100.

7. Clarke, *Penny in the Clouds*, 96.

Tunnel": "But surely there you have the Irish artist? Sitting fully dressed, innerly locked in the toilet of a locked coach where he has no right to be, resentfully drinking somebody else's whiskey, being whisked hither and thither by anonymous shunters, keeping fastidiously the while on the outer face of his door the simple word, ENGAGED?"[8]

As Cronaun's brightest pupil, Aidan would have to restore Cluanmore's intellectual renown by emulating MacOnan's academic rigor while avoiding the moral corruption triggered by learning in this heretical predecessor. Aidan is, of course, unaware of the potential Cronaun had seen in him, and his accidental journey of discovery leads him not only physically but also spiritually away from Cluanmore, away from academic learning and chastity and toward bardic lore and sexual liberation. The epic world of heroism and passion is much diminished in these Christian times, and the great tales of the Irish tradition are regarded with suspicion. Moran's wife, Blanaid, accuses the soldiers who abducted Aidan and brought him to her house of behaving "from morning to night as though we were all living in the days of Fionn MacCumhail and his seven battalions. What will the clergy say to-night when they see them here? What will they think of us?" (56). Her daughter, Ethna, loves the old tales, but her mother warns her "not to listen to those stories of the bad old days! Don't the clergy denounce them as immoral and injurious to young minds?" (59).

The old stories and the activity of storytelling are therefore subtly subversive, and the desire to hear them is a form of temptation. On their journey, Ethna tells Aidan the stories she knows, in particular the tale of Diarmuid and Grania, to whom the young lovers consciously compare themselves. This is one of the few stories overtly related in the book, but in all there are allusions to more than twenty-five stories and characters, not counting the titles of the books in the library at Cluanmore. Most of these are love stories in which the lovers defy the powers that stand in their way: "I could tell you of the courtship of Emer, of Lasara who fell in love and followed the track of great wheels far along a mountain road, and of Liadain who came south in the spring to meet Currither, of Etain, too, Fionnuala and Fedelma" (95). But there are also references to the encounter between Patrick and Oisín in texts like *Duanaire Finn,* and to *Buile Suibhne* ("The

8. Flann O'Brien, "A Bash in the Tunnel," in *Stories and Plays* (Harmondsworth, U.K.: Penguin Books, 1974), 206.

Madness of Sweeney"), both of which involve a confrontation between a pagan and a cleric—in which, ominously, the cleric ultimately prevails. Imaginative stories tempt the mind away from the rigors of clerical learning, but if, as Ethna and Aidan discover, stories are lessons too, which need to be studied until they are imaginatively understood and known by heart (96), these tales provide a counterforce to the Church's language of absolute authority, especially in its views on sexual love.

The epigraph to *The Bright Temptation* is also taken from an old story, "The Adventures of Connla the Fair," as translated by Standish O'Grady in *Silva Gadelica.* This story dates from the eighth century and relates how a woman of the Sídhe fell in love with Connla, son of Conn of the Hundred Battles, and invited him to the otherworld. She gave him an apple of which he ate but which never diminished, tempting him with immortality, and such longing for the woman seized him that he eventually gave in, leapt into her crystal boat, and was never seen in this world again. In the passage quoted in the epigraph to *The Bright Temptation,* the otherworldly girl explains to Teigue what her intentions were in inviting her beloved: "'I had bestowed on him true affection's love,' the girl explained, 'and therefore wrought to have him come to me in this land, where our delight, both of us, is to continue in looking at and in perpetual contemplation of one another; above and beyond which we pass not, to commit impurity or fleshly sin whatsoever.' 'That,' quoth Teigue again, 'is a beautiful and at the same time a comical thing.'" Teigue's dialogical observation approaches the lovers' position from two opposite angles. The romance view perceives idealized purity as beautiful; the satirical perspective, on the other hand, ridicules the denial of the material body. The romance between Aidan and Ethna should be regarded in this ambiguous light, too, for while Aidan's youthful innocence is, on the surface, depicted as touching and beautiful, it becomes ridiculous when his sexual inexperience is revealed as ignorance exacerbated by religious repression. The lovers' reenactment of the elopement of Diarmuid and Grania may be subversive in its pagan connotations, but it is highly idealized as befits a romance (indeed, Clarke claims to have sought in the early Gaelic elopement tales "a version of the Platonic ideal"[9]), and entirely bereft of the insurmountable sexual passion that formed the reason for the elopement of their precursors (even if its consummation

9. Clarke, *Black Church,* 122.

was, for a time, postponed). Ethna's version of the story also omits Finn's treachery and Diarmuid's death. In her quest for the ideal, Ethna regrets that "so many stories do not end as I want them to!" (95). The contrast between the two pairs of lovers in this respect is so great that Ethna's dreamy and innocent question, "I was wondering what Diarmuid and Grania did on a wet day" (172), becomes loaded with irony.

Romance consistently denies the physical side of existence; satire persistently emphasizes it. In *The Bright Temptation,* the lovers seek the path to purity, but are forever waylaid by the darker road. To find safety, Aidan and Ethna decide to head for the "holy glen where the culdees [from "Cele Dé" or "serving companion of God"] live in their small cells," where "among the hills, a saint lives alone" (84), and which is "far away from the wickedness of the world" (140). In their uncertain search for the glen, Aidan and Ethna chance upon the hidden path once followed by Diarmuid and Grania in their flight from Fionn. Sheltering in Diarmuid and Grania's cromlech, Ethna compares herself and Aidan to "two hermits, each in a cell" (121), without the faintest sense of irony. In romances, the enemy is typically "associated with winter, darkness, confusion, sterility, moribund life, and old age,"[10] and in the holy glen the natural world has become thwarted and menacing. What the lovers find there is a deserted, oppressive ruin:

Higher than their shoulders was the wilderness of fierce weeds that follow where the spade has been. There the penitential nettles were still bedded, heavy-seeded, ready with grey stings to beat down the flesh-rising which hermits fear. The humble, absolving dockleaf was hidden, but the thistles in barbaric companies were ranked above the companionable burrs. There, there, the purple-flowered fleabane, the plant against itch, had flourished, coarse leafage of the piss-mire shrub, piss-a-beds with those gaudy tops no children pull, beggar's wort and the viper's bugloss. In that wilderness of briars, of lurking stings, frail blossoms were unsmocked. Simples that had been brought from Europe to ease, to heal, were hidden amid the fierce tenantry that triumphs over man's eviction; they were lost as gentle thoughts in the harshness of religion, they were unthriven as kindness in the celibate minds of Ireland. (155)

The world of lovers is incompatible with that of culdees, but if Aidan is to become the hero of his romance, who is typically associated with "spring, dawn, order, fertility, vigor, and youth,"[11] he still has a long way to travel.

10. Frye, *Anatomy,* 187–88.
11. Ibid., 188.

Terence Brown has noted Austin Clarke's tendency in his poetry to examine the body and bodily functions, in particular in connection with sexual experience, from "strangely unexpected perspectives," for the same reason that he frequently uses images of mental breakdown: "[T]he poet as satirist proposes a version of life which offers marginality as the truest mode of being."[12] Aidan only knows the human body from its depictions in religious art, but these bodies were "interlaced in obscurities" through "the interstices of illuminated letters" (178): their complications are a delight for the intellect, not the senses. Aidan is so alienated from his own body that, when he catches a glimpse of it after falling into the river, his own knees "looked strange, as if they did not belong to him" (17); this is not surprising, since he has never before seen himself naked. Ethna, too, seems disembodied when he first meets her, like a ray of sunshine: "He seemed to be following that bright sky-maiden as in a dream" (79). Ethna is the *spéir-bhean* of Irish vision poetry, specifically of the love aisling, in which a man has a vision of a beautiful woman with whom he seeks to be united in love. Unfamiliar with the secular literary tradition, however, Aidan can only think of her as a "holy virgin" (83). In the course of their journey together, their relationship gradually becomes more physical. When Ethna shows herself to him naked, Aidan is as happy as he is confused, for, as the narrator explains, he has seen a rare sight: "Even in the Ireland of our own century the female form is as much feared by pious laymen as holy water is feared by the devil. Therefore no properly married woman would dream of allowing her husband to see her in *puris naturalibus*" (181). Immediately following this physical revelation, Aidan literally loses his way as he is looking for firewood, and finds himself close to the ruined hermitage. Its proximity is a reminder that mentally, Aidan has not yet freed himself from the notion that his feelings for Ethna are sinful and evil.

Aidan's predicament is reflected in the title of *The Bright Temptation*, which is a self-quotation from Austin Clarke's poem "The Young Woman of Beare" in his volume *Pilgrimage and Other Poems* (1929). In its turn, this poem is a creative response to the ninth-century Irish poem "Caillech Bérri," usually translated as "The Old Woman of Beare." The legendary Caillech Bérri was originally the sovereignty goddess of Celtic mythology. As the goddess of the land, she passed repeatedly through the cycle of youth

12. Brown, "Austin Clarke: Satirist," 134.

and old age, and each time it was sexual intercourse that transformed her from an old hag back into a beautiful young woman. In the ninth-century poem, composed after the introduction of Christianity in Ireland, the old woman has become "the Nun of Béarra Baoi" who has now been deprived of finding eternal renewal on earth by the newly introduced religious faith. She recalls the sensual delights of her youth, the food, the wine, and the beautiful company, especially the "pretty boys," all of which are now lost to her, while expressing regret at the present decrepit state of her body. Likening her life to the tides of the sea, she is resigned to the fact that, for her, no flood will come after the present ebb.[13] In Austin Clarke's poem "The Young Woman of Beare," the woman "is revitalised. The distance portrayed in the poem is not that between the felt present and the remembered past, it is that between the sensual woman rejoicing in sexual fulfilment, and her society made up of figures crowding anonymously to the bleak self-denying rituals of the church."[14] The textual transformation of the poem through the centuries mimics that of the woman herself: from being a fertility goddess in the pagan, matriarchal world of Celtic mythology the Old Woman is transformed into a nun in the early Christian Middle Ages, eventually to be restored to her former sexual self in the patriarchal world of Clarke's poem, where she is forced to express her sexuality covertly, with a mixture of guilt and defiance.

The theme of Clarke's poem, and of his romance, is the condemnation of natural, irrepressible sexual desire by the clergy as sinful:

I am the bright temptation
In talk, in wine, in sleep.
Although the clergy pray
I triumph in a dream.[15]

Unlike Ethna in the prose romance, however, the Young Woman of Beare has another side: "I am the dark temptation / Men know—and shining or-

13. See "Caillech Bérri" and its English translation, "The Old Woman of Beare," in *The Field Day Anthology of Irish Writing,* ed. Seamus Deane (Derry, Northern Ireland: Field Day, 1991), vol. 1, 32–34.

14. Peter Denman, "Austin Clarke: Tradition, Memory, and Our Lot," in *Tradition and Influence in Anglo-Irish Poetry,* ed. Terence Brown and Nicholas Grene (Totowa, N.J.: Barnes and Noble, 1989), 67–68.

15. Austin Clarke, "The Young Woman of Beare," in *Selected Poems,* ed. with introduction by Thomas Kinsella (Portlaoise: Dolmen Press, 1974), 7.

ders / Of clergy have condemned me."[16] In *The Bright Temptation*, however, the dark side of love, while present, is depicted not as pertaining to the book's heroes but as extrinsic and opposed to, even as a threat to, the heroic quest. The paradox is therefore that, while the romantic quest of Aidan and Ethna is for liberation from the fear of the body, in particular the sexual body, instilled by the clergy, that liberation is idealized and (supposedly) achieved without reference to and total acceptance of the body's functions. Direct references to physical matters are only present in *The Bright Temptation* when they are negative. Time after time Aidan is confronted with images of grotesque physicality and sexuality, by which he is consistently horrified. When he feels sexual arousal for the first time, he is "overwhelmed by secret shame and ignorance of what was attacking him" (168), but he vows that "he would fight that evil, and never again, now that he knew of it, would it conquer him" (169). Clarke implies that it is the shame that is evil rather than the sexuality itself, but the narrator nevertheless avoids direct, positive descriptions of physical pleasure. When Aidan is eventually reunited with his beloved at the end of his journey, having by now apparently come to terms with his sexuality, the narrator carefully omits any reference to the lovers' activities between sunset, when they are engaged in small talk, and the following sunrise, when we find them fast asleep: "Their naked arms were around one another, their dark and fair curls were entwined, and on their happy cheeks was the foxglove hue of the love-spot" (263). While this may be an appropriate ending for a romance, and leaves plenty of room for the imagination, the lack of explicitness is at the same time at odds with the objective of the quest of this particular romance. The narrator, who denounces the Church's condemnation of "the joy of the senses" (161) without himself overtly celebrating that joy, submits to a form of self-censorship. In the words of Maurice Harmon, "[T]he language of censure and accusation is more vibrant than the language of love."[17] Clarke would not find that "language of love" until much later in his career.

Clarke represents unmediated materialism and spirituality as opposite extremes that are both equally unacceptable. Blindly escaping from a group of xenophobic and inhospitable villagers, Aidan runs straight into the arms of his next captor, the huge, one-eyed Prumpolaun (from the Irish *priom-*

16. Ibid., 12.
17. Harmon, *Austin Clarke*, 137.

pallán, "dung beetle"). The model for this rogue figure is the *bodach,* or clown figure, in "Eachtra Bhodagh a' Chóta Lachtna," or "The Adventures of the Churl in the Grey Coat," which is itself probably modeled on "Eachtra an Cheithearnaigh Chaoilriabhaigh," or "The Adventures of the Narrow-Striped Kern."[18] The Prumpolaun's carnival appearance and his irreverent jokes suggest that he is a subversive figure, both comical and frightening: "Over the hairy slabs of the monster's chest, half hidden by his beard, were hung thick folds of frieze, which had been patched together with rope-ends and twists of iron spits. The tatters that flapped as the strange fellow shook with horrible merriment became less than their own gaps and rips. Rougher rags were knotted, bunched, into a kilt around the massed hair of his shanks, and he carried a large sack on his shoulder" (189). The Prumpolaun insists on bestowing his company and his "horrible generosity" on Aidan (194). He is a wanderer, a runner, "the great journeyman of Ireland" (190), who carries messages and takes with him the stray and the lost for company. Aidan is swept along on a whirlwind journey: "There was no sound in the mist now but that of the big man's shoes as they clattered and squelched between rock and heather. *Sin! Sin!* they seemed to say as they sped. Where was the Prumpolaun taking him? Where could he be going? They might have been sinners, both of them, hurrying from the fear of conscience to the cave-mouth of Purgatory in the north" (199). The Prumpolaun is a figure of grotesque and comical physicality, whose motto is "I run fast, I eat hard, and I lie soft" (195). Ever since ignoring his Easter duties for the earthly delights of a large flitch of bacon, eating has been his way of triumphing over the world:

He took out of his bag a hunk of bread large as the cauldron in a household of fifteen men, an enormous chunk of rancid bog-butter, a three-quarter wheel of griddle-bread and half a flitch of hard-rinded bacon.

He broke off great junks, of the bread and of the meal-cake, and with a knife he stripped the slices of striped, salt and mouldy bacon, tearing and eating ravenously as he did so with sucking, milling and rolling of his molars. (193–94)

Aidan's forcible journey with the all-too-earthy giant can be seen as an allegory, a nightmare concretization of his feelings of physical longing, escapism, and guilt.

18. Ibid., 30–31.

The Prumpolaun tells Aidan that he was not always a messenger but used to be employed by a saint as a strong man. One day, as he was carrying the saint across the Ford of Luan, he was bitten by the Devil in the shape of a black-crested eel and started running, with the saint still clinging around his neck. When he finally came to a stop the saint put a curse on him: "may you keep running for the rest of your life, you big galoot, and may your memory be always as bad as it was this day week when you forgot my instructions at the Ford of Luan" (200). Since then, whenever the Prumpolaun stops running, he forgets his message. The messenger can only remember his news when he is running fast enough, but then he has trouble sharing it with others. Perhaps in some way the Prumpolaun represents the Irish writer in exile who, bitten by the Devil and cursed and banned by a Church that he cannot manage to shake off his back, still attempts in vain to deliver messages to his countrymen. When he finally delivers it, the Prumpolaun's message—a warning that the Danes are coming—turns out to be valid enough, although Aidan is too confused to pay much attention to it.

The Prumpolaun suddenly abandons Aidan during a dizzying game of tig (or "tag") in which the boy "did not know whether he was pursuing the Prumpolaun or being pursued by him" (210). The strange and frightening place where he leaves Aidan turns out to be Glen Bolcan, the valley where the madmen of Ireland are traditionally wont to gather. This next episode has a nightmarish quality. Aidan is greatly disturbed by the ghostly figures he encounters in the moonlight: "Each of them seemed to be speaking to an unseen companion, pleading, expostulating. As they did so, they twisted their hands, they raised their faces in torment. What were they all terrified of; from what were they trying to escape? Why was each of them sunk in an awful loneliness of his own?" (217). The narrator of *The Bright Temptation* furnishes the reader with his private views on the matter: "Tempted by ignorance, driven by the moral rigor which forbids passion in Ireland, they succumb to the solitary sin, ever with insane hands, that they cannot keep from themselves, wasting their pale watery substance. Through the brakes went tortured things that had been men or women, crazied by scruples of conscience, by injustice, scandal or wrong, flying in fear of themselves, in fear of the rushing force that was once their minds" (221). Panic-stricken, Aidan flees, falls, and loses consciousness.

Bec-mac-Dé, the saint who finds Aidan lying unconscious a few hundred yards outside the valley, tells him that the vision was a warning to him not to give way to the same temptation. Bec-mac-Dé makes sure that Aidan knows which temptation he is dealing with:

"And did the Devil cause you to touch yourself? Did you make yourself weak, my child?"

Pious was that question and familiar to Aidan, for he had been asked it in Confession at Cluanmore. Still, still, in the dark confession-boxes of Ireland, the good clergy whisper that question to young penitents who admit of faults against the sixth commandment. Stammering, clasping their sinful hands in shame, the young answer Heaven's representative in a tremble, until the very moment of absolution. (229)

The saint suggests that fear of sinning can save Aidan from the fate of those in Glen Bolcan; the narrator, by contrast, suggests that it was precisely this fear of sinning that led to the condition of those in Glen Bolcan.

Bec-mac-Dé is a particularly austere saint who has given himself up to severe mortifications of the flesh, insists on the everlasting torture reserved for sinners, and refers to Christ variously as "the King of Pain" (233) and "the Man of Nails" (234). Bec-mac-Dé's austerity and denial of the body (except in suffering) are the reversal of the gross materiality of the Prumpolaun, but equally awe-inspiring: "He was a drover of demons, a chastiser of unchastity, and his frown could put the fear of God into the sinful." His eyes "seemed blackened and scorched by the spirit within them; they were wounds through which that mighty spirit showed itself" (224). The Prumpolaun and Bec-mac-Dé represent opposite but equally negative extremes of physicality and austerity, and just as Aidan found himself powerless to escape from the Prumpolaun's physical grasp, he is equally unable to free himself from the mental restraints of Bec-mac-Dé's rhetoric of fear.

Bec-mac-Dé claims to have been a great performer of miracles, the final one of which involved the cursing of a pagan king who tried to prevent Bec-mac-Dé from building a church on his land: "The king dropped his sword, he ran with a howl into the woods, seeking those glades where the mad congregate under the full moon. He became feathered from head to foot, so powerful was my word, and his abode was in tree-tops that have been twigged by the herons. I have heard from a pilgrim that he went at last over sea to converse in other forests with the madmen of Britain" (228). Aidan is readily impressed by the powers of the saint; he does not recognize that Bec-mac-Dé's story plagiarizes *Buile Suibhne,* the tale of the madness of the seventh-century king Sweeney, in almost every detail—the notable exception being that, where the enraged Suibhne "set out stark-naked in his swift career to expel the cleric from the church,"[19] Bec-mac-Dé modestly has the king jump out of bed "with only a shirt to his back" (227). In *Buile Suibhne,* the malediction is pronounced on Sweeney by Saint Ronan, a name conspicuously absent from Bec-mac-Dé's list of famous curse-uttering saints. Indeed, the holy man has a great deal in common with Ronan, who is described as "a man who fulfilled God's command and bore the yoke of piety, and endured persecutions for the Lord's sake. He was God's own worthy servant, for it was his wont to crucify his body for love of God."[20] To anyone familiar with *Buile Suibhne,* Bec-mac-Dé's claims may raise suspicions about his honesty and credibility; if *Buile Suibhne* is his source, he is a pious fraud whose telling of apparent falsehoods in order to enforce what he calls "holy purity" undermines the general validity of his opinions. At the very least, the similarity between the stories (for one can hardly speak of parody) is an indication that the Church's teachings commonly drive people insane, and that Aidan, like Sweeney, may find solace in poetry and the natural world.

Unfamiliar with *Buile Suibhne* and frightened out of his wits by the vision of the everlasting torture that results from yielding "even in thought to the desire of woman" (230) conjured up by Bec-mac-Dé, Aidan vows to stop thinking of Ethna (not so easy, since he keeps wondering why such beauty was created if it were sinful to his sight and would condemn him to eternal torment), and to return to Cluanmore, where "he would be safe from all temptation of passion" (241). The fear and obedience instilled in Aidan by Bec-mac-Dé create a single-mindedness that is tantamount to blindness. Aidan's total reliance on Cluanmore as a refuge and a place of salvation forms a single truth in his mind that allows him to see only the expected and blinds him to any other reality. The irony of this is profound,

19. J. G. O'Keeffe, trans. and ed., *Buile Suibhne (The Frenzy of Suibhne)* (London: Irish Texts Society, 1913), 5.
20. Ibid., 3.

for once he is back within the security of the monastic settlement every single one of his interpretations proves to have been wrong, and every time his
fears are eased by feelings of safety or familiarity these feelings turn out to
have been misguided. Instead of being disturbed by the strange fires and
unusual crowds he sees moving between Cluanmore's main buildings,
Aidan decides that it must be the feast day of Saint Nessan, the founder of
the settlement. A vision comes into his mind of Ethna warning him of im-
pending danger, but he dismisses it as a temptation from the Evil One.
Instead of running away, Aidan climbs over a wall into the enclosure of
Cluanmore: "He was safe at last. No violence or danger could reach him
now. His trials were over and he had conquered himself" (245).

Inside the enclosure, however, the world has been turned upside down.
Aidan finds himself in an unfamiliar part of Cluanmore, and he realizes
that he must be in the Trian of the Elders where students are strictly forbidden to go. Not only does his immediate transgression of the rules make
him feel uneasy, but the unfamiliarity of his surroundings causes him to
lose his bearings and to walk around in a circle. The sound of guttural,
foreign voices adds to his confusion. As he passes the Teampull Diarmuid
in the forbidden quarter, Aidan (who had earlier fancied himself as a
would-be Diarmuid) suddenly comes face to face with what he thinks is a
naked woman but is actually the sheela-na-gig on the outside of the church:

> The Devil was mocking him with an evil vision, for no female was ever permitted
> to enter the holy precincts of Cluanmore. But he knew instinctively that his eye
> could not have deceived him. Too clearly had he seen her repulsive face, seen the
> lewd smile she gave him as the torchlight swept over her shameless breasts and
> showed that their black tops were erect. The shadows in which she was dwarfed had
> hidden her abdomen, but he knew she was bow-legged and that her arms were
> akimbo. Never could he have imagined, even in Glen Bolcan, so horrible a sight. The
> woman vanished into the darkness again, but he still remembered her mocking
> smile. (247–48)

Austin Clarke's interest in sheela-na-gigs dated back to at least 1918,
when he went in search of the carvings with the help of a list compiled for
him by the historian Edmund Curtis.[21] The name "sheela-na-gig" has vari-

21. See Maurice Harmon, "Notes towards a Biography," *Irish University Review*, 4, 1
(1974): 17.

ously been explained as *Sighle na gCíoch* or "the old hag of the breasts"—
the interpretation favored by Clarke, who refers to the figure as "Cile-na-
gCich" (248)—or *Síle-ina-Giob,* meaning "sheela (an old woman) on her
hunkers."[22] It is likely that the figure has its origin in the Celtic matriarchal
goddess of creation and destruction, and as such is related to the *Caillech
Bérri,* another dualistic figure whose original potential for sexual renewal
was subsequently denied her in the medieval Christian version of the poem.
That denial was typical of medieval Europe, where "there developed a range
of exhibitionist figures . . . whose function was to alert the faithful to the
dangers of the sin of lust. . . . The emphasis on the genitalia—which are
usually enlarged—related to the Church's teaching that sinners were punished in hell through the bodily organs by which they had offended."[23] The
sheela-na-gig, the old hag with explicitly sexual features, is a grotesque, dualistic carnival figure of death and renewal: her bodily depths are ambivalent in that life "is shown in its twofold contradictory process; it is the epitome of incompleteness."[24] When Aidan sees the sheela-na-gig in *The Bright
Temptation,* the figure's abdomen is hidden in shadow, and her explicit sexuality is obscured. Even so, he shrinks from her in horror. Rather than a figure representing life-in-death, she has come to stand exclusively for death
and evil. For Aidan, Ethna represents the complete opposite of purity and
light. Earlier in the book, Aidan had thought that Ethna's face "reminded
him of one that had been carven on a cornice at Cluanmore" (103).
Ironically, however, Teampull Diarmuid conceals a carving of a dark counterpart to Aidan's bright angel. There is no middle ground: in *The Bright
Temptation,* the two extremes of light and dark, life and death, are never
reconciled in one figure.

Running from what he believes to be the work of the Devil, and no
longer safe from sin even in the holy enclosure, Aidan comes across other
signs of profanation and desecration. A sacred chalice is lying in the middle of the quadrangle, and when he enters the church he finds himself face
to face with yet another woman, this time made of flesh and blood and in-
decently enthroned upon the high altar: "her white arms were raised in ex-

22. Eamonn Kelly, *Sheela-na-Gigs: Origins and Functions* (Dublin: Country House/
National Museum of Ireland, 1996), 5.

23. Ibid., 10.

24. Bakhtin, *Rabelais,* 25.

ultation. Her breasts were of hammered metal, but each nipple was of gold. Her mailed body was half hidden by a broidered vestment of sea-purple, but her large thighs were naked, torched, as she leaned back upon that throne" (250). At first Aidan incongruously believes the Danes in the congregation worshiping before her to be monks gone mad, until the truth finally dawns on him and he realizes how misguided he has been all along: "Fool that he had been to have lost himself in vain thought, to have believed himself the victim of especial temptations during the last hours of his journey" (251). This time Aidan is forced to flee to safety *outside* the walls of Cluanmore. From afar he witnesses the sacking of the holy city and the torching of the refectory and the libraries. The destruction of the holy school by the Danes provides an ironic perspective on the abbot's earlier and evidently misguided insistence that the falling of the holy books should be interpreted as a sign not of the coming of the Danes, but of the scholars' sins against the holy purity of Ireland.

On his way to Monarua, where he had first encountered Ethna, and where he is eventually reunited with her, Aidan is led by voices to a small bardic college. There he hears for the first time the old Gaelic poetry of his native land, composed "before the cleric's bell was heard in the east dividing man from woman" (257). As the Ollamh speaks of the wisdom of nature, Aidan "longed to study the divisions of poetic knowledge, commit its commentaries to heart, and learn the Thousand Tales of Ireland. All night in his sleep he seemed to hear music that freed him from the shadowy fears of his early education" (257). Clarke implies that the Irish tales may present a natural compromise between the unacceptable extremes of body and spirit represented by the Prumpolaun and Bec-mac-Dé, but that middle ground is never overtly presented. The ending to *The Bright Temptation* is not without irony. When the "pagan sun" rises and discloses the young lovers to the members of Moran's household, naked in each other's arms, "no need of Gospel book had those scandalised match-makers at the sheiling to tell them that those youngsters must be sent to Confession as soon as possible and restored to Irish virtue by holy matrimony" (263). Earlier Ethna had exclaimed that "so many stories do not end as I want them to!" (95): this story does end happily, for the lovers gain each other and are blissfully united. The Church, however, is allowed to have the final word, and even though its ruling is presumably not one that the lovers would want to contest, the extent of their liberation from, and of their victory over, the restrictions imposed on them by the puritanical morality prevalent in Ireland is by no means clear. At this point it may be relevant to recall the ominous dream of Torbach in the opening scene of *The Bright Temptation,* in which he attempts in vain to find the tip of the dragon's tail: "at the end of his search he was no farther than he had been at the beginning" (3).

As an unadulterated romance, Austin Clarke's *The Bright Temptation* must essentially be a monologic text, since romance equals idealism. Aidan's journey is a learning process in which he is guided by the invisible Aongus, during which he can make mistakes but is ultimately convinced of the rightness of his feelings for Ethna and the wrongness of repression. This is the "truth" Aidan needs to discover, but it is a truth that is itself removed from the idealism and purity that are the objectives of romance. Because the hero's values are in the end explicitly at odds with traditional, institutional values, the romance tends all along toward the perspective of what Bakhtin would consider radical romantic satire. A further dialogic component in *The Bright Temptation* involves its narrative persona. Speaking insistently and didactically, the narrator does not deliver his message of anti-authoritarianism in a straightforward manner but through irony, in a voice that has ostensibly internalized the reigning ideology (the first-person plural includes the narrator), but which actually functions to convey the opposite viewpoint Clarke endorses himself.

Moral training in Ireland is severe and lasts until marriage. Even in childhood we are taught by the pious clergy to battle against bad thoughts, so that we may preserve our holy purity. In youth we learn the dangers of idle talk, the temptations of self-sin, the need of avoiding stories that may incite passion. For passion in Ireland is denounced as evil and obscene. Women are the snares set for us by the Devil. Even to think of a woman's body with pleasure is a mortal sin. Only by the practice of frequent confession, therefore, can the young fortify themselves against temptation. They should be careful and quick, however, when examining their conscience for faults against the sixth commandment, lest the Devil tempt them again.

But in holy matrimony all is changed, and we no longer can sin by look or touch. . . . Only the theologians, the pious clergy, can understand these great matters; the newly married are content to tickle and thump themselves into virtue. (135–36)

The narrator's tone echoes that of pious saints like Bec-mac-Dé, but whereas the latter's voice is monologic, the narrator's is dialogic, and involves a discrepancy between several types of diction. It is these stylistic lapses ("tickle and thump") that indicate the double-voiced nature of the discourse.

The ideal presented in *The Bright Temptation* is liberation from fear of physical love and passion, which Clarke equates with fear of nature itself. The idealizing romance format, however, prevents Clarke from depicting and celebrating that same sexual love in any concrete or graphic sense. The book's form is therefore, at least to some extent, ill-at-ease with its content, and the idealizing flow of the romance seems constantly to be impeded by a satirical undercurrent moving in the opposite direction. Several commentators have remarked upon this uneasiness, and wondered whether Clarke is entirely in command of his material. Susan Halpern, for instance, finds that the romance is "marred by the excessive satiric jibes at the Church's indoctrination which Clarke cannot seem to avoid."[25] It is as if the "bright" romance is conducting a dialogue with the "dark" elements it has consciously omitted but which are nevertheless a felt presence throughout the book. In *The Singing-Men at Cashel* Austin Clarke deals more consciously and overtly with these contradictions.

25. Halpern, *Austin Clarke*, 177.

chapter six

"Romances Are Complicated Affairs"

The Singing-Men at Cashel

Austin Clarke probably found the history of the tenth-century queen Gormlai, the protagonist of his second romance, in Eugene O'Curry's *Lectures on the Manuscript Materials of Ancient Irish History;* certainly O'Curry's information about her is more extensive than that given in any other source. O'Curry compiled the story of her life and her three marriages from several sources: references to Gormlai are found in the *Annals of Clonmacnoise* and, more accurately and elaborately, in the *Book of Leinster;* in addition, a list of historic tales in the *Book of Leinster* mentions a romance called *Serc Gormlaithe do Níall* (The love of Gormlaith for Niall), but no version of this text survives, although Clarke uses its purported existence for his own ends.

Clarke follows the events of Gormlai's life almost exactly as they are presented by O'Curry. The latter tells us that Gormlaith—the names are given here in O'Curry's spelling—was first betrothed to Cormac Mac Cullennan, bishop, scholar, and king of Munster, "but that marriage was never consummated, as the young king changed his mind, and restored the princess to her father . . . while he himself took holy orders. He . . . became subsequently Archbishop of Cashel, and was . . . the author of the celebrated Saltair of Cashel, as well as of the learned compilation since known as Cormac's Glossary."[1] Gormlaith was then married against her will to Cearbhall, king of Leinster. A short time later, Gormlaith's husband joined her father, Flann Siona, king of Meath, in a battle against Cormac, during which the latter was killed and beheaded. When Gormlaith protested

---

1. Eugene O'Curry, *Lectures on the Manuscript Materials of Ancient Irish History* (Dublin: William A. Hinch and Patrick Traynor, 1878), 132.

Cearbhall's gloating over the desecration of Cormac's body, Cearbhall "struck her so rude a blow with his foot, as threw her headlong on the floor."[2] Insulted by this indignity, Gormlaith insisted on a separation from her husband, whereupon her young kinsman Niall Glundubh, son of the king of Aileach (Ulster), asked for her hand; but it was not until after Cearbhall had been killed by the Danes in the following year that she consented to marry Niall.[3] Austin Clarke's romance ends shortly after Gormlai's wedding to Nial (Clarke's spelling), but not because he was unaware of the details of her later life. The manuscripts quoted by O'Curry give much more information about the queen's life until her death in 947; I will have cause to refer to this material later on in this chapter.

Although *The Singing-Men at Cashel* factually follows the events of the life of Queen Gormlai, Clarke has interpreted the feelings and motivations behind the characters' actions quite freely and personally. The book is therefore more than simply a historical novel. In this respect, Maurice Harmon has noted that Clarke's portrayal of the medieval world "is selective and sometimes inaccurate. His use of history tends to be sketchy, but he is intent on describing a world that is similar to his own and yet significantly different."[4] By depicting Gormlai's life from her perspective and in relation to her three husbands, Clarke highlights the Catholic Church's attitude toward sexuality and marriage—in this case, multiple marriages—and especially its hostile treatment of women. To quote Maurice Harmon again: "No other work in Clarke's entire output holds the mirror of the past up to modern Irish Catholicism with such force and accuracy."[5]

Austin Clarke interweaves the story of Queen Gormlai with the adventures of Anier Mac Conglinne, clerical scholar turned wandering poet, a figure he borrowed from another medieval tale, "Aislinge Meic Con Glinne" ("The Vision of Mac Conglinne"). He had already used the same figure in

---

2. Ibid., 133.

3. The *Annals of Clonmacnoise* give the marriages in a different order, stating that Gormlai "was first married to Cormack mc o'Cuillennann king of Mounster, secondly to king Neale, . . . and lastly shee was married to Kervell mc Moregan king of Leinster." Quoted in O. J. Bergin, "Poems Attributed to Gormlaith," in *Miscellany Presented to Kuno Meyer*, ed. Osborn Bergin and Carl Marstrander (Halle, Germany: Max Niemeyer, 1912), 343, note 33.

4. Harmon, *Austin Clarke*, 32.

5. Ibid., 35.

The Son of Learning (1927), a play whose plot is based more closely on the source text than the events depicted in *The Singing-Men at Cashel*. Anier is a subversive figure in the original satire, who turns away from a life of the spirit at Armagh—"the greatest of Ireland's seats of piety and learning at that time"[6]—toward a life of the senses:

The reason why he was called Anier was that he would satirize and praise all. No wonder, indeed; for there had not come before him, and came not after him, one whose satire or praise was harder to bear, wherefore he was called Anera (i. e., Non-refusal), because there was no refusing him.

A great longing seized the mind of the scholar, to follow poetry, and to abandon his studies. For wretched to him was his life in the shade of his studies. And he searched in his mind whither he would make his first poetical journey. The result of his search was, to go to Cathal mac Finguine, who was then on a royal progress in Iveagh of Munster. The scholar had heard that he would get plenty and enough of all kinds of whitemeats; for greedy and hungry for whitemeats was the scholar.[7]

Robin Flower describes Anier as "an example of the truant scholar, . . . the happy-go-lucky vagabond who goes singing and swaggering through the Middle Ages until he finds his highest expression and final justification in François Villon."[8]

Anier Mac Conglinne is a satirist, and "The Vision of Mac Conglinne" is a satirical text in which the hero criticizes in particular the Church and the monks of Cork who treat him less than hospitably. The monks put him on trial and the abbot of Cork tries to have him crucified, but a vision seen by Anier during the night, of a land in which everything is made of food, gives the abbot the idea that Mac Conglinne may be just the person to rid the king of the demon of gluttony that has taken possession of him. Anier manages to expel the demon by starving the king, restraining him with ropes, and eating a copious meal in front of him that eventually tempts the demon to leave the king's body and fly off to hell. The king rewards Mac Conglinne, and the text concludes by stating that similar rewards will be given both to

6. "The Vision of Mac Conglinne," in *Ancient Irish Tales,* ed. Tom Peete Cross and Clark Harris Slover (1936; reprint, New York: Barnes and Noble, 1969), 552.

7. Ibid., 553.

8. Robin Flower, *The Irish Tradition* (1947; reprint, Oxford, U.K.: Clarendon Press, 1978), 76.

whoever is able to recite the story of "The Vision of Mac Conglinne" and to those who will listen to the tale.

Cross and Slover call "The Vision of Mac Conglinne" "one of the wildest extravaganzas of all literature" in which the writer "composes an uproarious satire on hagiography, ecclesiastical mendicancy, and royal gluttony."[9] Apart from the satirical content, the text has many other characteristics of Menippean satire. Robin Flower points out that the tale

is one long parody of the literary methods used by the clerical scholars. At every turn we recognize a motive or a phrase from the theological, the historical, and the grammatical literature. A full commentary on the Vision from this point of view would be little short of a history of the development of literary forms in Ireland. And it is not only the literary tricks of the monks that are held up to mockery. The writer makes sport of the most sacred things, not sparing even the Sacraments and Christ's crucifixion. He jests at relics, at tithes, at ascetic practices, at amulets, at the sermons and private devotions of the monks; the flying shafts of his wit spare nothing and nobody. . . .

. . . It at once sums up and turns into gigantic ridicule the learning of the earlier time much in the same way as François Rabelais at once typified and transcended the learning of the later Middle Ages.[10]

In terms of a large part of its borrowed material, then, *The Singing-Men at Cashel* allies itself more closely and directly with satire than did *The Bright Temptation.*

While Austin Clarke's second romance closely follows the sources in depicting the events of Queen Gormlai's early life, its treatment of Anier Mac Conglinne is much more liberal and fragmented. Although the vagabond scholar is clearly based on the hero of the "Vision," and while Clarke borrows elements from that text, Anier's adventures in *The Singing-Men at Cashel* are inspired by the author from a variety of sources. The beginning of book 1 shows Anier suddenly becoming aware, in the middle of a lecture on the *Moralia* of Saint Gregory, of the world outside the religious school; he leaves the room "under the pretence of an urgent natural call" (12),[11] thus irreverently giving priority to the body over the spirit (which is, by im-

9. Cross and Slover, *Ancient Irish Tales,* 551.

10. Flower, *Irish Tradition,* 76–77.

11. Austin Clarke, *The Singing-Men at Cashel* (London: George Allen and Unwin, 1936); all page references in the text are to this edition.

plication, "unnatural"), throws away his slate, and sets out upon his travels. It is in this way that he comes upon the festivities for the wedding of Cormac and Gormlai. At this point, the narrative focus shifts to her, until Anier reappears toward the end of the narrative. Anier's final adventure in *The Singing-Men at Cashel* is initiated by his argument with five Ulster poets, who challenge him to venture into the cave entrance to the under-world of "Illan-na-Frugadory," better known as Saint Patrick's Purgatory in Lough Derg. The third part of Clarke's narrative is almost entirely devoted to Mac Conglinne's experiences in this cave.

The two story lines, of Gormlai and Anier, meet only tangentially. Most commentators on Clarke's work have regarded this as a flaw in the book. According to Susan Halpern, for example, while *The Singing-Men at Cashel* "is unquestionably the finest of the three romances, the subplot is not very effectively joined to the main thread of the story."[12] Maurice Harmon, too, argues that the book's "structural collapse at the end affects its ultimate suc-cess,"[13] in that "the last six chapters interrupt the narrative and the finely re-alised sequence of events that had characterised most of the novel up to then."[14] He also feels that *The Singing-Men at Cashel* is not very successful "in making the story of Anier Mac Conglinne intersect significantly with the story of Gormlai."[15] Benedict Kiely is even more disturbed by the book's seeming flaws and blames them on a poet's struggles with the "lowly" medium of prose; the elements of the story, he says, "are all tumbled to-gether in one book as blocks of priceless marble might lie in heaped con-fusion in a rich quarry."[16] Dissenting from this general view, however, Craig Tapping sees Anier's story as "the perfect contrast for the larger, more seri-ous story."[17]

The hesitations about the book's structure quoted above seem to be mainly the result of misguided "novelistic" expectations. Romance and satire are much more "loose-jointed"—to use Northrop Frye's term—in narrative terms than the novel, while in satire, moreover, fragmentation is common and contrasts, often violent ones to the point of contradiction, are

---

12. Halpern, *Austin Clarke*, 180.   13. Harmon, *Austin Clarke*, 92.

14. Ibid., 107.   15. Ibid., 109.

16. Benedict Kiely, *Modern Irish Fiction: A Critique* (Dublin: Golden Eagle Books, 1950), 68.

17. G. Craig Tapping, *Austin Clarke: A Study of His Writings* (Dublin: Academy Press, 1981), 133.

prevalent. As Frye points out in relation to another flawed novel, *Tristram Shandy*, "a deliberate rambling digressiveness . . . is endemic in the narrative technique of satire," and "an extraordinary number of great satires are fragmentary, unfinished, or anonymous."[18] In Bakhtin's words, such satire "loves to play with abrupt transitions and shifts, ups and downs, rises and falls, unexpected comings together of distant and disunited things, mésalliances of all sorts."[19] This is the case in Austin Clarke's second "romance," which may therefore be read more fruitfully in terms of Menippean satire.

In *The Singing-Men at Cashel*, there are no singular perspectives or single voices: everything is polarized and presented in terms of contrasting paired images or dialogic voices. Divisions are both external—between two or more characters—and internal—within the self. Duality is the controlling principle of the narrative, for no position, however trivial or unimportant, is presented as being the single truth. For every interpretation of reality there is an equally valid alternative, opposite view. Such a duality informs the relationship between the stories of Anier and Gormlai. At the beginning of the book, Anier resolves to leave Armagh, to "go to the Devil" (12), and to become a wandering scholar, thus liberating himself from the shackles of authority and allying himself with the dark side of life. Gormlai, by contrast, is virginal and obedient; her marriage to Cormac represents her submission to the laws, to the authority of the Church, and to the bonds of holy matrimony, which "is a victory over evil and the consequences of Original Sin" (32).

The bold unruly Anier and the chaste passive Gormlai of the opening passages of *The Singing-Men at Cashel* are each other's opposites, but in each case the external appearance is antithetical to the character's inner thoughts and feelings. Although Anier is outwardly only concerned with practical jokes, sex, and getting drunk, he is filled with self-hatred when he sees the chastity and loveliness of Gormlai on her wedding day; even before he deserted from the monastic school he had seen his own soul in a vision, "small and luminous, but already speckled by his sins" (18). Confronted with the queen, he feels corrupt and unable to overcome the "druidic waves" and darkness that assail him (29). At that same moment the bride herself, however, is feeling far from lovely and serene: "She scarcely heard

18. Frye, *Anatomy*, 234.
19. Bakhtin, *Dostoevsky's Poetics*, 118.

the clamour of the companies below, because of the clamour of her own mind. Embarrassment rang around her and somewhere lost in its remote tumult she waited, knowing that her cheek was fiery beyond control and that her temples were chill" (32). The division in Gormlai's mind is represented by conflicting private and public voices: remembering the morning's ceremony, "suddenly she seemed in the chapel. . . . Deep and treble voices were intoning the inspired words of Saint Sechnall, words that an angel had dictated to him. . . . Those pure voices were calling to her and her soul answered in joy. . . . The glory faded again as suddenly as it had come. . . . The tumult of the crowd came towards her, louder and more confusing. She was still in that lay-house, bewildered and without guidance" (36–38). This dialogic conflict between authority and freedom, certainty and uncertainty, spirit and body, reality and imagination governs not only the main characters but the entire structure of *The Singing-Men at Cashel.*

The Singing-Men at Cashel is divided into three books, each of which broadly corresponds with one of Gormlai's three marriages: at the beginning of book 1 she has just married Cormac; in book 2 she is already married to Carrol (Cearbhall); at the end of book 3 she is going through the wedding ceremony with Nial. Clarke depicts each relationship as different, following a basic thesis—antithesis—synthesis distribution in which Cormac represents the spirit, Carrol the body, and Nial the harmonious union of both. When Gormlai sees Cormac praying on their wedding night, "in a flash, she knew that her husband had the hands of a priest" (63). Her forebodings turn out to be justified: with the aid of a great deal of sophistry, Cormac manages to overcome his "lower desires," leaving his wife disappointed that she still remains unenlightened as to the secrets of married life that she had hoped would be revealed to her that night. While Gormlai's marriage to Cormac remains unconsummated, her marriage to the brutal Carrol is the opposite extreme, leading Gormlai to believe that she has discovered in her second marriage what her first husband Cormac had been protecting her from: "I, too, share your revulsion and loathing, Cormac. But it is too late, and I am alone" (226). The contrast between Cormac and Carrol is also expressed through their attitudes toward language and the written word. While Cormac is a scholar, Carrol despises books and learning to the degree that he even forbids monks to travel through his territory with their manuscripts. Cormac uses complicated arguments to convince his wife of his standpoint, but Carrol uses physical force. Both husbands are alike in frowning upon Gormlai's knowledge of poetry and imaginative literature, however, because neither has any use for the creative imagination.

During Gormlai's first marriage "the secret world of poetry which she guarded in her imagination dwindled before syllogisms and the truths of Revelation" (161). She comes to believe that there is other, secret knowledge available in texts elsewhere that will teach her about herself and about marriage: "What use was all her knowledge of poetry and story to her? There were secret Latin books which the clergy possessed in their schools, but no lay person would be permitted to read them, much less a woman" (56). What she finds when she furtively reads the books in the scriptorium, however, is "a bewildering world of vehement opinions, of strange anger, of stern ordinances. . . . There was some shame in womanhood and its periods, some mysterious corruption due to the Fall which she could not ascertain. Still in ignorance of the meaning of matrimony, she raced from page to page . . . ever in the hope of finding some precise definition that would reveal all to her" (162–63). The information she seeks, however, is not forthcoming; instead, she ominously reads about the adulterous nature of second and third marriages.

Gormlai's mixed feelings of guilt and defiance translate themselves into a nightmare, in which she sees people who are naked but sexless—the Blessed, she thinks—while she herself is naked and ashamed, and in which she is put on trial at the end of her life for having been married three times. Hers is a Kafkaesque trial she cannot win; she vehemently protests her innocence, but the very fact that she is protesting at all turns out to be the greater crime: "The next instant she knew that she had been tricked into condemning herself. In that dark flush of wilfulness she had laid bare her true nature, she had shown her rebelliousness against the subservient position of womankind" (186–87). Still rebelling, she finds herself falling down a precipice and into a river of blood. Clarke often uses dreams and a fall to initiate a character's transformation: the dream confronts the character with a test or an evaluation of the self, while the fall symbolizes a breaking free, consciously or unconsciously, from official rules and authoritarian constraints.

Cashel represented monastic, patriarchal learning. Gormlai is confronted with another, contrasting, and unwritten form of secret knowledge in the form of oral folk wisdom when she is living with Carrol at Naas. But although women are part of the latter tradition, the midwife—Clarke's *Ban Glúna Mór* or "Great Kneewoman"—who reveals this knowledge to her does not inspire confidence either: "I know what the clergy have hidden away in their books—the safe time between the horns of the moon and all the calculations. They say it's not a sin then to trick the Big Man. There's many a woman has tried to look over the priest's shoulder into those books but found they were written in Latin. But it's not safe, ducky. It's not as safe as the ways I know" (220–21). The secret contraceptive knowledge exclusively reserved for women makes Gormlai almost as uncomfortable as the misogynistic opinions contained in the patriarchal Latin books at Cashel. Both represent opposite extremes, ultimate positions that polarize men and women, and both are therefore equally sterile and life-denying. Poetry and romance, the forms of imaginative literature from which Gormlai is distracted by her first two marriages, represent healing and fertile alternatives to these extremes.

Cormac's thoughts are all for his soul to the detriment of the body, while Carrol's pleasures are all physical. The war between the two kings reflects the irreconcilable and polarized nature of the ultimate positions they adopt: they represent unhealthy and untenable extremes of soul and body, both of which are satirized and ridiculed by Clarke in that each of these positions can be justified only with the aid of convoluted reasoning. What is doubly ironic, however, is that in each instance the justification is provided by the Church. By using this strategy, Clarke circumvents the problem of how to satirize Carrol's physicality, since it is "much more difficult to satirize materialists than spiritualists because materialists have already appropriated the most effective strategy of satire."[20] Gormlai is already aware of the Church's perplexing attitude toward sex: "She knew indeed that it was a scandal for the married not to sleep together, just as it was a dreadful sin for the unmarried to do so. It was puzzling, but she knew that much" (133). Cormac, however, claims that there are other things to be taken into account in marriage, such as the spiritual law of compensation that will allow some people to atone for the excess of others: "it is possible, so to speak, to raise marriage to a higher level even than that of the unmarried state" by

20. Palmeri, *Satire*, 55.

sacrificing "what is permitted to all in matrimony. We can choose the spiritual alone and in that way achieve a victory of a very high kind over the nastiness of the instincts. . . . Some who found the temptations of a single life insufficient have even entered into the married state deliberately in order that they might submit themselves to a more difficult test of spirituality" (135–36). His argument puzzles and depresses Gormlai: "Marriage was more complicated and difficult than even she had thought" (136).

Gormlai's problems with the perplexing nature of clerical reasoning are compounded during her second marriage, when she finds herself rebelling with all her mind against her husband's physical presence. Her first husband, Cormac, had argued that abstinence was a virtue, but when Gormlai seeks spiritual guidance from Father Benignus because she has refused her second husband his "rights," she is told a different story: because Carrol has not asked her to act "contrary to the divine law," she has no reason to refuse him and, indeed, deepens her own state of mortal sin with each refusal. When Cormac felt attracted by his wife's nakedness, he shrank back in horror from his feelings of desire as if the Devil had tempted him by "presenting to his mind's eye a salacious image or eidolon" (65). Yet, when Gormlai shrinks from Carrol, not to escape from unholy desire, but in revulsion, Benignus diagnoses this, too, as a temptation from the Devil: "[I]n yielding to an impulse of natural disgust, you are allowing yourself to be beguiled by the Tempter. You must resist this instinct which is given to the unmarried to protect them, for in your married state it is sinful" (290). Moreover, Benignus argues, by putting the claims of natural affection above those of duty she is driving her husband into sin: "Your neglect may cause him to commit fornication and in that way you, alone, will be responsible for the loss of his soul, you, alone, will hurl him into the eternal flames" (291). The Church, through its representatives Cormac and Benignus, thus manages to argue that sexual abstinence within marriage is both the greatest virtue *and* the greatest sin. This is the familiar Catch-22 of Menippean satire: it is the "unresolved juxtaposition of conflicting frames of reference or systems of belief" characteristic of narrative satire,[21] with the added complication that the paradox here is to be found within the same system of belief.

Menippean satire typically creates an unresolved dialogue between opposed ideological alternatives, without authorizing either position, and ex-

21. Ibid., 1.

cluding a middle ground or synthesis. In *The Singing-Men at Cashel* there is, however, a third husband who potentially represents such a synthesis, for Gormlai's final marriage is depicted—insofar as it is depicted at all—as both spiritually and physically fulfilling. As Maurice Harmon points out, however, the book's "central issue is the conflict of mind and body which she experiences in her first two marriages and not the happiness which she enjoys in the third."[22] It is clear that "Clarke did not want to describe the third marriage, nor did he want to deal directly with Gormlai's recovery of imaginative faith."[23] In fact, the satirical impulses of Clarke's romance prevent the occurrence of such a synthesis; instead, the story of the third marriage is fragmented, displaced in time, and narrated indirectly through a number of textual layers. In other words, the middle ground between extremes is presented as incomplete and as fictitious rather than real.

As soon as the story arrives at the point where Carrol declares war against Cormac of Cashel, the narrative jumps forward about a hundred years in time, to focus on the eleventh-century scribe Ceallachan, who is copying a passage from a historic tract. The text he is copying describes how Cormac fell off his horse, broke his back and neck, and died piously. It "had been written in great haste almost a hundred years ago by one of Cormac's scribes" (308). Next, Ceallachan takes up the lay romance *Searc Nial do Gormflaith*—a reference to the lost text mentioned in the *Book of Leinster*—and comments on its dubious historical value: "This love-tale of Nial and Gormlai, set down hastily by some forgotten scribbler, was partly composed of traditional and imaginary episodes" (313). The text of the romance as it appears through Ceallachan's disapproving eyes in *The Singing-Men at Cashel*—which is the only information provided in the book as a whole about Gormlai's life after her wedding to Nial—is therefore doubly fictitious, doubly "untrue": the actual romance mentioned in the *Book of Leinster* is known to be lost, and therefore details about its contents, language, and structure must have been invented by Austin Clarke. Moreover, once it is placed into its new context, that invented story is presented indirectly by Ceallachan through fragmentary quotations and summaries and scornfully said by him to have been largely made up from borrowed and invented material.

22. Harmon, *Austin Clarke*, 99.
23. Ibid., 107.

The scribe begins reading at random a passage in the middle of the text that describes "the prosperous years which Gormlai enjoyed when Nial acceded to the High Kingship. Her son, Murrough, was then no more than five years old, and she was completely happy" (314). The narrator of the romance extols the queen's virtues and the aid she has given to the revival of secular art and poetry: "She had established new poetic colleges and endeavoured to give influence to those orders which had been deprived of their educational power long ago, by the ecclesiastical decree of Drumceat" (315). The pious Ceallachan reads these words with disapproval, but he is at the same time aware of Gormlai's success, for a literary and poetic revival is taking place throughout Ireland in his lifetime. He then reads the manuscript from the beginning, noticing that the storyteller had modeled Gormlai's flight with Nial on the old elopement tales, "interweaving his own fancies with the plain facts" (316). This is, of course, exactly what Austin Clarke is doing, too, in *The Singing-Men at Cashel.* Eventually darkness prevents the scribe from reading further, and, because we are reading through his eyes, the story of Nial and Gormlai breaks off at this point.

Austin Clarke's narratives often engage in a dialogue with other, existing texts. The elements he borrows from these texts frequently bear, in the words of Robert Welch, "what might be called a contrapuntal relationship to the original."[24] In *The Bright Temptation* Clarke created a complex counterpoint between the story of the mythological Old Woman of Beare, the medieval poem about the "Nun of Beare," his own poem "The Young Woman of Beare," and his treatment of similar thematic material in the prose romance.[25] A similar contrapuntal process is at work in *The Singing-*

24. Robert Welch, "Austin Clarke and Gaelic Poetic Tradition," *Irish University Review,* 4, 1 (1974): 41.

25. In this context it is interesting to note that James Carney has suggested an origin for Gormlaith similar to that of the Old Woman of Beare:

Gormlaith means either "Red Ale" or "Dark Sovereignty." Whichever meaning one chooses it is a perfect name for a kingship-goddess in her function as the pourer of the liquor of sovereignty. Gormlaith was a daughter of Flann Sinna, king of Tara and of Ireland. She married successively three kings: Cerball of Leinster, Cormac of Cashel, and finally Niall Glúndub, king of Ireland. Had the tradition of this woman come to us by hundreds of years of oral tradition, confused with other queens of the same name, we might easily hear that she had a dozen husbands, all kings, and that she allowed no one to be king who did not marry her.

See the "Introduction" by James Carney, in Eleanor Knott and Gerard Murphy, *Early Irish Literature* (London: Routledge & Kegan Paul, 1966), 16.

Men at Cashel, where Clarke creates a dialogue not only with O'Curry's version of Gormlai's story taken from the *Annals of Clonmacnoise* and the *Book of Leinster,* but especially with Clarke's own poem "The Confession of Queen Gormlai," published in *Pilgrimage* (1929), which in turn takes its cue from a collection of poems attributed to Gormlai herself. Both the poems attributed to Gormlai and Clarke's "The Confession of Queen Gormlai" are retrospective laments spoken by Gormlai herself at the end of her life.

O'Curry provides the full picture of Gormlaith's life in a scholarly and unbiased manner. He tells us that little is known of her life after she married Niall until his death at the hands of the Danes in the year 917, after which he was succeeded by Gormlaith's brother, who died in 942. O'Curry continues: "[O]n his death, the sceptre passed away from the house of her father and of her husband; and it is possible, or rather we may say probable, that it was then that commenced that poverty and neglect, of which she so feelingly speaks in her poems." In what O'Curry believes to be Gormlaith's last poem, "she details the death of her son, who was accidentally drowned in the county Galway during his fosterage, and the subsequent death of her husband; and in it is also preserved an interesting account of her mode of living."[26] The *Annals of Clonmacnoise* state that at the end of her life, Gormlaith "begged from doore to doore, forsaken of all her friends and allies, and glad to be relieved by her inferiours."[27] She died in 947 and an account of her death is provided in the *Annals of Clonmacnoise:* "[S]he dreamed that she saw King Niall Glunduffe; whereupon she got up and sate in her bed to behold him; whom he for anger would forsake, and leave the chamber; . . . she gave a snatch after him, . . . and fell upon the bedstick of her bed, that it pierced her breast, even to her very heart, which received no cure until she died thereof."[28] O'Curry claims that she composed her poems during her last illness.

The poems O'Curry speaks of were translated by Osborn Bergin in 1912. According to Bergin, however, "If any of these poems were really written by Gormlaith, they must have been greatly altered in transmission. Some of them appear to have been composed long after her time."[29] He adds that it

---

26. O'Curry, *Manuscript Materials,* 134.
27. Quoted by O. J. Bergin, in "Poems Attributed to Gormlaith," 343.
28. Quoted by O'Curry, in *Manuscript Materials,* 135.
29. Bergin, "Poems Attributed to Gormlaith," 344.

is tempting "to regard the whole collection as belonging to or founded on the lost historical romance called *Serc Gormlaithe do Niall,*" but that "in the absence of evidence as to their origin it is safest to class them with the many Middle Irish lyrics attributed to distinguished characters of an earlier period."[30] The poems, in other words, are not autobiographical but fictional.

In *The Singing-Men at Cashel,* Gormlai's dream of what lies ahead of her includes lines from Clarke's poem "The Confession of Queen Gormlai." The queen in the poem is old and destitute; her confession, actually more a personal reminiscence about her three marriages, is framed by two stanzas that describe her indigence and her distraught state of mind caused by the conflicting emotions of guilt and defiance:

> *Dawn, fielding on the mountains,*
> *Had found that hovel,*
> *And in the dark she lay there*
> *Whom kings had loved,*
> *Sharp on a shoulder-blade*
> *Turning in straw and rags;*
> *While, crossed from that clay threshold,*
> *Her flesh became a dagger.*

>   * * *

> *At sun, she lay forsaken*
> *And in black hair, she dragged*
> *Her arms, around the stake*
> *Of that wild bed, from rags*
> *That cut the gleam of chin*
> *And hip men had desired:*
> *Murmuring of the sins*
> *Whose hunger is the mind.*[31]

As in the case of *The Bright Temptation,* where the external materials relating to the Old Woman of Beare complete the picture presented in the romance, the events depicted in *The Singing-Men at Cashel* and the poems about Gormlai are complementary: while the romance provides only the

30. Ibid., 345.

31. Austin Clarke, "The Confession of Queen Gormlai," in *Collected Poems of Austin Clarke,* with an introduction by Padraic Colum (New York: Macmillan, 1936), 89–97.

happy conclusion to the early part of Gormlai's life, the poems concentrate solely on the unhappy end of her life after Nial's death, that is to say, on the aspects deliberately omitted from the romance.

The textual dialogue thus created is a complex one. In *The Singing-Men at Cashel*, Clarke presents the story of Gormlai's marriage to Nial only through fictionalized, romanticized, inaccurately remembered and hastily scribbled, incomplete embedded texts. Other texts from outside the context of *The Singing-Men at Cashel* can be used to complete the historical picture, but these texts are equally fragmentary, fictitious, unreliable, and (sometimes) contradictory. It is clear that Clarke deliberately creates a labyrinth around Gormlai and Nial that leads in several directions but never to just one answer or conclusion. To that extent, the purely fictional status of Gormlai's love for Nial forms a contrast with the much more straightforward, factual presentation of Gormlai's first two marriages. If the romance does create a middle ground between the single-minded extremes of Cormac and Carrol, it is a highly ambiguous and elusive one.

Throughout *The Singing-Men at Cashel* poetry and story are contrasted with religious tracts, the main difference between them being that poetry and fiction are multi-interpretable or dialogic, while religious texts are monologic—even when they ostensibly come in the form of a dialogue, such as the catechism. Religious texts are safe because they mean only one thing; poetry and romances are dangerous to the Church's authority because they raise the possibility that the truth is open to interpretation. In *The Singing-Men at Cashel* secular imaginative texts are dialogic and the domain of pagan bards, wandering scholars, and women; religious tracts are monologic, forbidden to women, and the territory of the male clergy. Cormac is well aware of the dangers posed to the authority of the Church and to its dogma by dialogic texts that allow for, indeed even require, the use of imaginative interpretation. He warns Benignus that there is a temptation in the study of such literature: "I cannot tell you how often I've heard a dozen answers to one question, how often I've forgotten the subject at hand and been beguiled by a pleasant story" (118). The copyist Ceallachan had been similarly beguiled by *Searc Nial do Gormflaith*. By contrast, the truth of Christian dogma is absolute and monologic: "We can live in certainty, for we know the object and purpose of our mortal existence. All that is left for us is to co-relate, to systematize our knowledge of the universe" (121).

The epigraph to *The Singing-Men at Cashel*—"*Gabhlánach an rud an scéaluidheacht,*" which Clarke translates as "Romances are complicated affairs"—underlines the centrality of a textual conflict of this sort to the book as a whole. The phrase is spoken by Saint Patrick to Caoilte in the *Acallam na Senórach* or "Colloquy with the Ancients," the dialogue between pagan heroes and representatives of Christianity that I have already discussed above in connection with Darrell Figgis's *The Return of the Hero*. Clarke's epigraph can be taken as a comment on the dialogic nature of secular romances in general or on the narrative complexities of *The Singing-Men at Cashel* in particular, in contrast to the dogmatic and single-minded vision of religious tracts. In this regard, the context in which Patrick originally made the remark in the *Acallam* is also of interest. According to Standish O'Grady's translation, a warrior of the Tuatha Dé Danann, Aillén mac Eogabail, fell in love with the wife of Manannán mac Lir; at the same time Aillén's sister, Áine, daughter of Eogabal, fell in love with Manannán, who loved her dearly in return. Aillén tells his sister of his secret love, and she claims to have the solution to their problems:

"'for Manannan is in love with me and, if he give thee his wife, I will as the price of procuring thee relief yield him my society.' They, Aillen and Aine, came away as far as to this *tulach*, whither Manannan too (his wife with him) arrived. Aine took her seat at Manannan's right hand, and gave him three loving passionate kisses; then they sought news one of the other. But when Manannan's wife saw Aillen she loved him—" Here Patrick interrupting said: "why this is a complicated bit of romance: that Aillen mac Eogabal's sister should love Manannan, and Manannan's wife fancy Aillen"; whence the old adage: "romancing is a complicated affair."[32]

This episode from the *Acallam* provides a relevant commentary on the story of Gormlai's complicated love life, as well as on the complex structure of Clarke's romance as a whole. It is, of course, ironic that in the *Acallam*, Ireland's patron saint himself should listen so earnestly to Caoilte's tale and merely shake his head in amazement and admiration at the complexities of love and love stories, without expressing moral disapproval, while the clergy in *The Singing-Men at Cashel* consider romances (both in the sense of "love stories" and of "love affairs") morally dangerous and a challenge to their authority.

32. *Silva Gadelica*, vol. 2, *Translation and Notes*, trans. and ed. Standish H. O'Grady (London: Williams and Norgate, 1892), 196–97.

The authority of the Church is based on a claim to absolute certainty: religion provides one answer to every question, whereas poetry and romance may provide as many as a dozen. Raised in the monastic tradition, the scribe Ceallachan finds himself tempted by the numerous possibilities of romance. Frustrated by the absence of light by which to read further in the love story of Nial and Gormlai, Ceallachan begins to fantasize about the continuation of the romance before he realizes the moral danger inherent in this activity: "He had been beguiled, despite himself, by one of those secular stories which are designed, under a pretended moral concern, to incite passion in the mind" (322). For this reason also the language of *Searc Nial do Gormflaith* does not please Ceallachan: "Absent was the severity which he liked and the monastic discipline of phrase, the brief logical sentence. Here was the rich many-sounding style of the oral tradition which, after centuries of use and embellishment, had degenerated into flowing sentences . . . designed to defeat the attention of the listeners even while flattering their ears" (313–14). What *The Singing-Men at Cashel* shows, however, is that the truth claimed by the Church is based on games of language and logic rather than the inherent absolute existence of truth.

Clarke draws attention to the problem of meaning and interpretation early on in *The Singing-Men at Cashel*. Describing the architectural features of Cashel, the book's narrator points out that the phallic shape of prayer towers in the East resembles that of the round towers of Irish monastic settlements, but that a similarity in form does not necessarily imply a similar significance: "unlike those structures, shaped to virgins' shame, about which the pagans performed their abominable rites, . . . the monastic towers were a refuge from danger, warners of invasion, bell-storied and raised in tribute to the Most High" (91). There is a subtle form of irony at work here: the narrator introduces the possibility of a phallic interpretation of the tower's shape, only in order to deny that such a reading is valid.[33] Bakhtin points out that the tall tower interpreted as the phallus was a common motif in carnivalized texts since antiquity: "[T]he monastic belfry, uncrowned and renewed in the form of a giant phallus" uncrowns the monastery itself, along with "its false ascetic ideal, its abstract and sterile

---

33. Austin Clarke read Henry O'Brien's *The Round Towers of Ireland* between 1913 and 1916, and was disturbed by its theory of phallic symbolism. See Harmon, "Notes towards a Biography," 15.

eternity."[34] A refusal to acknowledge such an interpretation does not alter the shape of the tower: meaning is not inherent in the thing itself. *The Singing-Men at Cashel* exposes the unreliable nature of language as a basis for claims to the absolute truth, because all use of language is subjective. The only way in which authority can be maintained is by ignoring or denying this fact. The Church claims authority because it always proves itself right; its authority—indeed, all authority—is based on an ad hoc refusal to accept at any time even the possibility of another interpretation or point of view that might undermine its position of power—even if it has to contradict itself in the process.

Cormac, the archbishop-to-be, is the main representative of this monologic cast of mind. When the thought strikes him at one point that "we perceive only through the mind," a notion that allows for the possibility of alternative perceptions or interpretations of reality, he dismisses the idea abruptly: "The Evil One was subtle in his attacks and was inveigling him into sophistry. Experience had long ago rendered him suspicious of those debates in which the mind argues with itself as with an unseen disputant" (171). When the dialogue inside his head—between fallen spirits who whisper "do" into one ear and angels who whisper "don't" into the other—becomes too heated, he resorts to flagellating himself to block out the words he does not want to hear. Gormlai's inner conflict is similarly externalized as a dialogue between her guardian angel, Caol, and the demon Iafer Niger: "'Your father forced you into this marriage,' spoke the voice at the foot of the bed. 'No, no. It was of your own free will you married Carrol. You know that you consented. Do not listen to the Tempter,' urged Caol" (231). The two spirits argue until Gormlai is totally perplexed: "Do not betray . . . accept . . . do not . . . betray . . . pray . . . do not pray . . . pray . . ." (235). Unlike Cormac, however, who sees the mind as a danger to authority, Gormlai eventually comes to regard it as a sanctuary: "'All, all is in the mind,' thought Gormlai, 'in the end, violence is powerless against it'" (276). Gradually she begins to realize that the inner voice of the imagination is more real and more important than the external voices of authority.

This development is best illustrated by a juxtaposition of the description of Gormlai's first wedding to Cormac and that of her third wedding to Nial,

---

34. Bakhtin, *Rabelais*, 312.

for in both instances the descriptions of the voices of the clergy and the words of the ceremony are virtually identical. Both occasions are marked for Gormlai by a sense of alienation. The first time, it is her husband's lack of individuality that is the source of her unease: "If she turned an inch, she knew that she would be able to see her husband. But she would not see him clearly, she would see him from an estranging angle of sight. She dared not turn towards him, even though they were now one in the sight of Heaven and man. In the confusion of her first glance, she had forgotten his features. Were she to see him coming towards her amid a company of scholars, she would not be able to recognize him with certainty, save by his noble demeanour and stature" (38). Cormac is a representative of the Church before he is a distinctive individual. During her third wedding, Gormlai feels much closer to her husband, and her unease stems instead from her awareness of being socially and morally suspect: "Strange thoughts troubled her mind and the past became so real to her that the present seemed a dream. . . . She had repeated the holy words of promise as if in a dream. Truly we can only know pure happiness when our desires are in conformity with divine and human custom. Yet she had found happiness in a secrecy of her own that none suspected" (381–82). Having placed herself beyond the boundaries of clerical approval by marrying three times, Gormlai comes to realize that true happiness is found only in the privacy of the imagination.

The Singing-Men at Cashel shows that *every* ideological position is masked by language, and that no language, as Bakhtin puts it, can claim to be "an authentic, incontestable face."[35] Reality is perceived through the individual mind, and absolute truth does not exist; as a depiction of reality, fiction therefore has more validity than monologic texts, because it allows for multiple "truths," none of which can claim authority over other truths. Clarke ridicules the extreme positions of Cormac and Carrol, but because satire undermines all forms of authority without exception, the deliberate fictionalization of the story of Nial and Gormlai prevents it from laying claim to the truth: it is "not real," even if reality itself is "all in the mind." The fiction therefore cannot claim to be more true than any other text—only more "truthful" in its depiction of the impossibility of absolute truth.

---

35. Bakhtin, *Dialogic Imagination,* 273.

For this reason the story of Anier Mac Conglinne dominates the end of *The Singing-Men at Cashel*. The more the book shows that reality and truth are language-bound, text-based, and ultimately the work of the imagination, the more the satirical nature and the Menippean characteristics of the book take over from its romance traits. The sudden transitions, the lack of coherence, the fragmentation of the narrative, and the falling apart of the book toward the end are actually the logical consequences of its own anti-authoritarian message.

The final episode concerning Anier begins with his arrival at Leacmore, where the southern poets are getting ready to compose a special satire against the Five Ulstermen, who have insulted them by claiming that the northern poets are better than they are. This incident is modeled on the seventeenth-century poem *Iomarbháigh na Bhfileadh*, the "Contention of the Bards": "The original challenge is thrown down in a poem feigned to be the work of Torna Éigeas, foster-father of Niall of the Nine Hostages. In this it is asserted that Corc of Cashel (standing for southern claims) submitted to Niall as his overlord. The challenge is taken up by a Clare poet, Tadgh Mac Dáire Mac Bruaideadha, who is answered by a Leath Chuinn poet, Lughaidh Ó Cléirigh, and several others join in. All the traditional learning of the poetic order is brought into play, legendary history, genealogy, ancient poetic rhapsodies, etymology, etc. Much of the argument seems frankly humorous."[36] A cynical contemporary commentary on the "Contention" suggests that the debate is all clever language and no substance: "Lughaidh, Tadgh and Torna, famous poets of our land; hounds are they with much learning, wrangling over an empty dish."[37] It is appropriate that Anier should meddle in such a hollow debate, and that he should do so claiming to be a catechist and an excellent reciter of sacred poems. He is, of course, neither a cleric nor an official poet, having placed himself beyond all official institutions.

When Anier's recitation of an interminable list of southern saints has pushed the representatives of the north to the brink of defeat, the Ulstermen strike back with their claim to "Illan-na-Frugadory, the Cave-entrance into purgatory and the lower regions, the only one in the world and famous far and wide" (346). Anier realizes he is defeated: when he fee-

36. Eleanor Knott, *Irish Classical Poetry*, in Knott and Murphy, *Early Irish Literature*, 88.
37. Quoted in Knott and Murphy, *Early Irish Literature*, 92.

bly counters that the cave is only a myth, he is invited to go and see the entrance to purgatory for himself. Clarke took much of the detail of what follows from various historical accounts of visits to Saint Patrick's Purgatory, such as those by Henry of Saltrey in 1185, Raymond de Perelhos in 1397 and Antonio Mannini in 1411. A note on Speed's Map of 1611 provides the following information about the site: "This is the cave which the inhabitants in these days call Ellan u'Frugadory, that is the Isle of Purgatorie and S. Patricks Purgatory," in which "the punishments and tortures which the godless are to suffer after this life might be then presented to the eye that so he might more easily root out the sins and heathenish errors that stuck so fast in the hearts of the Irish."[38]

During the Middle Ages Lough Derg was not the national pilgrimage destination it is today. "It was not the pious who were attracted to the Purgatory, but famous sinners, who could not get absolution otherwise, the type of misdoer who to-day finds his misdeeds reserved to the Grand Penitentiary of the Roman Church. Lough Derg was then the last throw of the desperate against the devil!"[39] How appropriate, then, that the lawless Anier should set out to undertake this journey. Far from desperate or penitent, however, Mac Conglinne merely uses the above-mentioned knowledge of the damned to bribe his way into the cave with a good story. The prior guarding the entrance asks him for letters of permission from his bishop, without which he cannot be admitted; Anier claims to have been assailed by the Evil One who stole his wallet and his documents. When this lie does not work, he claims to be in a state of sin, but "it is one of the five sins which cannot be absolved in Ireland" (360). It can only be absolved in Rome, but Anier claims to have taken a vow to descend into the pit at Lough Derg before going on that long journey. He promises to reveal the terrible sin to the prior in private on his return from purgatory. This promise gains him immediate permission to enter the cave.

As soon as he is sealed into the cave, Anier begins to learn the secret of the pit. Purgatory in *The Singing-Men at Cashel* is a place of alienation from

---

38. Quoted by Shane Leslie, in *Saint Patrick's Purgatory: A Record from History and Literature* (London: Burns Oates and Washbourne, 1932), xlv. Austin Clarke was clearly familiar with much of the material collected by Leslie and may well have used this book as a source of information.

39. Ibid., xvii.

the self, where the wholeness of a person is destroyed; it is a place on the brink of hell where body and soul become polarized and estranged from each other. At first, Mac Conglinne believes that there is an unknown watcher waiting for him in the dark trying to draw his soul from his body, but after a while he realizes that "his own soul was the dreadful watcher which was waiting within arm's reach of him" (368). In spite of his efforts not to move and to stay in touch with the door, he suddenly finds himself standing defenseless in the dark and on the brink of space. Groping his way back to the door, he realizes there is somebody in his place: "His hand was clasping a cold shin, clutching at a bony knee. The contact was repulsive and yet dimly familiar to him. An irresistible force flung him at the whole body and he knew that it was his own. While he was rushing from that horrible brink, his body had remained lying there at the door. His soul had become impatient and . . . taken him off his guard" (370). The conflict between soul and body, which in Gormlai's case is externalized through her marriages to Cormac and Carrol, is here internalized. Anier becomes a split personality. His sense of self is tied up with both his soul and his body, but never with both at the same time: first his "self" recognizes his soul as an "other," next it is his body that is perceived by the soul-self as a stranger.

A similar paradox occurs a moment later when Anier witnesses his own funeral and perceives himself as simultaneously alive and dead. He had apparently fallen asleep, for he is awakened by the sound of footsteps and finds that the monks are in the cave. They are carrying a coffin and find the body of Anier Mac Conglinne, dead three days. Anier wants to shriek that he is not dead, but his voice is gone. When he dashes past the "madmen," however, he hears demonic laughter: "Demons had assumed the form of monks in order to outwit him and the death-pale eidolon of himself which he had seen on the ground was only an enchanted stock. He had been tricked at last" (373). As his soul falls into the pit, Anier experiences simultaneously the presence *and* the absence of the body: "His soul had escaped from his body and his agony was caused by the absence of physical space, but there still remained all those capabilities of pain which come from the displacement of the senses" (373). In purgatory, he paradoxically experiences the states of being and not-being at the same time. To Bakhtin, the underworld "symbolizes the defeated and condemned evil of the past."[40]

40. Bakhtin, *Rabelais,* 391.

The netherworld in the folk tradition "becomes the symbol of the defeat of fear by laughter." And Bakhtin asserts that the fear is dual: "[T]he mystic terror inspired by hell and death and the terror of the authority and truth of the past, still prevailing but dying, which has been hurled into the underworld."[41] Anier's experiences in the underworld are not recorded, but the gaping hole that devoured him also allows him to be reborn. When he wakes up again he finds himself in a sunny guest room, none the worse for wear, having been found unconscious in the cave after twenty-four hours. His experiences have not left him more contrite or pious; indeed, they have not changed him at all: "Already his imagination was at work and he began to invent the horrible dragons, gridirons, and toothed instruments of torture which he would describe to the Abbot and the community. He would put the fear of God into them before he left the island. He would go far and wide, so that all would praise his great exploits and courage in the other world" (376–77). On this imaginative note Anier's experiences in the book end.

Anier's frightening experiences in the otherworld appear to have taken place exclusively in his mind and, like Gormlai's nightmarish trial, to have been induced by his own fear or guilt, or his own imagination. Thus, experience itself has no meaning; perception and imagination create meaning. Progress and change are not possible, it seems, except through the world of myth and poetry, where the fertile imagination re-creates experience to its own advantage. Anier's imaginative account of his descent into purgatory will make his reputation; Gormlai's happiness is found within herself, in "a secrecy of her own" (382) that eventually leads her to revive the ancient *Aonach Tailteann,* the month-long festival of the earth goddess, and to aid the revival of secular art and poetry.

The last sentence of *The Singing-Men at Cashel* reads: "So far, then, the love-story of Nial and Gormlai, set down by a poor clerk to keep body and soul together" (382). This is a fitting ending to a satire whose conclusions suggest that there are no conclusions and that fiction is the only reality and the only truth, for it is a punning and ambiguous statement open to a great deal of interpretation. "Clerk" may be read as "Clarke," and a metaphorical reading of the phrase "to keep body and soul together" suggests that Austin Clarke wrote the book as a potboiler and not because it contains any in-

41. Ibid., 395.

trinsic merit or deeply felt emotions. A literal reading, however, is also in order, for the alienation of soul and body—represented by Gormlai's first and second marriages, and by Anier's experiences in purgatory—lies at the heart of the narrative. Represented by the third marriage during which Gormlai aids the revival of secular art and poetry, by Anier's anticipation of his juicy account of his otherworldly experiences, as well as by *The Singing-Men at Cashel* as a whole, poetry and romance involve the fusion of both body and soul—of reality and imagination, of history and fiction.

Moreover, the suggestion that the "clerk" is also the scribe who hastily wrote down the love story of Nial and Gormlai identifies the writer of *The Singing-Men at Cashel* with the author of the lost *Searc Nial do Gormflaith*, the text referred to within the pages of *The Singing-Men at Cashel*. Clarke's romance is thus equated with this long-lost romance, or with the re-creation of it; but the irony is that the text never presents directly the actual romance of Nial and Gormlai; whatever *The Singing-Men at Cashel* may be, it cannot be adequately described as the love story of Nial and Gormlai. The "clerk" claims to have written a book which, to all intents and purposes, and in more ways than one, does not exist.

In addition, the suggestion that the poor clerk told the story for financial gain also puts him on a par with the narrator of the medieval satire "Aislinge Mac Conglinne," who states at the end of his tale that "the reward of the recital of this story is a white-spotted, red-eared cow, a shirt of new linen, a woollen cloak with its broach . . . to him who is able to tell and recite it."[42] The last sentence of *The Singing-Men at Cashel* in this way not only draws the whole of the text into the realm of fiction, but creates a clerk/Clarke who incorporates a triad of authors past and present who claim responsibility for the tale, while at the same time dismissing the story's importance. The fictional uncertainties of the book act as a disclaimer to any comments on and connections with the real world the reader may find in the text; at the same time, *The Singing-Men at Cashel* suggests that fiction is the only reality we have, and that the mind and the imagination create the only truth we know.

42. Cross and Slover, *Ancient Irish Tales*, 587. According to Joseph Nagy, this elaborate blessing is a parody of a form of closure frequently found in Old and Middle Irish texts, for example, in the Book of Leinster version of the *Táin*, and in *Altram Tige Dá Medar*. See *Conversing with Angels and Ancients: Literary Myths of Medieval Ireland* (Dublin: Four Courts Press, 1997), 16, note 41.

chapter seven

"Everything Next to Nothing"

The Sun Dances at Easter

Austin Clarke's prose narratives progress from the escapism of *The Bright Temptation,* via the bleak, condemnatory outlook of *The Singing-Men at Cashel,* to a more positive attitude of celebration in *The Sun Dances at Easter.* While *The Bright Temptation* can be characterized most accurately as romance, and while *The Singing-Men at Cashel* is dominated by the techniques of Menippean satire, the term most applicable to Clarke's third narrative, published sixteen years after the second, is carnival. Like satire, carnival is aimed at subverting authority and undermining hierarchical structures; unlike satire, however, it is not purely negative but includes a positive, celebratory aspect. According to Bakhtin, carnival and ritual laughter are linked with destruction and regeneration, and with symbols of the reproductive force: "Combined in the act of carnival laughter are death and rebirth, negation (a smirk) and affirmation (rejoicing laughter)."[1] In *The Sun Dances at Easter* carnival laughter ridicules the sterile forces of authority and celebrates the fertile powers of nature and the imagination.

Rejoicing laughter and reproduction form the core elements of Clarke's third narrative. The plot is as follows: Orla and Flann have been married for over two years, but in spite of their prayers Orla's dearest wish, to have a child, has not been fulfilled. A jolly, fat, wandering cleric (who later turns out to be the Irish god of love, Aongus, in disguise) promises Orla a son if she visits the Well of Saint Naal (or Natalis) and sees the Blessed Trout jump. The pagan god represents the material bodily principle of renewal and fertility, and his arrival causes a temporary suspension of the power of the official Church. In spite of Flann's objection to the pagan superstition,

---

1. Bakhtin, *Dostoevsky's Poetics,* 127.

Orla sets out on the journey. On her way she meets a young scholar called Enda, who closely resembles her husband; he is a student at a monastic school and also in search of a miracle, for his dearest wish is to see an angel. He decides to keep her company, and entertains her with two stories, both involving Aongus, which take up much of the book. Orla visits the well and sees the Blessed Trout jump, at which point Flann, who had been put on the wrong road by Aongus, finally catches up with his wife. In due course, Orla gives birth to a baby boy who looks exactly like his "father"; the identity of the latter—Flann, Enda, or even Aongus—is intentionally left open to speculation.

The essence of the book is captured in its title: *The Sun Dances at Easter*. It refers to a once popular superstition in Ireland that the sun, when it rises on Easter morning, dances with joy at the (re-)birth of Christ, man's hope of salvation.[2] The superstition has pagan origins and is probably connected with the return of the sun and the renewal of life in the spring. As a festival of material rebirth and renewal, therefore, Easter has important carnival connotations, which have largely been lost in modern times, but of which the medieval Church was fully aware. In his discussion of the *risus paschalis*, Bakhtin points out that Easter time in the medieval Church was traditionally associated with laughter, physical joy, and celebration: "During the Easter season laughter and jokes were permitted even in church. . . . The jokes and stories concerned especially material bodily life, and were of a carnival type. Permission to laugh was granted simultaneously with the permission to eat meat and to resume sexual intercourse (forbidden during Lent)."[3] Clarke, however, foregrounds the "intolerant, one-sided tone of seriousness" that Bakhtin claims is characteristic of official medieval culture, with its concomitant emphasis on "asceticism, somber providentialism, sin, atonement, suffering, as well as the character of the feudal regime, with its oppression and intimidation."[4] In *The Sun Dances at Easter* the aspect of laughter and material renewal is exclusively represented by the pagan Irish god Aongus.

2. In *Twice Round the Black Church*, Clarke relates how, as a child, "on Easter Sunday, my sisters and I had crept to the top landing window at six o'clock to see beyond the cattle-sheds and the slates the sun dancing for joy. Only once, however, did we see that wonder" (46).

3. Bakhtin, *Rabelais*, 78–79.

4. Ibid., 73.

To understand some of the motivation behind Clarke's depiction of the Church, it is important to know that the Irish Catholic bishops, beginning in the 1920s and throughout the 1930s and 1940s, persistently expressed their grave concern about the decline in sexual morality in the country, which they attributed largely to foreign influences: "New mass media—the cinema, the radio, and above all the English sensational newspapers . . . — were bringing unfamiliar values to the attention of their flocks."[5] The replacement of traditional Irish dancing by foreign dances which, in the words of Archbishop Gilmartin of Tuam, "lent themselves not so much to rhythm as to low sensuality,"[6] appears to have been one of their greatest worries. The Irish bishops voiced their fears in a joint pastoral in 1927: "The evil one is ever setting his snares for unwary feet. At the moment, his traps for the innocent are chiefly the dance hall, the bad book, the indecent paper, the motion picture, the immodest fashion in female dress—all of which tend to destroy the virtues characteristic of our race."[7] By making the "evil one" in *The Sun Dances at Easter* the indigenous Irish god Aongus, Clarke problematizes such racial arguments involving the inherent sexual purity of the Irish. As an antidote to such monologic thinking, the title of his book introduces an ambivalent juxtaposition of Christian and pagan elements characteristic of carnival: a two-faced, contradictory image that is repeated in the image of Aongus in the garb of a Christian monk.

The dance as an image of physical celebration is a recurring element in *The Sun Dances at Easter*. On the way to the well, Orla is distracted by twelve merry children who dance with her in a circle; as she moves round and round, troubled memories of her own childhood begin to flood her mind until "she was no longer dancing under the fairy thorn, she was being dragged around that other tree in the cold shadowy Garden of Eden where no children ever played. She was unbaptizing herself, searching into the false horrors of the soul" (40).[8] The fertile, joyful imagery of the pagan fairy dance is mirrored by the cold and sterile vision of the Christian Eden: in Paradise there is no celebration, and there are no children. Such inverted mirror images are typical of carnivalized literature because, as Bakhtin

---

5. Whyte, *Church and State*, 24–25.   6. Ibid., 25.

7. Ibid., 27.

8. Austin Clarke, *The Sun Dances at Easter* (London: Andrew Melrose, 1952); all page references in the text are to this edition.

puts it, "[T]hey unite within themselves both poles of change and crisis."[9] In other words, in their duality they contain both problem and solution. If Orla's wish to have a child is to be fulfilled, it will have to be with pagan assistance and in defiance of official Church doctrine.

The merry stranger who promises Orla that her wish will be fulfilled if she goes on the pilgrimage is himself the very incarnation of carnival ambivalence. When she sees him approaching from very far away, Orla at first thinks of the distant skipping dot as a sign from heaven, then as a gigantic flea or a goat, and finally as perhaps only a figment of the imagination. The shape-shifting wanderer who finally arrives may be all of the above:

He was cloistered beyond all charity in his own findings: scraps of frieze, loom-droppings, patches of fur, pelts that a ragpicker would have thrown away; and these treasures of his were tied and twisted with *sugaun,* pinned to their quadragesimal knots with huge thorns, skewered and pothooked from shoulder to muddied hem. He was out at the knees and in at the elbows. He was so enormously fat that the entire collection clung to him or clambered about him in fleshly bulges and bursts of frightened modesty. He was a standing humiliation and a holy show. But as he chuckled and clucked to himself, some of the tattings, the taggles, shook with little jokes of their own, despite their insecurity, and bobbed the hundreds of withered burrs which they had caught in last year's woods. His chesty beard wagged beneath the goatskin hood which almost hid his red face. His paunch rumbled with such mirth beneath an enormous hairy hand-grasp that at one moment his robes were all holes, at the next moment all mendings, and the moment after that the seams had changed places again and the uncountable rips went into little stitches of laughter (14).

The cleric's patchwork outfit and his merriment associate him with the clown or rogue figure of traditional folklore who plays an important part in carnival: such figures laugh at themselves as they are laughed at by others; they are both ridiculous and subversive at the same time. The cleric's ever-changing motley costume of found bits and pieces represents this ambiguous lack of unity in his identity. Orla's reaction to the cleric's appearance and his encouraging words to her—she wants to dance and kneel in prayer at the same time, and laugh and cry simultaneously—is as dualistic as the "disgraceful sanctity" of the monk himself (15). Bakhtin describes

9. Bakhtin, *Dostoevsky's Poetics,* 126.

similar characters in medieval Latin literature: "The character of the monk is either complex or intermittent. First, as a devotee of material bodily life he sharply contradicts the ascetic ideal that he serves. Second, his gluttony represents the parasitism of a sluggard. But, third, he also expresses the positive, 'shrove' principles of food, drink, procreative force, and merriment. The authors offer these three aspects concurrently, and it is difficult to say where praise ends and where condemnation starts."[10] The stranger is indeed a "holy show" in that his person, like the title of the book, unites the sacred with the profane in true carnival fashion.

Both Orla and Enda are in search of fulfillment. When Enda was seven years of age he witnessed the miraculous passing of the last Irish saint escorted by a bright flight of angels, since which time there have been no more miracles. Enda's dearest wish is to see an angel, but his only attempt so far to witness the sacred had resulted in an experience of profanity. He had tied himself to a stone where an angel was supposed to appear at night, and awoke to a sensation of falling dew and rustling wings: "[A]n enormous bird rose from the pillarstone into the moonlight with a croak. I tore up handfuls of the blessed grass and raved as I wiped the bird-filth from my head" (52). This grotesque experience is not necessarily merely negative, however, but serves as an example of what Bakhtin calls "positive negation," that is, a deliberate mixing of hierarchical levels (reversal of top and bottom, the head in contact with excrement) to free the object from all hierarchical norms and values, in order to create a new conception of the world.[11] Such degradation "has not only a destructive, negative aspect, but also a regenerating one."[12] In other words, it is the first step toward the granting of Enda's wish. As they set out on their journey, Orla assures him that the hermit who promised her a son will make his dream come true as well.

According to Bakhtin, carnivalization, "with its joy at change and its joyful relativity, is opposed to that one-sided and gloomy official seriousness which is dogmatic and hostile to evolution and change, which seeks to absolutize a given condition of existence or a given social order."[13] Whereas festive laughter "was linked with the procreating act, with birth, renewal, fertility, abundance," medieval seriousness "was infused with elements of fear, weakness, humility, submission, falsehood, hypocrisy, or on the other

---

10. Bakhtin, *Rabelais*, 294.
12. Ibid., 412.

11. Ibid., 403.
13. Bakhtin, *Dostoevsky's Poetics*, 160.

hand with violence, intimidation, threats, prohibitions."[14] The Church in *The Sun Dances at Easter* is depicted as an institution corrupted by hypocrisy: "The pious leave their wealth to religion so that our churches may be fair and ornamented, and they are rewarded in the future life. Virgins who take the veil and become heavenly brides must bring with them to their community an earthly dowry. Riches are dangerous, but the clergy hold them in trust, so that those who live in the world may be spared from further temptation" (127). It is in this context of double standards that laughter and mirth confront the high seriousness of church and state. In that sense, laughter represents a force of renewal that liberates from dogmatism, falsehood, and intolerance.

Clarke frequently depicts such moments of liberation in combination with a fall, a physical reversal of top and bottom that deliberately mixes the hierarchical levels and places the character outside all norms and values. When Orla notices how attractive Enda is and how much he resembles her husband, "a ridiculous thought skipped into her mind and she could not help laughing at its impudence. She should have been ashamed of herself, but instead, she shook so mirthfully that she almost sprawled off her mount, and had to grab wildly at flank and mane" (57). Orla's impudent thought, her laughter, and her near-fall are more genuine, and therefore ultimately more fruitful, than her attempts to please heaven through severity and abstinence: "During the seven weeks of Lent she had kept to her own half [of the bed], in order that Heaven might be favourable at last to her husband and herself" (19). As Craig Tapping points out, "[T]he assumption that conception is associated with sexual repression motivated by Christian asceticism suggests that Christianity has somehow overturned the natural order."[15]

The narrative of *The Sun Dances at Easter* incorporates two stories based on medieval sources but substantially altered by Clarke. They are both related by Enda to Orla and are of direct relevance to the main plot and its outcome. Clarke calls his first story "The House of the Two Golden Methers" (a mether is a drinking cup). It is based on the fourteenth-century *Altram Tige Dá Medar*, translated by Lilian Duncan as "The Fosterage of the Houses of Two Methers." The tale "shows native Irish Christianisation

14. Bakhtin, *Rabelais*, 94–95.
15. Tapping, *Austin Clarke*, 143.

of a pagan Celtic magic-vessel story"[16] and juxtaposes the old gods of Ireland, the Tuatha Dé Danann, or Áes Sídhe, and the new religion introduced by Saint Patrick—not in a genuine dialogue, however, but only in order to justify the coming of Christianity: "'Is there a god over our gods?' said Aengus. 'There is, indeed,' said Manannán, 'the one God Almighty who is able to condemn our gods, and whom they are not able to despoil.'"[17] According to the story, this new God takes all who are obedient to him into his heaven, and puts all those who are against him in prison for punishment. The entire tale is a parable illustrating the power of the new religion over the old and the sad but inevitable demise of the Tuatha Dé Danann.

In the original story, the old gods and the representatives of Christianity confront each other over the possession of the soul of Ethne, Aengus's foster child. Manannán explains that Ethne can only drink the milk of a cow she herself milks into a golden cup, and cannot eat the food of the Sídhe because one of their company had insulted her, and at that moment "'her accompanying demon went (from) her heart and an angel came in its stead, and that does not let our food into her body, and she will not revere magic or wizardry henceforth, and it is for that reason she drinks the milk of that cow, for it was brought from a righteous land, i.e. India. . . . and it is the . . . three-personed Trinity which will be the God of worship for that maiden,' said he."[18] Soon after the arrival of Saint Patrick in Ireland, the otherworldly Ethne becomes visible to the cleric Ceasan, who instructs her in the Christian faith. One day Aengus and the other Áes Sídhe come to look for her to take her back. Ceasan prays for help and Saint Patrick himself arrives to confront Aengus. When Ethne hears Aengus's people lamenting her loss, she falls ill; she asks Patrick to baptize her and to pardon her sins, for, "Though there be many cries and weepings / among the womenfolk of the Brugh, / I prefer the cry of clerics round my head, / protecting my soul from Hell."[19] Having uttered this lay, she dies piously, whereupon Patrick ordains that her tale will have many benefits and virtues for those who listen to it, among them happiness and fertility in marriage, safety, liberty, and prosperity: "every one who has this elegy / he shall win the goal."[20]

---

16. Gerard Murphy, *The Ossianic Lore and Romantic Tales of Medieval Ireland,* in Knott and Murphy, *Early Irish Literature,* 168.

17. *Altram Tige Dá Medar,* trans and ed. Lilian Duncan, *Ériu,* 11 (1932): 210.

18. Ibid., 216.   19. Ibid., 223.

20. Ibid., 225.

The version of the story Austin Clarke puts into the mouth of Enda is a parody of the original in that its intention is directly opposite to that of its source, and yet for Orla the tale appears to carry all the blessings of the original. In Enda's carnivalized version of Eithne's story (Clarke's spelling), Christianity is the religion of suffering and fear described by Bakhtin in *Rabelais and His World*, while the Áes Sídhe represent happiness and laughter; the emphasis is not so much on Eithne's conversion to Christianity as on Ceasan's increasing longing to join the Sídhe. Eithne vaguely remembers coming from a place of happiness and peace, but now she wants only to learn how to be a good Christian, which means banishing all joy, concentrating on suffering and pain, and submitting to the Church's authority: "I will never look at a book again, I will submit my reason, knowing that complete and unquestioning faith is all, that we must be guided by the heart and not by thought. You have said that the training and exercise of the intellect is necessary only in order that the false arguments of the pagan philosophers may be confuted. . . . Have you not said that Ireland will be renowned in the future before all other lands, that faith will prosper there and be known by the threefold sign of obedience, simplicity and total ignorance?" (116). Aongus approaches Eithne, but she refuses to return to the otherworld; afterward she remembers "only that there was some wonderful happiness near me, and yet I knew that I must avoid it. Was it wrong of me to struggle against it, Ceasan, to want sorrow instead?" (106–7). Ceasan does not know the answer: the more Eithne questions him, the more he begins to question the Church's one language of truth.

From the moment he first meets Eithne, Ceasan feels guilty at the pleasure she brings him and the temptation she represents. She tells him to eat the salmon he has caught but "he was uneasy, feeling that he must not yield to the pleasures of appetite" (86). Later he watches her sleep and realizes too late that this makes him guilty of shameful curiosity: "His eye had been held by its own immodesty and was taking a wrongful pleasure against his will" (89). While his instructions guide Eithne toward religious obedience, her presence guides him toward material and physical pleasure. He begins to forget to say his prayers, and when he does try to pray, it is as if "the Adversary was deliberately distracting him, snatching away the right words in order to defeat his purpose" (98–99). Instead, he longs to see Aongus, to "tell him I am half mad for that unending happiness, for that knowledge which is its cause" (113). Ceasan feels his mind sinking into pagan superstition, but when he goes in search of guidance from Patrick he is literally caught in a storm: he steps into a quagmire, stumbles—in another liberating fall—and has to return when he finds that he cannot cross the flooded ford that divides him from the monks on the other side. Sensing the danger they are in, Eithne insists that Ceasan baptize her, but when he begins half-heartedly to pronounce the rite, she disappears: ". . . and, then, from the cliff-wood, came, in echo, his own cry of disbelief" (131).

Whereas in the original version of the story there is no question about the superior power and authority of the Church over the Tuatha Dé Danann (who themselves also concede God's greater strength), Enda's version is much more ambiguous. Ceasan is confused by the juxtaposition of different worlds, by the conflict between body and soul, superstition and faith, happiness and suffering, and asks himself the agonized question, "but why was everything next to nothing?" (128). Ceasan is caught in what Bakhtin calls *carnival ambivalence*: "[E]verything lives on the very border of its opposite. . . . opposites come together, look at one another, are reflected in one another, know and understand one another."[21] Instead of the single vision of the original story, Enda's version creates a duality typical of carnivalized literature that evades a "conclusive conclusion."[22]

Enda's version of "The House of the Two Golden Methers" sets up a duality between a joyful pagan religion and a severe Christian religion of pain and suffering. Although Orla does not comment on the story directly, her encounter with the comical hermit has convinced her of the importance of religious joy, a joy lacking in the official representatives of the Church: "I knew then that all true religion is happy, for he laughed with me, and when he nodded my soul was filled with joy. Indeed when he shook with that holy laughter, even his rags danced so that I thought they were a lovely bird-flock which was trying to fly over his head" (140). She does not yet realize that the birds and the dance represent Aongus, the god of love. When Orla arrives at the women's hostel there are more images of carnival and fertile celebration; six mummers in corn masks and bibs dance a wild reel, and during the dance she sees men and women disappearing into the bushes.

---

21. Bakhtin, *Dostoevsky's Poetics*, 176.
22. Ibid., 176.

She begins to understand the ancient secret of the Well of Saint Naal, but just as she herself is about to give in to the spirit of the occasion, Enda appears beside her to take her further on her journey.

Almost immediately Orla and Enda find themselves wandering around in a circle, caught in a fairy-ring. In Enda's first story, Ceasan had wondered: "Were there many worlds, each with their own order of invisible beings, known in dream or delirium by the different races of mankind?" (111). Now, for Orla and Enda, the boundaries between these different worlds begin to dissolve. At first they take shelter from the rain in a small hut and fall asleep; when they wake up they make their way to a hall, where two small golden methers appear to them, filled with mead. Orla remembers the story of Eithne and Ceasan, and Enda recalls that "part of the story is lost, and I've never been able to find it in any manuscript" (162): it appears that they themselves are living the missing part, for it is no longer clear whether their experiences are taking place in their own reality, in the otherworld, or in a dream. Ultimately, of course, they exist only within the pages of a work of fiction. If, as Bakhtin contends, carnival celebrates a temporary liberation from the established hierarchical order, and frees human imagination for new potentialities, then this principle also, and perhaps especially, applies to the narrative levels of Clarke's text, whose elements begin to intermingle freely as their hierarchical division is temporarily suspended.

Orla suspects she is falling in love with Enda and he with her, and to distract them both from this disturbing development, she asks him for another story; this time, inspired by the comical hermit and the lessons of the previous story, she insists on a merry tale. Enda's story, "The Only Jealousy of Congal More," is loosely based on *Eachtra Chléirigh na gCroiceann* ("The Adventures of the Skin-Clad Cleric"). Robin Flower summarizes the original story as follows:

Aonghus an Bhrogha comes to the court of Congal Cindmagair (king of Ireland 705–710) in hideous guise as a cleric of S. Patrick's company to demonstrate to the king that his boast of his wife's excelling chastity is premature. He transforms the king into a goat, which he sells to the queen, and the king, thus transformed, witnesses his wife's lightness. Afterwards the king is brought back to his natural shape on the hill of Howth and is taken overseas to a fairy island. From the island he brings a magic cup by means of which his wife, her lover, the prior of a monastery, and various other characters are caught in a compromising situation, the hands of the queen and her lover adhering to the cup and the other characters adhering to them.[23]

In Austin Clarke's version, the serious ideological intent of the tale is carnivalized as its outcome is reversed and its main character debased. In Enda's story, King Congal More is married for the second time, to his late first wife's sister, a practice that would normally be frowned upon by the medieval Church. In this case, however, the second marriage was blessed by the clergy because Congal gave land and stock to the religious orders; Congal himself, meanwhile, is the staunchest supporter of the severely moralistic abbot-bishop in upholding standards of decency in his kingdom. Congal's disguise as a goat backfires to the extent that he comes to regard his bestial and humiliating experiences as a punishment for spying on his wife. The pious king's grotesque transformation into an animal traditionally associated with lechery and satanism exposes him to ridicule, and symbolizes the hypocrisy of the moralistic attitude he adopts to gain favor with the abbot-bishop.

In the story about Congal Clarke uses explicit carnival motifs when he contrasts the official serious representatives of church and state with the laughing figure of the roguish monk. Like the grotesque personification of the Catholic fast, King Lent, in Rabelais, the bishop represents "a personification of the bias against natural processes characteristic of medieval ideology:"[24] "It happened on a sunny day in Spring that the Lord Abbot-bishop of Midhe and his white-clad clergy were approaching the slopes of Tara. Behind every bush, as they passed, the birds went into hiding, reeds shook, tiny pleasure-seekers clambered down from the grass-stalks and took to their heels. Every thicket, every pool was still, for the reverend Macuad was the most renowned moralist in Ireland, and wherever he went he was both feared and respected" (171–72). As the abbot-bishop begins to preach to a large public gathering, he denounces all amusement and worldly pleasures: "Traditional stories and poems that incite passion have become widespread and we are threatened with a new era of paganism. In consequence the moral law is openly flouted, and there has been a disgraceful laxity of con-

23. Robin Flower, *Catalogue of Irish Manuscripts in the British Museum* (London: Trustees of the British Museum, 1926), vol. 2, 367.

24. Bakhtin, *Dialogic Imagination*, 175.

duct" (173). As discussed earlier, Macuad's view is a partial reversal of the position of the Irish bishops of the early twentieth century, who saw the threat of this new paganism in the influence of foreign media rather than in traditional Irish stories and poems.

The Lord Abbot-bishop is not just a stock depiction of a moralistic clergyman: Macuad is a thinly veiled satirical portrait of the Most Reverend John Charles McQuaid, who was appointed archbishop of Dublin in 1940 (he retired in 1972). Archbishop McQuaid was uncompromising on matters of sexual morality. As late as 1971 he wrote in a letter to be read in all churches of his diocese: "Given the proneness of our human nature to evil, given the enticement of bodily satisfaction, given the widespread modern incitement to unchastity, it must be evident that an access, hitherto unlawful, to contraceptive devices will prove a most certain occasion of sin, especially to immature persons. The public consequences of immorality that must follow for our whole society are only too clearly seen in other countries."[25] For several decades Archbishop McQuaid was the bane of Irish writers. John McGahern, for example, claims that he lost his teaching job after his novel *The Dark* was banned because the archbishop "had an absolute obsession about what he called impure books."[26] Brian Moore, whose novel *The Lonely Passion of Judith Hearne* was banned in 1955, similarly remarks that Archbishop McQuaid "was a heavy-duty banner, and it was his say-so in the fifties which books were put on the Irish index."[27] The climate following the Censorship of Publications Act of 1929 was not conducive to literary expression, and all writers automatically came under suspicion. Austin Clarke was in outspoken disagreement with the Church on many issues, and his third prose narrative, like the previous two, was banned shortly after its publication in 1952. The ban on *The Bright Temptation* was removed in 1954, but an appeal a year later to have *The Sun Dances at Easter* removed from the index was unsuccessful.

The sacrilegious monk who sent Orla on her journey, and who represents the incarnation of the paganism and pleasure so forcefully denounced by Macuad, appears as a character with a similar mission in Enda's second

25. Quoted in Whyte, *Church and State,* 406.

26. John McGahern, interview with Julia Carlson, in *Banned in Ireland: Censorship and the Irish Writer,* ed. Julia Carlson (Athens: University of Georgia Press, 1990), 56.

27. Brian Moore, interview with Julia Carlson, in Carlson, *Banned in Ireland,* 113.

story. As Macuad begins to preach, guffaws interrupt his diatribe against immorality, and as the crowd sways back he catches a glimpse of their instigator,

a fat monk with a red foolish face, whispering merrily to those around him. His listeners were nudging each other as if he were telling them a dirty story they had never heard before, and they grabbed at their bigger lip to keep in the bursts of laughter. . . .

All could see the monk now, for he had wagged his big head out of its hood and was gabbling like a booby. Never indeed has such a ridiculous figure frolicked at Tara from that day to this. The puckers of his goatskin habit were unmatched-and-patched among themselves. . . . Neighbours were elbowing strangers knowingly as his jokes went by them, the young were giggling, the old were wheezing and clawing their leather, for they remembered the good times they had had in the past. Strong men staggered into fits of laughter until their legs could support them no more, and women could not help wetting themselves, so quickly did the tears run down their cheeks. Lookers who were looped outside the crowd were no luckier, for when they lay down in their mirth, they were tickled again by the grass. (174–75)

Bakhtin explains the role of the clown as that of a carnival figure who exposes the underside and the falseness of a situation: "These figures carry with them into literature first a vital connection with the theatrical trappings of the public square, with the mask of the public spectacle; they are connected with that highly specific, extremely important area of the square where the common people congregate; second—and this is of course a related phenomenon—the very being of these figures does not have a direct, but rather a metaphorical, significance."[28] Elsewhere, Bakhtin describes the form of life represented by clowns and fools as "real and ideal at the same time."[29] The subversive nature of the irreverent monk's infectious laughter becomes evident as the king's soldiers in vain attempt to capture the culprit, but only manage to strike out at themselves and each other, so that the situation deteriorates into slapstick comedy. The laughter drives a wedge between the crowd and the solemn representatives of authority: "Huge was the merriment of the people and their cheers raced neck to neck. Only Congal, the Lord Abbot-bishop and the clergy sat there with dooming faces" (176).

28. Bakhtin, *Dialogic Imagination*, 159.
29. Bakhtin, *Rabelais*, 8.

In his rage, Congal pursues the fleeing monk on horseback, but loses control of his horse and is hurled to the ground. His fall brings him face to face with the monk, who now reveals himself as Aongus. The god tells Congal that his wife is betraying him with another man (cuckoldry is a popular festive form of uncrowning), and helpfully offers to disguise the king so that he can spy on the adulterous lovers. Before Congal realizes what is happening, he has been turned into a goat. The grotesque transformation provides Congal with a split personality, for "events of the grotesque sphere are always developed on the boundary dividing one body from the other and, as it were, at their points of intersection."[30] The two halves of Congal's persona are fused and yet in conflict with each other: inwardly, to himself, Congal is still the same piously moralistic king, but externally he looks and sounds just like an animal. The king's wife calls him a "stinking brute," an insult Congal humbly takes to heart before realizing that, as far as his wife is concerned, she is not addressing her husband but chasing away a goat. Even when his wife and her lover go after him with a knife, Congal still believes that Aongus has given him this shape "so that my wife might see the image of her own lust in me" (186).

The most poignant confrontation with himself-as-other for Congal, staunch supporter of what Bakhtin calls "the poetics of the medieval church, of 'the one language of truth,'"[31] is through the loss of that unitary language. Congal can still think, but he cannot translate his thoughts into meaningful words, and all his attempts at communication are misinterpreted as the very opposite of what he is trying to say. Looking for help, he sneaks into the scriptorium and appeals to Father Ruadan, his spiritual confessor. The astonished priest, however, only hears a bleating noise:

He gaped with surprise when he saw a goat looking up at him. Congal tried to smile, but as the lips curled back from his pointed teeth in a bestial leer, the holy father dropped his book, slowly rose and backed away in terror.

Congal moved towards him, but he crouched closer to the wall.

"Do you not recognize me, Father?" he bleated hopefully. (194)

Ruadan, however, is under the impression that the Devil himself is speaking to him in Hebrew. Congal's confrontation with Macuad is equally am-

---

30. Ibid., 322.
31. Bakhtin, *Dialogic Imagination*, 271.

biguous; as the goat-king totters forward on his hind legs, bleating piously at his "protector and soul-friend" (196), the abbot-bishop sprinkles him with holy water in an attempt to exorcize the Devil. The scorching pain Congal feels when the water touches him suggests that he has indeed, in some way, become what the others see in him.

Congal's goatish disguise has the function of decrowning the hypocritically pious and moralistic king and confronting him with his own natural instincts, which the Church's teachings reject as being more bestial than human. Bakhtin argues—in connection with Rabelais—that it is in fact these hypocritical teachings themselves that debase the natural functions of life: "The healthy 'natural' functions of human nature are fulfilled, so to speak, only in ways that are contraband and savage, because the reigning ideology will not sanction them. This introduces falsehood and duplicity into all human life. All ideological forms, that is, institutions, become hypocritical and false, while real life, denied any ideological directives, becomes crude and bestial."[32] Congal is humiliatingly confronted with the ideology he has himself endorsed when he is caught and put into a pen with a frisky nanny goat, for the king had supported the abbot-bishop in his campaign "to remove all direct and indirect incitement towards passion," and Macuad had "made it a reserved sin for anyone to bring a cow to the bull, let a mare be served, or loose a raddled ram within the fold except under cover of darkness" (205). Still convinced that, as a human being, he is above such animal passions, and realizing his "shameful and ridiculous predicament," Congal tries to get as far away as he can from the "ill-smelling creature" (204). As a human being, the king has every reason to feel humiliated and outraged at being fancied by an animal—and yet one can hardly blame the goat for being deceived by his appearance; Congal's censuring of the goat's natural behavior by applying the dubious moral standards of human beings is much less defensible.

Like Eimar O'Duffy, Clarke employs the common satirical device of equating sexual appetite with the hunger for food: both sex and eating are natural urges necessary for the survival of the species, but only one is considered sinful in the ideology of the Church. As his animal nature begins to take effect, Congal's human desires and taboos are gradually being replaced

32. Ibid., 162.

by more goatish ones. A naked girl bathing in a stream cheerfully waves at the goat without realizing that she is giving great offense to the king, who has no way of expressing his indignity. The next moment, however, he has forgotten his sense of moral outrage at the girl's lack of inhibition as he himself is about to give in to temptation: "He closed his eyes but he was unable to overcome his wild feeling of desire. He struggled against the temptation in vain: cautiously, cutely, he opened his eyes and peeped once more" (215). The temptation comes in the form of the girl's silk underwear—which Congal proceeds to eat greedily. Still hungry, he begins to take bites out of the clothing of girls lying in the bushes with their lovers, thereby causing great scandal, because the girls are under the impression that they are being assaulted by their young men. Ironically, now that, as a goat, Congal no longer cares about sexual morality, his "bestial urges" are the cause of such a "roar of morality" that for a long time afterward "he could still hear that rumble of morality moving through the night as the old pursued the young" (221).

Congal's victory over a number of rival bucks in a fight over a she-goat completes his transition toward bestiality. But as he proudly stalks toward his prize, completely lost in his new identity, the day suddenly darkens: "Devil-headed, he stood there, seeing through the mist the pale forms of the clergy and the stern face of the blessed Macuad. A curse came to his bestial lips and, lost in darkness, he heard the voice of his wife calling him gently" (227). The king wakes up in bed, much relieved at being himself again. The function of dreams in carnivalized literature is to "make ordinary life seem strange," to force one "to understand and evaluate ordinary life in a new way."[33] Congal's dream turned the king into another being, a decrowned double of his real self; he realizes that everything exists on the border of its opposite, and that he must never be jealous of his wife again. Apart from this lesson in tolerance, however, the revolutionary extent of the king's reformation is limited, given the temporary nature of carnival decrowning, and given that each decrowning implies an imminent crowning, and vice versa: "Neither carnival, nor the serio-comic genres it informs, can therefore be truly subversive, for to be so they would have to declare free interplay among people as always superior to the current ruling authority. . . .

33. Bakhtin, *Dostoevsky's Poetics*, 147.

Bakhtin's account of the relationship between authority and carnival ultimately reifies authority, and on aesthetic grounds. . . . freedom is aesthetic
freedom, a liberty predicated on a monolithic, dominating centripetal force
pervading society."[34]

This predominantly aesthetic freedom is evident in the plot about Orla
and Enda, who are still trapped in the land of enchantment, where reality
and imagination (in the form of storytelling and wishful thinking) are in-
distinguishable, where time is suspended, where every wish is granted, and
"where all that can be imagined is true" (238). Using their free will, they escape from the otherworld, only to find themselves in bed together: "They
were still under the enchantment of Aongus and their real wish had been
granted to them" (242). Soon thereafter, Enda's dearest wish, to witness a
miracle, is fulfilled: he sees a flight of angels and follows it, the shining light
illuminating his naked body. It is clear that Orla's wish is also about to be
granted by Aongus, and that its fulfillment, too, will be miraculous and
mysterious. When Orla and Enda wake up once more in the hut where they
had taken shelter from the rain, they wonder whether the otherworld had
been just a dream—but if so, it is a dream they both remember. As soon as
they embrace each other again, the narrative becomes deliberately ambiguous: Is Aongus giving Orla a chance at having a child, or is Saint Natalis
testing her worthiness? Must she resist the temptation, or should she give in
to it? The story of Orla and Enda, like that of Ceasan and Eithne, is incomplete, and part of it is not found in any written manuscript: its resolution is
a task for the creative imagination. The imagination is fertile, for Orla's
wish is granted: "[I]n due course she presented her husband with a fine
bouncing boy" (255).

The prevalent ideology of the Church in *The Sun Dances at Easter* does
not accept that it can exist side by side with other beliefs, for its authority
("the truth") is dependent on its position of uniqueness. The Church therefore always depicts the world in terms of either/or (that is to say, true/false)
oppositions, whereby one term in the equation excludes or denies the other. As Ceasan tells Eithne, "after the Great War in Heaven, the material
world was created and since then all thoughts and conditions had their op-

34. Craig Howes, "Rhetorics of Attack: Bakhtin and the Aesthetics of Satire," *Genre*, 18 (Fall
1986): 237.

posites" (80). Thus, or so Enda tells Orla, the pious view of Saint Brendan's legendary voyage (a tale, incidentally, much liked by Rabelais) is that the saint was allowed to see the Earthly Paradise, the Islands of the Blessed, not to experience their happiness, but only in order that he might refute the legends of Oisín and other pagans who sailed across the ocean to the Land of Promise (72). Clarke's narrative, on the other hand, blurs such binary oppositions. It never becomes clear, for example, whether the nightly church builders Orla sees at the holy house at Glan are angels, or members of the Sídhe, or merely apparitions in a dream; nor is the mystery of the conception of Flann Jr. ever revealed. Carnivalized literature is inclusive: it embraces the ambiguity of both/and, and the existence of multiple possibilities; it refuses to be pinned down on one single conclusion, or to be identified with one single moral or ideological conviction. Aongus, the Celtic god who appears in various guises, among them that of a Christian monk, and whose presence and influence are felt at all levels of the narrative, personifies this carnival element.

In *The Sun Dances at Easter* carnival laughter ridicules the solemn, monologic, and inflexible dogma dictated by the Catholic Church and supported by the Irish state. In 1952, the year of the book's publication, the Irish Taoiseach (prime minister) was Éamon de Valera, who had been largely responsible for the Irish Constitution of 1937, a document which, according to N. S. Mansergh, attempts "to reconcile the notion of inalienable popular sovereignty with the older medieval conception of a theocratic state."[35] Opposite this single-minded, closed (and, Clarke would argue, barren) doctrine of *one* answer and *one* truth, Austin Clarke posits a creative view that offers several equally possible alternatives, without closure and with no single answer, culminating in the fertile image of a birth, a new beginning. As such, the spirit of the book reflects what Bakhtin considers to be carnival's fundamental principle: "It frees human consciousness, thought, and imagination for new potentialities. For this reason great changes . . . are always preceded by a certain carnival consciousness that prepares the way."[36]

If this is so—after all, the change in climate in Ireland did not begin to happen until the late 1950s—*The Sun Dances at Easter* is a passive reflection of this spirit rather than an active instigator of social change: its truly lib-

35. Quoted by Lyons in *Ireland since the Famine*, 538.
36. Bakhtin, *Rabelais*, 49.

erating process takes place entirely on a textual level, within the closed system of the book itself. On that level, the textual carnival of *The Sun Dances at Easter* can be seen as a subversion of the legitimizing master narratives of Irish religious and political discourse. The book does not fundamentally attack the authority it mocks; rather, it illustrates the view that "carnival is most vital when institutional authority is most powerfully present as well."[37] The decades following the creation of the Irish Free State produced many carnivalized and satirical texts, many of which were banned in Ireland by the very authorities they sought to ridicule. Rather than fulfilling a truly subversive social function, self-contained carnivalized texts like *The Sun Dances at Easter* reflect the paradoxical double bind of the author writing in the vacuum created by official censorship, seeking to engage his audience in the dethroning of the very authorities by whom he is deprived of his audience.

37. Howes, "Rhetorics," 237.

part four

Flann O'Brien

(1911–1966)

When he calls Flann O'Brien "an author often taken to be a precursor of postmodernism,"[1] Theo D'haen sums up what was the most prevalent critical attitude toward the author of *At Swim-Two-Birds* before recent publications began to reassess O'Brien's place within the modern canon in general, and within Irish literature in particular. The scope is sometimes wider, as when Rüdiger Imhof places O'Brien in a broad "tradition of comic-experimental, or, preferably, meta-novelists, which ranges from the anticipants of the Sternesque novel to B. S. Johnson and other contemporary practitioners,"[2] but generally speaking, O'Brien has been regarded as a postmodernist *avant la lettre* and therefore something of a rarity, an odd man out in the world of Irish and international letters who happened to hit upon the notion of metafiction at least twenty years before its subversive conventions became de rigueur in the realm of experimental literature.

The formal techniques of postmodernist literature and those of Menippean satire overlap to a large extent, such that O'Brien's work can

1. Theo D'haen, "Popular Genre Conventions in Postmodern Fiction: The Case of the Western," in *Exploring Postmodernism*, ed. Matei Calinescu and Douwe Fokkema (Amsterdam: John Benjamins, 1987), 172.

2. Rüdiger Imhof, "Two Meta-Novelists: Sternesque Elements in Novels by Flann O'Brien," in *Alive-Alive O! Flann O'Brien's* At Swim-Two-Birds, ed. Rüdiger Imhof (Dublin: Wolfhound, 1985), 162.

be illuminated from either perspective, but only a few commentators have noted, and then only in passing, the similarities between O'Brien's brand of satire and that of (near-) contemporary Irish writers other than the ubiquitous James Joyce. Benedict Kiely discusses O'Brien alongside Austin Clarke, Mervyn Wall, and Eimar O'Duffy in the same chapter of his *Modern Irish Fiction: A Critique* (1950), and in what is still one of the better articles on O'Brien, J. C. C. Mays argues that O'Brien pursued a vein of fantasy similar to that of O'Duffy, Wall, and Clarke, although he did so "in his own inimitable way and for his own private reasons."[3] *The Oxford Companion to Irish Literature* speculates that *At Swim-Two-Birds* may have been influenced by O'Duffy's Cuanduine trilogy "in placing mythological characters in contemporary contexts."[4] It is not without interest in this regard that the technique adopted by O'Brien (as "Brother Barnabas") in a 1931 article in the student magazine *Comhthrom Féinne*, of inverting common surnames for humorous purposes ("Mr. Yhaclum," "Mr. Tnek"[5]), was also frequently used by O'Duffy. Arguments concerning the common (Menippean) concerns of O'Brien and these other writers, however, have seldom been consistently pursued. Keith Booker makes a convincing case for classifying O'Brien's novels as Menippean satires on a formal basis,[6] but his discussion largely disregards the literary and sociopolitical context that contributed to the satire. Several recent articles, one by Kim McMullen, who offers a dialogic reading of *At Swim-Two-Birds*,[7] and another by Joshua Esty, who provides a postcolonial interpretation of that same work,[8] have opened up the debate about the nature and extent of O'Brien's sociopolitical engagement. Keith Hopper's book-length study of O'Brien, too, while placing his work in a postmodernist framework, per-

3. J. C. C. Mays, "Brian O'Nolan: Literalist of the Imagination," in *Myles: Portraits of Brian O'Nolan,* ed. Timothy O'Keeffe (London: Martin Brian and O'Keeffe, 1973), 84.

4. *Oxford Companion to Irish Literature,* 427.

5. "The 'L and H' from the Earliest Times," *Comhthrom Féinne,* 15 May 1931; quoted by Thomas F. Shea in *Flann O'Brien's Exorbitant Novels* (Lewisburg, Penn.: Bucknell University Press, 1992), 21.

6. M. Keith Booker, *Flann O'Brien, Bakhtin, and Menippean Satire* (Syracuse, N.Y.: Syracuse University Press, 1995).

7. Kim McMullen, "Culture as Colloquy: Flann O'Brien's Postmodern Dialogue with Irish Tradition," *Novel: A Forum on Fiction,* 27, 1 (1993): 62–84.

8. Joshua D. Esty, "Flann O'Brien's *At Swim-Two-Birds* and the Post-Post Debate," *Ariel,* 26, 4 (1995): 23–46.

suasively discusses O'Brien as an Irish writer responding to and affected by the social and religious ideology of the emerging independent state.[9]

Flann O'Brien was born as Brian O'Nolan on 5 October 1911 in Strabane, in what is now Northern Ireland, the third of twelve children. His family spoke Irish at home at the instigation of his father, and since no Irish schooling was available, the three eldest boys were initially, somewhat haphazardly, tutored at home. All the same, they knew "as much English as any other children" because their mother's family spoke only English, and "hardly a day passed when we were not in their house in the Main Street or in one of the shops—places where only English was spoken."[10] Another brother remembers that they "were constantly delighted at the vividness and economy of language casually practised by our Strabane elders, and at a great range of strange words like 'hochle' and 'boke' which seemed more expressive than the ordinary words to be found in books."[11] Brian's bilingualism provided him with a sensitivity to language, which doubtless lay at the root of much of the wordplay in his writing, especially the puns and language games in his "Cruiskeen Lawn" column in the *Irish Times,* and of his ability to detach linguistic form from semantic content.[12] Bakhtin points out that this kind of linguistic awareness and versatility is possible only in bilingual and multilingual societies, since "it is possible to objectivize one's own particular language . . . only in the light of another language belonging to someone else, which is almost as much 'one's own' as one's native language."[13] During his entire life O'Nolan remained fascinated by the creative possibilities of homonyms, homophones, acronyms, and spelling conventions in both Irish and English, and the literal meaning of dead metaphors, just as he was consistently outraged by bad grammar, sloppy usage, and faulty translation.

---

9. Keith Hopper, *Flann O'Brien: A Portrait of the Artist as a Young Post-Modernist* (Cork, Ireland: Cork University Press, 1995).

10. Ciarán Ó Nualláin, *The Early Years of Brian O'Nolan/Flann O'Brien/Myles na gCopaleen,* trans. Róisín Ní Nualláin, ed. Niall O'Nolan (Dublin: Lilliput Press, 1998), 23.

11. Kevin O'Nolan, "The First Furlongs," in *Myles: Portraits of Brian O'Nolan,* ed. Timothy O'Keeffe, 15–16.

12. For a discussion of this characteristic of his work, see my article " 'Still Life' versus Real Life: The English Writings of Brian O'Nolan," in *Explorations in the Field of Nonsense,* ed. Wim Tigges (Amsterdam: Rodopi, 1987), 161–81.

13. Bakhtin, *Dialogic Imagination,* 62.

Brian O'Nolan completed a master's degree in literature at University College, Dublin (UCD), before entering the civil service in the summer of 1935, a year after Mervyn Wall had embarked on a similar career. During his student days he had been active as a debater, and had been a frequent contributor of increasingly outrageous material to the college magazine *Comhthrom Féinne,* acquiring a reputation among his peers as an intellectual, wit, and satirist. His professional persona as a civil servant, however, required seriousness of demeanor and dress. At least in his early years in the service, before his drinking became a growing problem, he appears to have been a model of efficiency, being promoted in 1937 to a more demanding position as private secretary to the minister of local government. Unlike Mervyn Wall, who detested the civil service from the very beginning, O'Nolan did not initially adopt an adversarial attitude: "[U]ntil a much later period in Brian O'Nolan's personal history there is no suggestion of a conflict in which the claims of freedom or free expression had to be balanced against other claims. When he did feel anything of the kind, it was too late."[14] O'Brien's way of coping with these various and conflicting demands was appropriately Menippean: he split himself into several different and sometimes elaborately constructed personas, a practice he had started when he wrote in *Comhthrom Féinne* under the alias "Brother Barnabas." Thus, the straitlaced civil servant Brian O'Nolan (or Brian Ó Nualláin in the Irish version, which he came to prefer), expeditor of the minister's authority, had subversive alter egos in Flann O'Brien the novelist and Myles na gCopaleen (later simplified to Myles na Gopaleen) the "Cruiskeen Lawn" columnist. This incongruous combination of personas was itself a source of literary inspiration. Seamus Deane mentions O'Brien's talent for adapting the language and formulas of the civil service as conversation in his fictions, a discourse both predictable and strange with a high potential for satire because "it contains within itself an inversion; the written word, the documentary procedure, the obituarist's format, has become the speech of the common populace."[15] O'Nolan's fictitious identities, as well as some of the disinformation he provided vis-à-vis events in his own life (such as the mysterious visit to Germany in

14. Anthony Cronin, *No Laughing Matter: The Life and Times of Flann O'Brien* (London: Paladin, 1990), 89.

15. Seamus Deane, *Strange Country: Modernity and Nationhood in Irish Writing since 1790* (Oxford, U.K.: Clarendon Press, 1997), 161.

the early 1930s, when he purportedly "met and married 18-year-old Clara Ungerland, blonde, violin-playing daughter of a Cologne basket weaver"[16]), were taken seriously by more than one commentator on his work, and helped protect his private life; much of what constituted the "real" Brian O'Nolan remains elusive to this day.

O'Nolan wrote four books in English, *At Swim-Two-Birds* (1939), *The Third Policeman* (completed in 1940 but unpublished until 1967), *The Hard Life* (1961), and *The Dalkey Archive* (1964), and one in Irish, *An Béal Bocht* (1941), published in an English translation by Patrick Power as *The Poor Mouth* (1973). *An Béal Bocht* is a true Menippean satire, but precisely because of the nature of the work the translation cannot do it full justice and is "but a mere ghost of the original text."[17] As Breandan Ó Conaire puts it, to appreciate

the full force and complexity of this creation it is necessary to have some knowledge of a number of specific themes and modes in Irish literature, a good grasp of modern writing in Irish and a reasonable acquaintance with some of the most characteristic aspects of modern Irish society, say, from the late nineteenth century to [the] late nineteen-thirties. To savour all the innuendoes, barbs, references, insinuations and word-magic something approaching a running commentary is probably necessary, on the lines, for example, of Samuel Putnam's edition of Rabelais. As in the case of much humour and satire, knowledge of an original is often required: it is the difference that counts. The intermedium is the message.[18]

The gap of over twenty years between the early novels and those of the 1960s is as wide as the division between their respective styles: the later novels move toward realism and away from the ludic textual elements of metafiction, hierarchical inversion, parody, and paradox that characterize the early works. For these reasons, my discussion of Flann O'Brien in the context of Menippean satire in postindependence Ireland will be confined to *At Swim-Two-Birds* and *The Third Policeman*.

---

16. O'Nolan provided this "biographical" information in an interview with Stanford Lee Cooper, published in *Time* magazine in 1943; quoted in Peter Costello and Peter van de Kamp, *Flann O'Brien: An Illustrated Biography* (London: Bloomsbury, 1987), 48.

17. Jane Farnon, "Motifs of Gaelic Lore and Literature in *An Béal Bocht,*" in *Conjuring Complexities: Essays on Flann O'Brien,* ed. Anne Clune and Tess Hurson (Belfast: Institute of Irish Studies, 1997), 89.

18. Breandan Ó Conaire, "Flann O'Brien, *An Béal Bocht* and Other Irish Matters," *Irish University Review,* 3, 2 (1973): 130.

chapter eight

"Answers Do Not Matter So Much as Questions"

At Swim-Two-Birds

Flann O'Brien's *At Swim-Two-Birds* has most often been discussed by critics as a metafictional novel, concerned with exposing the artificiality of the conventions of realist fiction. For a writer in 1930s Ireland, however, a preoccupation with literature per se was not necessarily merely a display of the degree of his modernity or vanguardism, although the literary heroes (Eliot, Joyce, Huxley, Hemingway) of O'Brien and his fellow students at UCD were all in the forefront of the literary avant-garde. Literature itself was under suspicion in Ireland, and anyone engaged in producing it was regarded as potentially subversive; as a result, much of the literature of the period "is concerned with the problem of the effects of inhibition on the individual and on the country. Keenly aware of the forces that curtail freedom, the writers give imaginative portrayal to characters, situations, and themes that select, evaluate, and judge the moral consequences of an overrestrictive environment."[1] That environment, a product of "the relationship between the Irish Ireland ideology and the exclusivist cultural and social pressures . . . bore fruit in the enactment of the Censorship Bill of 1929."[2] Rather than making traditional forces of authority, such as church and state, the object of his criticism and attacking their inflexible attitudes outright, Flann O'Brien moves straight to the heart of the matter, making literature itself both the vehicle and the focus of his satirical critique. The ex-

1. Maurice Harmon, "The Era of Inhibitions: Irish Literature 1920–1960," in *Irish Writers and Society at Large*, ed. Masaru Sekine (Gerrards Cross, U.K.: Colin Smythe, 1985), 36.
2. Terence Brown, *Ireland: A Social and Cultural History, 1922 to the Present* (Ithaca, N.Y.: Cornell University Press, 1981, 1985), 54.

perimental techniques of *At Swim-Two-Birds* subvert the country's censorship laws in subtle ways without overtly engaging them in a head-on collision.

At Swim-Two-Birds has all the outward trappings of Menippean satire, of which metafictional elements are, of course, an important attribute. In *Problems of Dostoevsky's Poetics* Bakhtin sums up the fourteen main characteristics of Menippean satire, and the presence of most of these can easily be demonstrated in O'Brien's oeuvre. *At Swim-Two-Birds* is about a student at UCD who is writing a book about a writer named Dermot Trellis, who is also writing a novel, but whose characters turn against him and conspire to write a story of their own in which their creator is tortured and almost destroyed. The layered construction of *At Swim-Two-Birds,* plus the fact that all the writers it contains are in the habit of borrowing heavily and indiscriminately from existing literary works, allows for great freedom of plot and invention, the creation of extraordinary situations, the wide use of inserted and borrowed texts as well as parodies of existing texts, and a consequent mésalliance of sharply contrasting themes, characters, styles, and registers. As a dialogic text, *At Swim-Two-Birds* "explicitly engages prior inscriptions of Irish identity in a scrutiny that is necessarily historicized and political, exposing the 'authored, prosaic, and historical' basis of the Celtic Revivalists' romantic antiquarianism and the cultural protectionists' essentialism"; as such, it is a text "which *both* values *and* interrogates tradition, and which deploys formal innovation as an agent of ideological critique."[3] In Menippean satire, the purpose of creating unusual, even fantastic, situations is to provide a setting within which a truth or philosophical idea can be tested. *At Swim-Two-Birds* raises questions about the nature of moral authority in the world, and more particularly in the book as world.

The starting point for what O'Brien called the "erudite irresponsibility"[4] of the book's antiauthoritarian message is its narrator's much-quoted conviction that traditional novels unfairly cause readers "to experience a real concern for the fortunes of illusory characters," and that in order to avoid such emotional involvement, "a satisfactory novel should be a self-evident sham to which the reader could regulate at will the degree of his credulity"

---

3. McMullen, "Culture as Colloquy," 75.

4. Letter to A. M. Heath and Co., 3 October 1938, in "A Sheaf of Letters," ed. Robert Hogan and Gordon Henderson, *Journal of Irish Literature,* 3, 1 (1974): 66.

(25).[5] This sounds like a perfectly logical attitude to adopt for a writer who is about to be engaged in the composition of a metafictional narrative, were it not that he immediately pulls the rug from under his own feet by paradoxically accommodating not only the reader but also the novel's "illusory" characters under his antiauthoritarian umbrella, and discussing them as if they were real people with rights and needs: "It was undemocratic to compel characters to be uniformly good or bad or poor or rich. Each should be allowed a private life, self-determination and a decent standard of living" (25). In a similar egalitarian vein, the narrator opines that "one beginning and one ending for a book was a thing I did not agree with" (9), and he proceeds by providing three separate openings. For a book to have three simultaneous beginnings is, of course, a physical impossibility.[6] The very fact that the narrator's beginnings are labeled the "first," the "second" and the "third" opening makes it clear that at least two of them are not openings at all, given that numbers two and three by definition follow number one; and the "first opening," which begins "The Pooka MacPhellimey . . . ," is not actually the opening of the book at all, for *At Swim-Two-Birds* begins with the words of the narrator's biographical frame story: "Having placed in my mouth sufficient bread for three minutes' chewing . . ." (9). It is evident that the narrator, for all his lofty intentions, cannot escape from the linear demands of his narrative. He is himself an example of the kind of "despotic" author he seeks to satirize in the figure of Trellis, and he is ultimately always the one who dominates and manipulates the various strands of the narrative. The pun of which the student is so proud that he utters it twice, "the conclusion of your syllogism . . . is fallacious, being based on licensed premises" (21, 47), is in fact an accurate description of his own brand of fallacious logic, in which an acceptable supposition or premise is followed by a logically unacceptable conclusion.

Trellis follows in his creator's footsteps by also adopting the student narrator's notion that characters should be interchangeable between books,

---

5. Flann O'Brien, *At Swim-Two-Birds* (1939; reprint, Harmondsworth, U.K.: Penguin Books, 1967); all page references in the text are to this edition.

6. John Barth presents readers with a similar predicament in chapter 20 ("Calliope Music") of *The Floating Opera* (New York: Bantam, 1972), which he feels he must begin "in two voices, because it requires two separate introductions delivered simultaneously" (168). He provides two columns of text side by side, for simultaneous reading.

and that the modern novel should be "largely a work of reference" (25), thereby supporting an encyclopedic approach to literature that is typical of Menippean satire. Since Trellis only reads green books and regards all other colors as symbols of evil, most of his reading material concerns Irish history and antiquities (the green-bound publications of the Irish Texts Society being an example); it therefore stands to reason that two of the main characters in the green book Trellis is writing, Finn MacCool and the Pooka, are derived from Irish mythology and folklore. His other characters are borrowed predominantly from the works of William Tracy, a writer of western romances with titles like *Flower o' the Prairie*. Since Trellis's own book is set in contemporary Dublin, the literary method he adopts forms the basis for a whole series of incongruous juxtapositions of characters and settings, such as the episode in which cowboys borrowed from Tracy go after a herd of cattle "rustled across the border in Irishtown by Red Kiersay's gang of thieving ruffians" (54). Since the student narrator of the biographical frame story is also in the habit of quoting at random from the ancient and modern books on his bookshelf, the result is a wide variety of styles and registers, inserted texts, quotations and parodies of quotations, on all levels of the narrative.

This narrative "involves several planes and dimensions" (101), whose boundaries are, however, highly unstable. Characters move from one plot into another, crossing the line that separates one narrative level from another, and even one book from another, for the "borrowed" characters in Trellis's plot still remember their adventures in other stories. Lamont, for example, recalls "an adventure which once befell him in a book when teaching French and piano-playing to a young girl of delicate and refined nature," while Shanahan relates his experiences "as a cow-puncher in the Ringsend district of Dublin city" (52–53). Not content with being fictional characters, especially in a book they dislike, they encourage Trellis's semi-literary offspring, Orlick, who has been instructed by the Pooka MacPhellimey in "evil, revolt, and non-serviam" (150), to punish his father by making him a character in a story. Shanahan, Furriskey, and Lamont, reluctant characters in Trellis's narrative, are themselves fictionally embellished by Orlick and introduced into his story, in which Trellis is now a character, so that they can violently attack their erstwhile creator. Finn MacCool, meanwhile, who was borrowed by Trellis from Irish mythology to act as the father of the domestic servant Peggy, but who assailed her virtue instead while his master was sleeping, tells the story known as "The Madness of Sweeny," or *Buile Suibhne*. The mad bird-king of this tale falls out of a tree in which he is roosting and tumbles stark naked into the plot occupied by Trellis's characters; Orlick, meanwhile, borrows the plot Sweeny has thus inadvertently vacated for the story in which he tortures Trellis. Structural topsy-turviness and contrariness of this kind undermine the hierarchical division of plot and subplot, author, narrator, and charac-ter that traditionally obtains in literary texts: boundaries between texts and textual levels dissolve, authors become characters, and characters turn into authors. *At Swim-Two-Birds* is a literary textual carnival staged in opposi-tion to the official world of the book.

At Swim-Two-Birds derives its title from a phrase in "The Madness of Sweeny," which is told in the book by Finn MacCool, one of Trellis's bor-rowed characters. Patricia O'Hara argues that *At Swim-Two-Birds* presents "several Finn MacCools: Finn as a character within a fiction as well as a cre-ator of a fiction, Finn of the tribal Celtic past as well as Finn of the seedy boarding house present. Out of these several portraits emerges a kind of double vision of Finn that is simultaneously heroic and anti-heroic."[7] Anne Clissmann likewise characterizes the Finn of *At Swim-Two-Birds* as "both hero and buffoon."[8] But the traditional Finn figure, too, existed both at the center and on the margins of his world. A poet, seer, and wise man, Finn lived with his band of warriors, the Fianna, in the wilderness, on the fringes of society and outside of tribal institutions. In both capacities (as seer and outlaw) he existed on the threshold between worlds, a liminal position symbolized by his frequent and effortless crossings into the otherworld.[9] In traditional Irish ideology, nature is the boundary zone between this world and the otherworld; this may explain why the gathering of all the diverse characters from all the different textual planes (or "worlds") of *At Swim-*

---

7. Patricia O'Hara, "Finn MacCool and the Bard's Lament in Flann O'Brien's *At Swim-Two-Birds*," *Journal of Irish Literature*, 15, 1 (1986): 56.

8. Anne Clissmann, *Flann O'Brien: A Critical Introduction to His Writings* (Dublin: Gill and Macmillan, 1975), 128.

9. These and other aspects of the Finn character are discussed in Joseph Falaky Nagy's *The Wisdom of the Outlaw: The Boyhood Deeds of Finn in Gaelic Narrative Tradition* (Berkeley and Los Angeles: University of California Press, 1985).

Two-Birds takes place in an archetypal forest. When asked to tell a story, Finn complies willingly and at length, as long as he can relate tales of his own wisdom and heroism and of the greatness of his fellow Fianna. However, he refuses outright to tell satirical tales, such as the story of the feast of Bricriu, and becomes angry when the request is for stories that show Finn and his people in a bad light, such as "the story of the Churl in the Puce Greatcoat," which Finn characterizes as an "Evil story for telling" (18). There are, then, it seems, good and evil stories: the good ones are heroic and can be told, the evil ones, which also display a more adventurous imagination, must be suppressed. This had also been the thinking of the minister for justice of the Irish Free State, who in 1926 had set up the Committee of Enquiry on Evil Literature that would eventually lead to the Censorship Bill.

According to Finn, however, the real culprit is not the story, but the storyteller:

"Who but a book-poet would dishonour the God-big Finn for the sake of a gap-worded story? . . . Who could think to turn the children of a king into white swans with the loss of their own bodies . . . changing the fat white legs of a maiden into plumes and troubling her body with shameful eggs? Who could put a terrible madness on the head of Sweeney [*sic*] for the slaughter of a single Lent-gaunt cleric, to make him live in tree-tops and roost in the middle of a yew, not a wattle to the shielding of his mad head in the middle of the wet winter, perished to the marrow without company of women or strains of harp-pluck, with no feeding but stag-food and the green branches? Who but a story-teller?" (19–20)

Paradoxically, these complaints do not prevent Finn from telling the story of Sweeny from beginning to end, and from thereby perpetrating the literary evil of which he himself also claims to be a victim. However, his story meets with little appreciation from its modern listeners, who prefer Jem Casey's working-class "pomes" to the "real old stuff of the native land" (75). When Finn and Sweeny walk into the present, they have the same effect as Cuchulain when he is introduced into the twentieth century by Eimar O'Duffy in *King Goshawk and the Birds:* larger than life and completely incongruous in what they say and do, these figures highlight what is wrong with the present-day world without themselves being able to act as viable and imitable role models.

"The Madness of Sweeny" is an appropriate story for Finn MacCool to tell, for it contains themes frequently encountered in Menippean texts, such as transgression, madness, and animal transformation, and, on the textual level, a mixture of styles and genres. Sweeny attacks the authority of the Church in the person of the church-builder Saint Ronan and his symbols: his book, which Sweeny deposits at the bottom of the lake, and, on a later occasion, his bell, which he breaks. When he attacks the psalter, "Sweeny challenges the emblem of the priest's Christian devotion and earthly authority. If the Word is God, language becomes monologic and absolute, its repository the unchanging, because scripted, holy text."[10] For this transgression, Sweeny is cursed and condemned to live in madness, "on a par with fowls" (65). For years Sweeny flies and leaps across Ireland, composing nature poetry wherever he goes while lamenting his fate, until he arrives at All Fharannáin, where Saint Moling resides. The holy man feeds Sweeny until one day the bird-king is mortally wounded by a jealous herd, whose sister had falsely accused the madman of adultery. Moling forgives and anoints Sweeny, after which he dies, much lamented by the saint, who writes down his story. Sweeny's rebellious life is thus immortalized by the very authority against which he rebelled, just as his salvation is accomplished by the same forces that evoked his rebellion in the first place. Sweeny and the Church depend on each other: without conflict there would be no reconciliation, but more important, without it there would be no story. This mutual dependence of conflicting forces upon each other for their effectiveness and survival lies at the core of Flann O'Brien's satire, and forms the philosophical "truth" his Menippean text seeks to explore.

Numerology plays a large part in the construction of this argument of mutual dependence in *At Swim-Two-Birds*. Numbers are assigned moral significance, truth being an odd number and evil being even. The proponents of this wisdom are the Pooka, "a member of the Devil class" (9) and hence a representative of evil, and his opposite number, the Good Fairy (who was originally to be referred to as the "Angel"[11]). The numerical con-

10. McMullen, "Culture as Colloquy," 80.

11. In a letter to A. M. Heath and Co. dated 3 October 1938, O'Brien wrote that "this change is desirable because 'Fairy' corresponds more closely to 'Pooka,' removes any suggestion of the mock-religious and establishes the thing on a mythological plane"; see Hogan and Henderson, "A Sheaf of Letters," 66.

ception of good and evil goes back as far as Aristotle and was developed by later philosophers like Boethius: ethics may be a philosophical discipline, "but its nature in many medieval works of literature is conditioned by the study of the mathematical sciences of the Liberal Arts."[12] Such thinking also pervaded the Catholic dogma that dominated O'Brien's education, particularly at Blackrock College, which was run by the Holy Ghost Fathers: "In Catholic apologetics there was an emphasis on the Aristotelian prime mover or first cause, St Thomas Aquinas's principal proof of God's existence."[13] The "good" numbers one and three that dominate *At Swim-Two-Birds* are those of the One God and the Trinity. Anthony Lamont, however (that is, Orlick's erudite, rewritten version of Anthony Lamont), espouses a different theory in which only evil is measurable, for he argues that "God is the root of minus one. He is too great a profundity to be compassed by human cerebration. But Evil is finite and comprehensible and admits of calculation" (190). The notion that numbers account, according to one of the conclusions of *At Swim-Two-Birds,* "for a great proportion of unbalanced and suffering humanity" (217), is derived from the concept of harmony in the world order: tragedy occurs when the order of the universe, the human body, or human emotions is disturbed or maladjusted.[14] Lest we take the idea of numerical ethics entirely seriously, however, *At Swim-Two-Birds* makes its readers solemnly aware of "this curious circumstance, that a dog as to his legs is evil and sinful but attains sanctity at the hour of his urination" (178–79). In other words, what appears basest may in actuality be most saintly. This is also why Trellis's book can be "salutary," even though it contains "plenty of smut" (35).

Good (odd numbers) and evil (even numbers) have no absolute significance and must be seen in relation to each other, as the Pooka explains to the Good Fairy:

"Are you aware of this, that your own existence was provoked by the vitality of my own evil, just as my own being is a reaction to the rampant goodness of Number One, that is, the Prime Truth, and that another pooka whose number will be Four must inevitably appear as soon as your own benevolent activities are felt to require

12. Michael Masi, *Boethian Number Theory: A Translation of the* De Institutione Arithmetica (Amsterdam: Rodopi, 1983), 40.
13. Cronin, *No Laughing Matter,* 34.
14. See Masi, *Number Theory,* 41.

a corrective? Has it never flitted across your mind that the riddle of the last number devolves on the ultimate appearance of a pooka or good spirit who will be so feeble a force for good or bad (as the case may be), that he will provoke no reagent and thus become himself the last and ultimate numeral—all bringing us to the curious and humiliating conclusion that the character of the Last Numeral devolves directly on the existence of a party whose chief characteristics must be anaemia, ineptitude, incapacity, inertia and a spineless dereliction of duty? Answer me that!" (109–10)

This mutual dependence is crucial, and means that no single force can ever achieve *complete* authority and domination over another without extinguishing itself in the process. This perpetual suspension of the truth between extreme opposites serves intellectuals "as a bottomless pretext for scholarly dialectic" (190). The narrator of *At Swim-Two-Birds* is warned by his friend Brinsley that, in spite of the number of characters in his book, their voices speak largely in monologic unison: "true dialogue is dependent on the conflict rather than the confluence of minds" (160). In such a dialogic universe (which, as Brinsley suggests, the narrator, in his "despotism," fails to create convincingly in his book), questions are preferable to answers: "Answers do not matter so much as questions," the Good Fairy says, there being "no answer at all to a very good question" (201). Menippean satirists by definition create paradoxical, insoluble situations that are designed to ask fundamental questions, but to make answering them impossible.

At Swim-Two-Birds fittingly concludes with a rhetorical question: "But which of us can hope to probe with questioning finger the dim thoughts that flit in a fool's head?" (217). The book reaches no firm conclusions about anything, apart from demonstrating that everything is part of a binary opposition, and that each "number" depends for its existence on its opposite, and thus inherently contradicts itself. The Pooka and the Good Fairy, prime representatives of this theory, are themselves therefore paradoxical figures: the Pooka represents evil but is courteous, polite, and philosophical, whereas the Good Fairy is selfish, bad-tempered, and practical. Being pure spirit, the latter can nevertheless smoke, travel in the Pooka's pocket, and get sick from its smell. The "evil" Pooka disapproves of gambling; the "good" Fairy insists on playing cards for money but disgraces himself when he loses and turns out to have lied about his financial solvency. Such paradoxes are common in satirical texts, in which the rebel against the status quo frequently makes his own position untenable by being so extreme in his views as to end up mirroring that which he most fulminates against. The narrator of *At Swim-Two-Birds* advocates democracy in the novel, but turns out to be a "despotic" manipulator of his plot, while his own character Trellis, who is supposed to advocate absolute control over the characters in his book, actually falls asleep and loses his authority before his evil story has had a chance to get under way. When the student narrator passes his exams and receives praise and a reward from his uncle, who had previously been the object of his ridicule in his "biographical reminiscences," and who had served as a partial model for Trellis (the other part being, paradoxically, the student himself), he remorsefully saves Trellis from the murderous hands of his characters by having his servant, Teresa, throw her master's manuscript on the fire, thereby destroying Furriskey, Orlick, and the other tormentors.

Trellis (and, by extension, the chastened narrator) has learned an important lesson. Observing Teresa's figure moving up the stairs ahead of him, Trellis concludes that literature should perhaps not, after all, be a self-evident sham:

The edge of her stays, lifting her skirt in a little ridge behind her, dipped softly from side to side with the rise and fall of her haunches as she trod the stairs. It is the function of such garments to improve the figure, to conserve corporal discursiveness, to create the illusion of a finely modulated body. If it betray its own presence when fulfilling this task, its purpose must largely fail.

Ars est celare artem, muttered Trellis, doubtful as to whether he had made a pun. (216)

In *At Swim-Two-Birds* Flann O'Brien writes a metafictional, Menippean satire in which he concludes that such texts are self-defeating and paradoxical; as Joseph Devlin observes: "A remarkable aspect of this rejection of experiment is that it questions O'Nolan's own comic method."[15] The book's conclusions run counter to its own form: throughout, *At Swim-Two-Birds* flaunts the nuts and bolts that hold it together as a literary text, only to determine that, by doing so, the novel fails as a work of art. The author, more-

---

15. Joseph Devlin, "The Politics of Comedy in *At Swim-Two-Birds*," *Éire-Ireland*, 27, 4 (1992): 103.

over, has been caught in a trap of his own devising. In order to liberate his narrative from authorial control, a writer would have to obliterate himself, in which case there would be no author to write the book, and hence no book. This is, in essence, what happens when Trellis is kept permanently asleep: his salutary, smutty book is never written. For all its (post)modernity, therefore, *At Swim-Two-Birds* is profoundly conservative in its conclusions—another instance where the satirist can have his cake and eat it, too.

In *At Swim-Two-Birds* books and the activity of writing them are associated with the forbidden and the indecent, although the licentious connotations of literature are merely hinted at, as if even the suspicion of what literature really represents cannot be uttered aloud in polite society. If plays are "consumed in wholesome fashion by large masses in places of public resort," the novel, being "self-administered in private" (25), is by implication associated with unwholesome activity. The student narrator of *At Swim-Two-Birds* prefers to conduct his spare-time literary activities in the privacy of his bedroom with the door locked, although his uncle would prefer him to work more openly in the dining room; on several occasions the uncle expresses skepticism regarding the activities of his nephew: "O I know the game you are at above in your bedroom. I am not as stupid as I look, I'll warrant you that" (12). If the uncle tacitly equates writing with masturbation, his nephew connects it in a similarly unspoken fashion with other forms of forbidden sexuality, describing his fellow students as being devoted variously to English letters, Irish letters, "and some to the study and advancement of the French language" (48)—the other meaning of "French letters" being, of course, condoms, and birth control being a forbidden subject in the context of the Irish Censorship Law. As Keith Hopper suggests, "Such clever manipulation of language evades censorship, but tacitly affirms it by that very cleverness."[16] At the same time, deliberately avoiding the use of the phrase "French letters" in this harmless context highlights its second meaning as much as it suppresses it. In addition to connecting literature with sexual innuendo, *At Swim-Two-Birds* also provides it with scatological associations. Defecation is satire's favorite "material" metaphor: "proud, self-delusional man ever aspires to elevate himself and his dignity, whereas the satirist destroys such upward mobility by reducing man to defecating ani-

16. Hopper, *Portrait*, 81.

mal before our eyes."[17] When Jem Casey, "Poet of the Pick and Bard of Booterstown," is discovered in the bushes by the motley company of literary characters on their way to the Red Swan Hotel, a suggestive dialogue ensues:

My hard Casey, said Slug. Tell me, what were you doing in that clump there?
     What do you think, asked Casey. What does any man be doing in a clump? What would *you* be doing?
     Here Shorty gave a loud laugh.
     By God I know what *I'd* be doing, he laughed.
     Approximately half of the company at this stage joined their voices together in boisterous noises of amusement.
     We all have to do that, roared Shorty at the end of his prolonged laugh, the best of us have to do that. (119)

Casey is not amused: "Well I will tell you what I was doing, he said gravely, I will tell you what I was at. I was reciting a pome to a selection of my friends. That's what I was doing. It is only your dirty minds" (120). It is, of course, our dirty minds that O'Brien is counting on for doing his "dirty" work for him, for, typically, his satirical method is indirect and relies on insinuation for its effect. The dirty minds come into their own later on, when Shanahan, in a conversation that includes references to blackheads, pimples, boils, and bedsores, also cautions against "our old friend pee-eye-ell-ee-ess," spelling out the word to protect the delicate sensibilities of Mrs. Furriskey while providing "a private wink for the entertainment of his male companions" (160). The only other time he deems it necessary to avoid uttering a word by spelling it is when he refers to "the bee-double-o-kay-ess" in a conversation with Orlick (168): "book" is, after all, a four-letter word.

     O'Brien's literary formation while a student at UCD took place in a restrictive climate whose confines seem to have been accepted without too many questions: the students periodically tested the boundaries of the permissible in inventive ways, but appear not to have seriously challenged the concept of censorship itself. The college magazine's way of making fun of censorship was to "censor" its contributors, including Brian O'Nolan, in tongue-in-cheek fashion: in May 1932, for example, the editors of *Comhthrom Féinne* announced that "'Mr Ua Nualláin's opinion of college women, coming under the Amendments (Censorship of Publications) Act

17. Clark, *Satiric Grotesque*, 116.

. . . was very reluctantly blue-pencilled but may be seen on application at our office.'" On another occasion, the magazine declared "that it could tell its readers about Brian O'Nolan 'but our censor won't pass it.'"[18] One (probably apocryphal) story has it that O'Nolan wrote a description of contemporary Dublin life in Old Irish, in the manner of the *Decameron,* and that the *Comhthrom Féinne* editor was subsequently charged by the president of the college with publishing obscene matter in a college magazine. Since neither the president nor the editor could read Old Irish, however, the matter was not pursued any further.[19] True or not, the story demonstrates the ambiguity of the writer's position in a censorship culture, which provides him with the unenviable choice of either submitting to the rules, or else circumventing them in ways so obscure or convoluted as to exclude virtually all readers, thereby largely defeating the rebellious purpose. It is interesting in this context to note that Bakhtin faced similar restrictions under the Stalinist regime: James Joyce was officially condemned, and faced with the choice of either attacking or ignoring him, Bakhtin opted for the latter and consequently never mentions Joyce, even though his works are prime examples of carnivalized and Menippean texts.[20]

Like other satirists of his time, O'Brien found ways in *At Swim-Two-Birds* of including forbidden topics without mentioning them, by making the prohibited subject simultaneously present and absent, in fact, by using the conspicuousness of its absence as a means of drawing attention to it. The literary "birth" of the character Furriskey as the result of "aestho-autogamy" is an example. Having awoken "as if from sleep," and consumed by doubts as to his own identity, Furriskey investigates the nature of his body by examining "his stomach, lower chest and legs."

What parts did he not examine?
His back, neck and head.
Can you suggest a reason for so imperfect a survey?
Yes. His vision was necessarily limited by the movement of his neck. (43)

The humorous logic used to explain the incompleteness of Furriskey's survey may sidetrack readers enough to prevent them from inquiring why

18. Quoted in Cronin, *No Laughing Matter,* 68.
19. See Cronin, *No Laughing Matter,* 59–60.
20. See Booker, *Menippean Satire,* 4.

Furriskey's curiosity did not extend to the parts of his anatomy situated between his lower chest and his legs. A similar informational lacuna can be perceived in the *"Relevant excerpt from the Press"* concerning the Dublin cowboys and the abduction of the black maids, whose presence in Ireland is accounted for by the "old Dublin custom of utilizing imported negroid labour for operating the fine electrically equipped cooking-galley" (56)—a fanciful notion based on a punning conflation of the American negro "slave" and the Dublin "slavey." When the gun belonging to Shorty Andrews is found in the bed of one of the maids, he is unable to explain its presence there but speculates that "she appropriated the article in order to clean it in her spare time in bed (she was an industrious girl) or in order to play a joke." The press excerpt concludes that "the former explanation is the more likely of the two as there is no intercourse of a social character between the men and the scullery-maids" (55). While the text censors our options by offering only two possible explanations for the incident, the qualifier in the phrase "intercourse of a social character" at the same time suggests the possible existence of other types of "intercourse," which the text studiously avoids mentioning. Hopper calls O'Brien's system of symbols built on the ambiguities of language "metonymic discourse," and regards it as the "central evasive tactic" of *At Swim-Two-Birds*: "[A]ll formal discourse on the subject [of sexuality] is deferred, with the author preferring the anonymity that the metonymic mask allows."[21]

Anthony Cronin regards this form of duality as typical of the intellectuals of O'Brien's generation: "You were in an ambiguous, not to say dishonest position, morally, socially and intellectually. You were a conformist among other conformists in terms of the most important social or philosophical questions you could face. But yet you knew about modern art and literature. You had read most of the great moderns and, above all, you had read James Joyce. That was what marked you out as different, the joke you shared against the rabblement of which you were otherwise a part."[22] As a result, "literature tended to become an in-joke, a badge of superiority and a freemason's clasp."[23] The slipperiness of the language and of the plot of *At Swim-Two-Birds* allow O'Brien to be socially and politically subversive

---

21. Hopper, *Portrait*, 78, 79.
22. Cronin, *No Laughing Matter*, 53–54.
23. Ibid., 56.

without admitting responsibility for his views, and the same is true of his adoption of several personas, none of which can ever be taken at face value: the use of the mask "creates an impossible flux of shifting perspectives which clash and interact unpredictably, and evoke different responses in different readers, so as never to rest on any 'true' meaning."[24]

At Swim-Two-Birds engages with the censorship culture of the late 1930s in ways that are subtle (perhaps too subtle, given that commentators on the book have until recently largely missed the presence of such elements) but pervasive. This is made especially clear by a closer look at the specific censorship concerns of two Irish organizations of O'Brien's day—organizations that had orchestrated much of the public demand for the 1929 Censorship Bill.[25] The Irish Vigilance Association issued a statement in 1926 objecting in particular to "the sale in Dublin shops of books by James Joyce, D. H. Lawrence and Warwick Deeping; the sale of books which advocated 'Race Suicide'; the publication of 'revolting details of sexual crimes and of divorce cases'; the 'whole tribe of little magazines for girls, devoted to stories of a highly sentimental character . . .'; and sporting and betting papers (betting being described as 'one of the major evils of the day in Ireland')."[26] A Catholic Truth Society pamphlet of the same period contained chapters on the banning of "Neo-Malthusian Birth Control Propaganda," "Newspapers open to Objection," "Books of an Immoral, etc., Tendency," "Newspapers and Magazines which give Stories of Passion, etc.," and "Photographic, etc., Prints of the Nude or Semi-Nude."[27] *At Swim-Two-Birds* manages to be provocative on all these fronts, and even if O'Brien's attitude is not overtly critical, the very act of including so many references to forbidden topics is subversive and indicative of the extent of his involvement with the censorship issue.

When he is not idling his time away in bed, the student narrator of *At Swim-Two-Birds* primarily occupies his time with his "spare-time literary activities," drinking, and betting on the races—although the mail he receives from Newmarket specifically bars "minors or persons at College"

24. Hopper, *Portrait*, 35.

25. See Brown, *Ireland*, 55.

26. Michael Adams, *Censorship: The Irish Experience* (University: University of Alabama Press, 1968), 27.

27. See Adams, *Censorship*, 28.

from doing so (13). Without doubt these were common activities among students at UCD: O'Brien became a heavy drinker in the course of his college days, and spent a lot of time with his friends in Grogan's public house; during the same period he was also employed on Saturday nights as a scrutineer at the turnstiles of the Shelbourne Park dogtrack.[28] For O'Brien's generation, the combination of, not to mention excessive indulgence in, all these practices amounted to a defiance of the values prevalent in de Valera's Ireland. One biographer of the latter noted that "his strictures extended beyond the evils of drink to the evil of jazz, the evils of betting on the races, the dangers from indecent books, and he concurred in the Government's Bill to censor publications."[29] Similar concerns were expressed in pamphlets of the time, which typically deplored foreign games, foreign papers, and foreign dancing, forms of which, "not in conformity with either Christian or Irish standards, have come into this country from abroad in recent years. These negroid imitations, and their many undesirable associations . . . have ramified through every corner of the Country." Irish dances, by contrast, "are modest, graceful, stylish and distinct," and have the added benefit that "the nearest approach to contiguity is the joining of partly out-stretched hands."[30] In At Swim-Two-Birds these values are upheld by the narrator's uncle and his friends: the uncle deplores the country's declining morals, wondering "what the world is coming to" (11) and expressing the opinion that Christian doctrine "is very necessary in the times we live in" (93), while his friend Mr. Corcoran represents de Valera's brand of sentimental nationalism by recommending Irish dancing over foreign imports like the waltz, which he claims are disapproved of by the Gaelic League and the clergy and should be left "to the jazz-boys" (133). The narrator derides his uncle behind his back, but, like O'Brien himself, does not openly bite the hand that feeds him; he hides his vices by locking himself in his bedroom, and on the one occasion when he does his writing in the dining room, his uncle surprises him by arriving home unexpectedly, so that he is forced to cover hastily "such sheets as contained reference to the forbidden question of the sexual relations" (91–92).

28. See Cronin, No Laughing Matter, 66.

29. Mary Bromage in De Valera and the March of a Nation; quoted in Adams, Censorship, 43.

30. Josephus Anelius, National Action: A Plan for the National Recovery of Ireland (Dublin: Gaelic Athletic Association, December 1942), 103.

The nameless narrator of *At Swim-Two-Birds,* like its author, is well versed in contemporary literature, and has in his possession "works ranging from those of Mr Joyce to the widely read books of Mr A. Huxley, the eminent English writer" (11). The love-hate relationship between O'Brien and Joyce has been much discussed. In spite of a notable anxiety of influence, O'Brien proudly sent Joyce a copy of *At Swim-Two-Birds,* and frequently expressed his admiration for the master in print, although his praise was not without reservations. In a revealing review written in 1950, O'Brien expresses appreciation of "the intimacy of Joyce's reportage and, above all, his gigantic status as the comic of the age," but goes on to say: "As a man who was undoubtedly high-minded, he shows exceptional lack of moral judgment in imagining that his salacities, many of them intrusive, are therapeutic. . . . The sad thing about the situation is that it has repelled so many people in this country who would, had there been more moderation, have given Joyce's immense genius recognition at home where . . . he was almost mortally concerned to have it."[31] O'Brien himself went out of his way to practice the moderation he preaches here, and ultimately came to resent the parallels that were too easily, and often inaccurately, drawn between Joyce's work and his own, to the point where he eventually exclaimed in exasperation that, if he ever heard the word "Joyce" again, he would "surely froth at the gob."[32] The inspiration O'Brien derived from Aldous Huxley's *Point Counter Point* for the writing of *At Swim-Two-Birds* has also been convincingly demonstrated; Keith Hopper discusses both the moral influence of Huxley's work on O'Brien's critique of science and philosophy in *The Third Policeman,* and the fact that *Point Counter Point* was the source of his theory of despotic authorship in *At Swim-Two-Birds.*[33]

Another clue to O'Brien's choice of Joyce and Huxley, however, quite apart from their prominence, may lie in the narrator's reference to the books of the "eminent English writer" as "widely read." For in the 1930s, when O'Brien was writing his book, Huxley could not be "widely read" in Ireland at all: *Point Counter Point* had the dubious distinction of being in-

---

31. Myles na gCopaleen, review of *The Sacred River: An Approach to James Joyce,* by L. A. G. Strong, in *Irish Writing,* 10 (January 1950): 71–72.

32. Letter to Timothy O'Keeffe, 25 November 1961, in Hogan and Henderson, "A Sheaf of Letters," 79.

33. Hopper, *Portrait,* 238–39.

cluded among the books on the Censorship Board's first list of prohibited publications, and was banned on 13 May 1930. So were Huxley's other books: *Antic Hay* (banned 1930), *Brief Candles* (1930), *Brave New World* (1932), *Eyeless in Gaza* (1936), and *After Many a Summer* (1940).[34] Joyce was never officially banned in Ireland, but his reputation was one of notoriety, and his works were virtually unobtainable. O'Brien's contemporary Mervyn Wall recollects how his own copies of *Dubliners* and *Portrait* were burned by his father, who had probably condemned them without reading them.[35] In the "Cruiskeen Lawn" column for Bloomsday, 1954, Myles na Gopaleen summed up the reputation of *Ulysses* by saying that, although the book was not banned in Ireland, this meant "simply that any person asking for it in a bookshop would probably be lynched."[36] He also made a point of mentioning that it was in fact the English customs authorities who first burned confiscated copies of *Ulysses* (in 1923), and he expressed satisfaction that Joyce was at last beginning to be recognized in both Ireland and England, having finally "shed the silly mantle of purveyor of erotica."[37] Fifteen years earlier, however, things were different, and by making the works of Joyce and Huxley central to his narrator's library, and inspirational to his own fiction, O'Brien staged a quiet revolt against censorship. These tactics may also explain why he sent a copy of *At Swim-Two-Birds* to novelist Ethel Mannin, an action that puzzled Anthony Cronin: "*At Swim-Two-Birds* was . . . a highbrow book; but Ethel Mannin was an expert sentimental and popular author who was probably a judge of public acceptability but little else."[38] This assessment sells Mannin short: she was a prolific writer of fiction and nonfiction, concerned, as a feminist and an atheist, with freedom of the individual and with social change, first as a Marxist, later as a pacifist. In *Young in the Twenties* (1971), she describes herself as "an emancipated, rebellious, and Angry Young Woman" who fought against the banning of books like *Ulysses*.[39] When O'Brien wrote to her, she

---

34. See Appendix 2, "A Selection of Books Prohibited 1930–1946," in Adams, *Censorship,* 240–43.

35. Letter from Mervyn Wall to Julia Carlson, in Carlson, *Banned in Ireland,* 9–10.

36. Reproduced in Costello and Van de Kamp, *Illustrated Biography,* 16.

37. *Irish Times* column reproduced in Costello and Van de Kamp, *Illustrated Biography,* 103.

38. Cronin, *No Laughing Matter,* 103.

39. See *The Feminist Companion to Literature in English: Women Writers from the Middle Ages to the Present,* ed. Virginia Blain, Patricia Clements, and Isobel Grundy (New Haven, Conn.: Yale University Press, 1990), 709–10.

was "at the height of her notoriety":[40] nine of her titles were banned in Ireland between 1930 and 1946.[41] Since his own book was being published by the English publishing house Longman's, O'Brien may have hoped for a similar fate; as Lynn Doyle explained in his book *The Spirit of Ireland* (1935), "an Irish writer whose chief circulation was in England could snap his fingers at the ban of the Censors and would even gain by the notoriety."[42] O'Brien may have believed that Mannin, a successful, best-selling author in England, many of whose works were prohibited in Ireland, might be sympathetic to a book he described as "a belly-laugh or high-class literary pretentious slush."[43] But Ethel Mannin did not really understand what she referred to as the "wilful obscurity" of "those Birds," and gave him no encouragement.[44]

The fact that a book was banned in Ireland did not necessarily mean that it was never available in the country. Because of the system whereby indecent works were submitted to the Censorship Board by vigilante members of the public, years could pass between a book's publication and its banning. In a letter to the *Irish Press* in February 1937, in which he explained his resignation from the Censorship Board only a month after he had been appointed a member, Lynn Doyle pointed out that "between a book's issue and its banning the more cultured and the more hardened readers have read it. The unsophisticated have not in general got to know about it."[45] O'Brien had read Joyce, Huxley, and other banned writers, and the general unavailability of their works merely added a certain prestige.[46] Copies of *Ulysses* were almost impossible to obtain in Dublin, which "increased the snobbery attaching to an acquaintance with *Ulysses* and the feeling of being part of a select circle when eventually you got hold of the book and read

40. Costello and Van de Kamp, *Illustrated Biography,* 64.

41. See Adams, *Censorship,* 241.

42. Ibid., 72.

43. Letter from Flann O'Brien to Ethel Mannin, 10 July 1939, in Hogan and Henderson, "A Sheaf of Letters," 69.

44. Letter from Ethel Mannin to Flann O'Brien, 13 July 1939, quoted in Sue Asbee, *Flann O'Brien* (Boston: Twayne, 1991), 19.

45. Quoted in Adams, *Censorship,* 73.

46. J. J. Horgan noted in *Round Table,* 20, 80 (1930), that "one bookseller who had six copies of Mr Huxley's book [*Point Counter Point*] which he could not sell, sold them all on the day the censorship of that volume was announced, and also received orders for twelve additional copies" (834); quoted in Brown, *Ireland,* 60.

it."[47] A copy of the book circulated among students at UCD, until O'Brien supposedly appropriated it. The elitist nature of a familiarity with literature, especially in a censorship culture that worried about cheap publications with a mass circulation more than it did about the availability of expensive editions of banned books, is also part of the literary theory espoused by the narrator in *At Swim-Two-Birds*: "A wealth of references to existing works would acquaint the reader instantaneously with the nature of each character, would obviate tiresome explanations and would effectively preclude mountebanks, upstarts, thimbleriggers and persons of inferior education from an understanding of contemporary literature" (25). Such class arguments were widespread in the censorship debate. When the 1929 Censorship Act came under revision in the Seanad in 1945, Senator Campbell (Labour Panel) felt that new legislation was unnecessary: "[T]he working class do not want it but the pseudo-intellectuals tell us that we must let up on censorship. They are making a mistake if they think that the plain people are going to stand for a reintroduction of the vicious type of literature which the original Act was largely successful in keeping out."[48] Literature for pseudointellectuals is all very well, but, as Shanahan says, "the man in the street, where does he come in? By God he doesn't come in at all as far as I can see" (75).

By merely inserting references to Joyce and Huxley into his novel, O'Brien makes a statement against censorship; an equally subversive method he uses is quoting passages by other authors on prohibited subjects. Many of the quotations come from the "forty buckskin volumes comprising a Conspectus of the Arts and Natural Sciences" which the narrator of *At Swim-Two-Birds* keeps on his mantlepiece, and which "retained in their interior the kindly seed of knowledge intact and without decay" (11)— that is, uncensored. Among many other fragments of texts, O'Brien includes an erotic poem by Catullus—"so often would love-crazed Catullus bite your burning lips, that prying eyes should not have power to count, nor evil tongues bewitch, the frenzied kisses that you gave and got" (38–39)— and extracts from *The Athenian Oracle* relating to, among other subjects, conception (immaculate or otherwise) and abortion. These literary plunderings "stress the ideological obsessions of a Catholic culture which priv-

47. Cronin, *No Laughing Matter*, 54.
48. Quoted in Adams, *Censorship*, 106–7.

ileges the ideal of virgin birth, and which denies even the mention of abortion through its rigid censorship laws—mentioning abortion by quoting another text is a clever evasion of this."[49] A debate in the Irish Seanad in November 1942, sparked by a public controversy about the banning of Eric Cross's *The Tailor and Ansty,* Shaw's *Adventures of the Black Girl in Her Search for God,* and Hemingway's *For Whom the Bell Tolls,* indicates just how subversive the use of quotations could be. To prove the unfairness of the prohibition of these works and others (including Kate O'Brien's *The Land of Spices*), Sir John Keane read out passages from the banned publications in the House, "justifying his doing so on the basis that the Minister was responsible for the banning and that for this reason the matter was being raised in the Oireachtas [House and Senate]. Senator Professor Magennis, Chairman of the Censorship Board and one of the protagonists in the debate, insisted that an instruction be given to the official reporters not to record the quotations: 'Otherwise we shall have some of the vilest obscenity in our records, and the Official Reports can be bought for a few pence.'" [50]

Sir John reminded the House of the wording of the 1929 Censorship Bill, which provided for the banning of publications that were in their general tendency indecent or obscene, and argued that a book "can be fairly condemned only when in its whole course it makes for evil, . . . when . . . it is systematically indecent."[51] Such a reminder was not superfluous, for in practice the Censorship Board took little notice of this amendment to the law; in fact, it was the Censorship Board's systematic disregard of this aspect of the Censorship of Publications Act that led to Lynn Doyle's untimely resignation, as he explained in his letter to the press: "The books are sent to the Minister by private objectors in different parts of the country. A permanent official marks, by writing folio numbers on a card, passages that he thinks come under the Act. The marked books are then sent to the members of the Board in turn. Now the Board is required to make recommendations according to the general tendency of the book. It is nearly impossible to report on general tendency after reading the marked passages. Even when one reads the book through afterwards one is under the influence of

---

49. Hopper, *Portrait,* 84.
50. Adams, *Censorship,* 85.
51. Ibid., 85.

the markings."[52] If one bears in mind the wording of the Censorship Bill, the fragmentary nature of *At Swim-Two-Birds* is in itself a playful way of creating problems for the Censorship Board, in spite of the book being replete, like Trellis's proposed novel, with "plenty of smut" (35). Even while, or perhaps because, its narrator conveniently "marks" individual passages for the reader with captions such as *"Description of my uncle"* or *"Nature of mime and ejaculation"* (30), it is difficult to say of a book like *At Swim-Two-Birds* what its "general tendency" is, or even whether it *has* a general tendency. Like Trellis's smutty novel, it could even be intended as a "salutary book."

At Swim-Two-Birds displays a strong awareness of the contemporary debate on birth control and the stance adopted by its adversaries. By 1920, as Mary Lowe-Evans points out, "the birth-control movement, Social Darwinism, and the eugenics controversy had gained international notoriety and influence. Counterforces such as the Catholic church and the populationists responded. The world became an arena where Neo-Malthusianism and the cultural mandate of Genesis ('increase and multiply') vied for dominance."[53] The language of Trellis's explanation of "aestho-autogamy" in *At Swim-Two-Birds* directly echoes this debate, but by making Trellis a "psycho-eugenist," O'Brien manages to remove the problem of reproduction from the realm of the physical: "Aestho-autogamy with one unknown quantity on the male side . . . has long been a commonplace. For fully five centuries in all parts of the world epileptic slavies have been pleading it in extenuation of uncalled-for fecundity. It is a very familiar phenomenon in literature. The elimination of conception and pregnancy, however, or the reduction of the processes to the same mysterious abstraction as that of the paternal factor in the commonplace case of unexplained maternity, has been the dream of every practising psycho-eugenist the world over" (40–41). Hopper argues that in *At Swim-Two-Birds* fiction itself "becomes the idealised response to the problem of a reproductive process which is contingent on sexual union—sex can be by-passed and a male can reproduce by himself, without reference to a female. The only female is the text itself . . . where the act of writing metaphorically be-

---

52. Quoted in Adams, *Censorship*, 72–73.
53. Lowe-Evans, *Crimes against Fecundity*, 54.

comes an act of sexual intercourse."[54] The assumptions underlying the passage about aestho-autogamy, that the birth-control debate is about the "elimination of conception and pregnancy" (that is, sex) rather than about population control, shift the focus of the debate toward the elimination of the socially and morally unacceptable: "Many social problems of contemporary interest . . . could be readily resolved if issue could be born already matured. . . . The process of bringing up children is a tedious anachronism in these enlightened times. Those mortifying stratagems collectively known as birth-control would become a mere memory if parents and married couples could be assured that their legitimate diversion would straightway result in finished breadwinners or marriageable daughters" (41). Writer William Tracy was the first to achieve a "successful act of procreation involving two unknown quantities" (41), but his literary method of eliminating sex and pregnancy (that is to say, his act of censorship) without removing birth itself only heightens the potential for immorality. When his own wife is "delivered of a middle-aged Spaniard" by means of aestho-autogamy, Tracy is immediately faced with a new moral problem: being a man who "carried jealousy to the point of farce, the novelist insisted that his wife and the new arrival should occupy separate beds and use the bathroom at divergent times" (41).

The Irish Vigilance Association's concern about the reporting of "revolting details of sexual crimes" is echoed in *At Swim-Two-Birds* by Trellis, who is "appalled by the spate of sexual and other crimes recorded in recent times in the newspapers—particularly in those published on Saturday night." Trellis is a hypocrite, however, for in order that his work will be read by all "he is putting plenty of smut into his book" (35). On the wall of his hall, moreover, hangs a picture of a handsome girl who "stood poised without her clothes on the brink of a blue river" (33): the kind of *Photo Bits* picture "of the Nude or Semi-Nude" that Leopold Bloom has in his bedroom, and to which the Catholic Truth Society objected in its censorship pamphlet. Trellis's salutary book of smut leads to indecent (even incestuous) assaults on the character Peggy by Finn MacCool—hired to act as her father and moral protector in the book, but more used to "rummaging generous women" (15)—and by Shanahan, because "Trellis's powers are suspended

54. Hopper, *Portrait,* 82.

when he falls asleep and . . . Finn and Shanahan were taking advantage of that fact" (61). Trellis himself, moreover, is so blinded by the beauty of his newly created character Sheila Lamont that he assaults her himself in his bedroom. None of the "revolting details" of these sexual crimes are included in *At Swim-Two-Birds*, however, for at precisely this point the narrator discovers to his consternation that several pages of his manuscript are missing, and that the remainder of the passage lacks structural cohesion. He decides therefore "to delete the entire narrative and present in its place a brief résumé (or summary) of the events which it contained" (60). This means not only that the whole of Trellis's novel, the raison d'être of most of the characters in *At Swim-Two-Birds*, is summarized in just over one page of text, but that the narrator's act of self-censorship makes his own literary method as hypocritical as the authorial practices he is deriding in the figure of Trellis.

Like the other writers and poets in the book, Trellis is a dualistic figure: he is a creative writer as well as a dogmatic authority figure. As someone who regards all colors except green as evil, he is a representative of the brand of prescriptive cultural nationalism that attempts to alter and regulate people's behavior, and to turn them into something they are not, and do not want to be. However, in the hands of Orlick, an even more "despotic" figure, the tables are turned on Trellis: he is the creative writer under siege, forced to defend himself in a surreal, nightmarish trial, during which his words are censored and his actions misrepresented. The charges against him are not clear and incomplete, but there are "several" of them, and in any case, it is sufficient that the prisoner "looks a very criminal type" (193). The same characters make up the judges, the jury, and the witnesses, who are in any event only there "for the sake of appearance" (208). Trellis's lawyers cannot speak, and he can barely be heard himself. The outcome of the trial is a foregone conclusion. Many Irish writers whose works were banned in Ireland must have felt that the methods by which the censorship laws were enforced resembled such a mock trial, in which the writer was accused, misrepresented, unable to defend himself, and silenced by a dubious, arbitrary tribunal working without regard for the spirit of the law. In *At Swim-Two-Birds*, Trellis is saved unexpectedly from certain execution when his servant Teresa burns his manuscript; this implies that, in order to survive the trial, the author must destroy his text. The Trellis plot is revised in this sudden manner by the student narrator because he himself has unexpectedly been presented with the gift of a watch by his uncle (a model for Trellis) in congratulation for the passing of his exams. If *At Swim-Two-Birds* is a book about rebellion against all forms of authority (and itself, as a Menippean text, also constitutes such a rebellion), it ultimately ends, on all levels, in submission to that authority. One may say the same about O'Brien's attitude toward censorship: there are numerous indications of protest against it in his work, but his ultimate attitude is one of compliance.

At Swim-Two-Birds includes some overt and numerous veiled references to every subject objected to by the Irish Vigilance Association and the Catholic Truth Society, and more: it mentions "private acts" in lavatories, piss, excrement and vomit, vermin, male and female underwear—sometimes "the worse for wear" (49)—bodily functions and body parts (including buttocks, testicles, and pubic hair), condoms, suicide, homosexuality, rape, incest, prostitution and abortion, artificial insemination, obscenities, expletives and dirty jokes, and graphic violence. Because of the book's indirect method, however, the effect is not nearly as shocking as this list might suggest, and O'Brien himself was quite happy to tone down anything that might cause offense. In a letter to his literary agent shortly before the book's publication he announced: "Coarse words and references have been deleted or watered down and made innocuous,"[55] the alleged coarsenesses being rather innocent in the first place.[56] He displayed a similar willingness to bowdlerize the manuscript of *An Béal Bocht*, informing his publisher that he had "cut out completely all references to 'sexual matters' and made every other change necessary to render the text completely aseptic and harmless."[57] O'Brien never adopted a completely unequivocal stance against censorship. As Myles na Gopaleen he was, on the one hand, dismissive of the Irish xenophobia that led to the banning of all things foreign, and poured scorn "on the 'mystical relationship' which was said to exist, 'between the jig, the Irish language, abstinence from alcohol, morality and salvation.'"[58]

55. Letter to A. M. Heath and Co., 3 October 1938, in Hogan and Henderson, "A Sheaf of Letters," 66.
56. See Cronin, *No Laughing Matter*, 96.
57. Letter to Browne and Nolan, 16 April 1941, quoted in Cronin, *No Laughing Matter*, 140.
58. Myles na gCopaleen, Cruiskeen Lawn, 15 March 1943, quoted in Cronin, *No Laughing Matter*, 137.

On the other hand, in the Cruiskeen Lawn piece for Bloomsday, 1954, he wrote, apparently quite seriously: "I ask—though no Bowdler I—is it not a great pity that an expurgated edition of 'Ulysses' is not published, *virginibus puerisque?*"[59]

The same ambivalent attitude is evident in O'Brien's apparent desire some twenty years later to provoke the Censorship Board into banning *The Hard Life* (1961) and, when that plan failed, *The Dalkey Archive* (1964). He believed that the name of Father Kurt Fahrt S. J. in *The Hard Life* would be enough to "lead to wirepulling behind the scenes here to have the book banned as obscene,"[60] while in the case of *The Dalkey Archive* "the nitwits will consider part of it blasphemous and ban it without further thought."[61] In each instance O'Brien was spurred by financial motives rather than principle, the idea being that he would appeal the decision and sue the Censorship Board for damages, on the grounds that "there is no other statutory ground for a ban than advocating birth control."[62] O'Brien's interpretation of the law was inaccurate, but he was right when he assumed that books were often banned for the wrong reasons, notably for adopting a critical attitude toward the Church. This had been mainly the case in the 1950s, however, when book banning was at its peak; by the 1960s, fewer books were banned, and those that were (such as Edna O'Brien's Country Girls trilogy and John McGahern's *The Dark*) were prohibited because of their sexual explicitness. Given the absence of overt sexuality in any of O'Brien's novels, his chances of being banned in the 1960s were extremely slim. Whether he really believed that his plan would work or not, "his hopes reveal that tendency, evident in his character since student days, to want to outrage and annoy without suffering any real personal damage as a result."[63] Like other satirists of his day, O'Brien is ultimately aware of the profound paradox of his position: in order for his satire on censorship to be read, it must be able to pass muster with the censor. In such an untenable

59. Reproduced in Costello and Van de Kamp, *Illustrated Biography,* 16.

60. Letter from Brian O'Nolan to Timothy O'Keefe, 1 September 1961, quoted in Cronin, *No Laughing Matter,* 234.

61. Letter to Timothy O'Keeffe, 27 November 1963, in Hogan and Henderson, "A Sheaf of Letters," 83.

62. Letter from Brian O'Nolan to Timothy O'Keeffe, 1 September 1961, quoted in Cronin, *No Laughing Matter,* 234.

63. Cronin, *No Laughing Matter,* 234.

position, a satirist typically justifies his own lack of principles by adopting the mask of misanthropy. On one occasion in the *Irish Times,* that "weary, lovable old person" Sir Myles na Gopaleen responded to an article on the paper's literary page that argued in favor of the right of adults to choose their own books and films: "How has this paragon of animals shown that he must not be guarded like an infant? Is his faculty for falling into the fire not embarrassingly perennial? How has he benefited by his . . . adult status, his 'right' to make up his *own* mind, to 'choose'—delicate euphemism!—his own rulers. Where is he at the present moment—or have I said the wrong thing?"[64]

64. Myles na Gopaleen, *The Best of Myles* (London: Picador, 1977), 256.

chapter nine

"Unimaginable Dimensions"

The Third Policeman

Flann O'Brien started writing *The Third Policeman* immediately after completing *At Swim-Two-Birds* in 1939. In September of that year he wrote to William Saroyan: "I'm writing a very funny book now about bicycles and policemen and I think it will be perhaps good and earn a little money quietly."[1] On 14 February 1940 he wrote again, saying: "I've just finished another bum book. I don't think it is much good and haven't sent it anywhere yet. The only thing good about it is the plot."[2] O'Brien showed the typescript to some of his friends, including Mervyn Wall, and eventually submitted it to Longmans, who rejected it on the grounds that it was too fantastic. He subsequently regaled his friends with various accounts of how he lost the manuscript—he claimed at different times that he had left it on a tram, misplaced it in the Dolphin Hotel, or that the manuscript had been blown, page by page, out of the boot of his car during a trip to Donegal— and he clearly considered the book a failure. However, in 1959 he showed it to some of his friends again, dismissing it as being no good but at the same time saying it had good things in it. Mervyn Wall believed that O'Brien subsequently "apparently worked on it, disciplining and improving it beyond all measure,"[3] and that it was this revised version that was published in 1967, a year after his death—a fitting moment, perhaps, for a book recounted by a posthumous narrator.

Unlike *At Swim-Two-Birds*, with its many "planes and dimensions" and interlinking story lines, *The Third Policeman* has a seemingly straightfor-

---

1. Hogan and Henderson, "A Sheaf of Letters," 70.
2. Ibid., 71.
3. Mervyn Wall, "A Nightmare of Humour and Horror," *Hibernia*, September 1967, p. 22.

ward, one-dimensional plot, within the framework of which there is room for fantastic occurrences. The book's protagonist whose name, even while he still remembers it, we are never told, murders old Philip Mathers with the help of his housemate, John Divney, in order to obtain the money for the publication of the definitive "De Selby Index," a compilation of commentaries on a scientist with whose work the narrator is obsessed. Divney hides the money, but after four years he allows his fellow murderer to collect the black cashbox from under the floorboards of Mathers's house. When the narrator touches the box he undergoes strange sensations, and the box disappears. There follows a nightmarish sequence of events, set in motion by two policemen whose help the narrator has sought to retrieve the cashbox. Only at the end of the book does it transpire that the box under the floorboards was a bomb planted there by Divney, and that the narrator has been dead all along and residing in a strange, cyclical otherworld. O'Brien thought this revelation was the best element of the plot and felt that "the idea of a man being dead all the time is pretty new."[4] Divney dies of fright when confronted with the ghost of his long-dead companion, and together they embark again on the same journey the narrator has already experienced once, although he no longer remembers it at this point.

While *The Third Policeman* contains numerous Menippean elements, the book's closed, self-contained plot appears to contradict the tendency of Menippean satire to challenge all such completed systems, which suggest a single perspective of whatever "truth" is being presented. *The Third Policeman* engages in few of the frame-breaking strategies commonly employed by Menippean satire, with the exception of elaborate footnotes to the primary text that effectively subvert the text's hierarchy and interrupt the reading process. Keith Hopper points out that "the mock-footnote is the perfect vehicle for a menippean satire: a condemnation of rationalist methodologies, using those very methodologies as its principal satirical weapon."[5] These parodies of scholarly meta-discourse first appear in chapter 2 of *The Third Policeman*, but begin to proliferate in chapters 8 and 9, the latter of which contains as much footnote text as it does primary text.

4. Letter to William Saroyan, 14 February 1940, in Hogan and Henderson, "A Sheaf of Letters," 71.
5. Hopper, *Portrait*, 196.

In one instance part of the note covers an entire page, entirely displacing the primary text, while chapter 11 has a single note running along the bottom halves of seven pages. The device introduces a form of textual topsy-turviness, but the conjunction of text and notes also works as an instrument of simultaneity, since the text splits itself and becomes literally "double-voiced." This forces a reader to make an awkward and unsatisfactory choice: either to abandon the primary discourse and become absorbed in the note, or to leave the note temporarily and return to it after finishing the chapter. Either way, the reading process is interrupted and the authority of the primary text subverted.

Hierarchical inversion can also be found in the narrator's preoccupation with specific details, without the benefit of a general context to explain the significance of such particulars. Attention is given to the microscopic without the benefit of the big picture, and what we see is consequently not enlightening but completely meaningless. This is analogous to viewing an object through Policeman MacCruiskeen's magnifying glass, which enlarges to the point of invisibility: "It makes everything so big that there is room in the glass for only the smallest particle of it" (137).[6] For example, the narrator explains that he first heard about de Selby on "the seventh of March" (9) and that the day after he returned home to the farm was "Thursday" (10). Since there is no mention of a particular year, and since both March and Thursday recur on a cyclical basis, the precision is pointless. The narrator's father "would mention Parnell" on "Saturdays" (7), but as there is no indication whether Parnell is alive or has been dead for years, this information is equally unhelpful in dating the events. The contextually disconnected markers of time in the text point to the conundrum of a narrator who is dead and therefore not subject to time, but caught in a revolving hell where the repetitive sequence of events nevertheless suggests the passing of time.

Numbers and statistics are used in a similar way to give the misleading impression of accuracy. Sergeant Pluck and Policeman MacCruiskeen worry a great deal about their daily "readings" of the underworld eternity; these readings ("'Ten point five' . . . 'Five point three' . . . 'Two point three'") are taken from something involving a "pilot," a "lever," and a "beam"; may in-

---

6. Flann O'Brien, *The Third Policeman* (London: Hart-Davis, MacGibbon, 1967); all page references in the text are to this edition.

volve a "fall" (with or without "lumps"); and may be adjusted by tightening the "shuttle" or putting "charcoal" in the "vent" (103–4). In a footnote, the narrator explains that he is able to provide, "from a chance and momentary perusal of the Policeman's notebook . . . the relative figures for a week's readings. For obvious reasons the figures themselves are fictitious" (103). The meaninglessness of the highly specific figures is exacerbated by the narrator's assumption of obviousness, for nothing about this information is "obvious," unless the reader takes the reference to be to the "obvious" fictitiousness of the text of *The Third Policeman* itself, within whose pages the reference is contained. The footnote accompanying a passing reference to de Selby and "the extraordinary affair of the water-box" (95) is equally self-referential. The note refers the reader to a secondary source: "See Hatchjaw: *The De Selby Water-Boxes Day by Day.* The calculations are given in full and the daily variations are expressed in admirably clear graphs" (95). The note purports to refer the reader to a point outside the text of *The Third Policeman* for an "admirably clear" explanation of the mysterious water-boxes, but since Hatchjaw is a fictitious character invented by O'Brien the reference can only lead back into the text of *The Third Policeman*. The logic of the book suggests explanation while simultaneously defying interpretation and analysis: the text is a closed system and entirely self-referential.

The Third Policeman uses a logical paradox to undermine the apparent cohesion of its narrative structure. The logical conundrum contained in the book's overarching frame is created by the fact that the narrative is related in the first-person singular by the nameless protagonist himself, in the past tense: he remembers the murder and what happened to him at the hands of the policemen, and he also recollects his fear of dying, as well as the revelation from the mouth of John Divney at the end of the book that he is already dead; he then describes how his mind went blank and how he started again on his circular journey. As the writer or narrator of the story, the protagonist is therefore external to it, able to observe and distance himself from the events: he can describe his hopes and fears, even the blankness of his mind. As the character in the story, however, he is a passive, hapless participant in the events, manipulated at will, and apparently in perpetuity, by the conniving policemen. Although the first-person narrative forces us to conclude that character and narrator are the same entity, logically this cannot be the case: as the character, he is caught in a repeating loop at the same time that, as the narrator, he is out of the loop. Indeed, the protagonist of *The Third Policeman* seems strangely aware of his own duality: at one point he makes a sound and hears his own voice "as if I was a bystander at a public meeting where I was myself the main speaker" (159). As Sue Asbee puts it, "[T]here is no provision in the text for the 'space' from which the story is recounted."[7] *The Third Policeman* presents a self-contained, fictional universe framed by a paradox.

The paradoxical nature of the book's framework is directly relevant for the questions it raises about the nature of the universe, or more specifically, the knowableness of the universe, particularly through language. *The Third Policeman* therefore continues the investigation of the book as world and the world as book that O'Brien began in *At Swim-Two-Birds,* but the focal point has shifted away from literary techniques and toward scientific theory, specifically quantum physics, which was emerging in the 1930s as "a consistent new way of viewing the world."[8] Quantum mechanics changed the status of science as a fact-based method of discovering the unchanging nature of things, showing its aims and methods to be more akin to those of the arts than was traditionally thought. Max Planck observed in 1936 that science "means unresting endeavor and continually progressing development toward an aim which poetic intuition may apprehend, but which the intellect can never fully grasp."[9] In this view, "[P]hysics does not study the universe but rather our knowledge about the universe."[10] O'Brien took an interest in physics and was familiar with the theories of Einstein, Planck, and others, and whether quantum mechanics is the origin of it or not, "mechanical" is the operative word in the otherworld of *The Third Policeman.* This world rings in the narrator's ear "like a great workshop. Sublime feats of mechanics and chemistry were evident on every side" (125). The act indirectly responsible for bringing him to this place, the murder of Mathers, had been carried out "mechanically" (16); when the narrator regains his faculties in Mathers's house after closing his hand "mechanically" on the black box (23), he "noticed several things in a cold mechanical way," notably Mathers's eyes which were like "mechanical dummies" (24). However, *The*

7. Asbee, *Flann O'Brien,* 55–56.

8. Andrzej Duszenko, "The Joyce of Science: Quantum Physics in *Finnegans Wake,*" *Irish University Review,* 24, 2 (1994): 272.

9. Quoted in Duszenko, "The Joyce of Science," 274.

10. Ibid., 282.

Third Policeman uses the language and concepts of quantum mechanics "not programatically but eclectically, creating a universe even more incomprehensible and erratic than it would be if only classical and relativistic theories were the basis of the novel."[11] One might argue, nevertheless, that O'Brien's premise in the book echoes Haldane's suspicion that the universe is not only "queerer than we suppose," but "queerer than we *can* suppose."[12] More important, it is also "queerer" than we can *say*.

For the narrator of *The Third Policeman*, who believes that there is a (mono)logical explanation for even the most irrational phenomena, and who believes that everything can be rationally and definitively interpreted, such an unspeakable universe is hell. O'Brien himself was more accommodating of ambiguity and disorder, and in fact took scientists to task for often ignoring the irrational side of existence. In the guise of Myles na Gopaleen, O'Brien called theoretical physics "not a science but a department of speculation" because "elements incapable of human observation are excluded." The column continues: "Physicists are deluded by the apparent orderliness of the universe. They do not realise that the forces of disorder—being energies residing in the human brain—are immensely more powerful than those of order and are such as to reduce planetary and other examples of order to inconsequence. The human mind is the paramount contemporary mystery but it cannot be investigated as a preliminary to reform owing to the absence of extra-human investigators. With that mystery untouched, however, it is a futility to fiddle with the matters known as 'physics.' It is also manifest vanity." Myles concludes that no aspect of the world "can be investigated or even observed without a simultaneous regard to the whole, and particularly to the gigantic abstractions known as thought, feeling, imagination, impulse. True and useful science must therefore be a synthesis of all the sciences, a thing that is generally called omniscience." Only half-jokingly, Myles deplores the absence of "omniscience" from the curriculum of the national schools, thus leaving young people "completely unequipped for . . . death."[13]

11. Mary A. O'Toole, "The Theory of Serialism in *The Third Policeman*," *Irish University Review*, 18, 2 (1988): 216.

12. J. B. S. Haldane, "Possible Worlds," in *Possible Worlds and Other Papers* (New York and London: Harper and Brothers, 1928), 298.

13. Myles na Gopaleen, *Further Cuttings from Cruiskeen Lawn*, ed. Kevin O'Nolan (London: Hart-Davis, MacGibbon, 1976), 98–99.

Flann O'Brien's knowledge as well as some of his misgivings about aspects of modern science may have derived at least in part from his contacts with Erwin Schrödinger, the Austrian physicist and philosopher responsible for the theory of "wave mechanics," one of the twin pillars of mature quantum physics along with Heisenberg's "matrix mechanics." Schrödinger won the Nobel Prize for Physics in 1933, but his outspoken anti-Nazism forced him to flee his country in that same year. He came to Dublin in 1939 to direct the School of Theoretical Physics of de Valera's newly created Research Institute, but also immersed himself in the city's literary life, speaking, for example, at gatherings in Desmond MacNamara's studio.[14] O'Brien knew about Schrödinger's wave equation, and makes Policeman MacCruiskeen in *The Third Policeman* explain the notion of "omnium" in terms of waves: "Light is the same omnium on a short wave but if it comes on a longer wave it is in the form of noise, or sound. . . . Everything is on a wave and omnium is at the back of the whole shooting-match" (110). Schrödinger was always deeply concerned with philosophical questions, particularly those that pertained to essentially humanistic issues, and fully recognized the limits of science in that regard. He believed that, to obtain a complete world picture, one required the union of all knowledge, that is, the insights achieved in all disciplines, including theology—what Myles na Gopaleen called "omniscience."[15]

The narrator of *The Third Policeman* is, in Keith Hopper's words, "a rationalist observer making simple cause-effect assumptions."[16] Hopper sees the book as O'Brien's encounter with the specter of Descartes, "the author-god of western thought,"[17] and its protagonist as "a godless Cartesian"[18] who, in spite of his faith in reason—*Cogito ergo sum*—does not in fact exist. He is also a modern Doctor Faustus, complete with wooden leg, who pays the price of hell for his ambitious desire for knowledge beyond the boundaries of the human imagination. The satirical scope of *The Third Policeman* is therefore very broad, in that it explores and deflates "the Western drive for knowledge" and "the confident pretensions of Cartesian

---

14. See Andrew Spencer, "Many Worlds: The New Physics in Flann O'Brien's *The Third Policeman*," *Éire-Ireland*, 30, 1 (1995): 146.

15. The information about Schrödinger is from *The McGraw-Hill Encyclopedia of World Biography* (New York: McGraw-Hill, 1973), 462–63.

16. Hopper, *Portrait*, 204.   17. Ibid., 264.

18. Ibid., 265.

epistemology to be able to reach (and recognize) Truth."[19] O'Brien was interested in the Faust motif and used it again, much more narrowly this time, to satirize the workings of Irish local politics in his play *Faustus Kelly*, which he wrote not long after *The Third Policeman* and which was staged at the Abbey in January 1943. In the play, the Faustian emphasis is on Kelly selling his soul to the Devil for personal gain; in *The Third Policeman*, the emphasis is on the quest for knowledge and the nature of knowledge itself. Marlowe's Faustus envisages that "All things that move between the quiet poles / Shall be at my command," and that his dominion will stretch "as far as doth the mind of man."[20] When the narrator of *The Third Policeman* discovers the possibilities contained in the box of omnium he is pursuing, his reaction is the same: "Sitting at home with my box of omnium I could do anything, see anything and know anything with no limit to my powers save that of my own imagination. Perhaps I could use it even to extend my imagination. I could destroy, alter and improve the universe at will" (189). The narrator does not realize that he will never be able to move beyond the limits of his own world, that is, the confines of his own mind, however far he might be able to "extend" it, and as such his quest is ultimately futile and hubristic.

It should be remembered that the narrator embarks on his murderous adventure for the sake of his obsession with de Selby. The narrator's depiction of the savant is curiously ambiguous, not least because he is frequently portrayed indirectly through the eyes of the many "commentators" on his work, who often violently disagree with each other. As for de Selby's scientific experiments, the narrator points out that it is "difficult to get to grips with his process of reasoning or to refute his curious conclusions" (117). On the one hand, the narrator tells us that de Selby, like all the great thinkers, "has been looked to for guidance on many of the major perplexities of existence" (144); on the other hand, he reveals that when the savant "deals explicitly with bereavement, old age, love, sin, death and the other saliencies of existence," he does so in a mere six lines in which he asserts "that they are all 'unnecessary'" (93). De Selby embodies a paradox, in that his theories

19. Booker, *Menippean Satire*, 48.

20. Christopher Marlowe, *Doctor Faustus*, 2.1.54–55, 59, in *The Literature of Renaissance England*, ed. John Hollander and Frank Kermode (New York: Oxford University Press, 1973), 351.

challenge established notions about the "truth" of the nature of things, thus opening up these phenomena to multiple interpretations, while at the same time he is completely dogmatic about his own scientific methods and explanations: "It is a curious enigma that so great a mind would question the most obvious realities and object even to things scientifically demonstrated (such as the sequence of day and night) while believing absolutely in his own fantastic explanations of the same phenomena" (52). Not all commentators agree about the "greatness" of de Selby's mind: du Garbandier argues that reading de Selby "leads one inescapably to the happy conviction that one is not, of all nincompoops, the greatest" (92). The narrator, however, is consistent in defending de Selby's shortcomings as being further evidence of his genius, thus proving his own logic to be on a par with de Selby's: "The humanising urbanity of his work has always seemed to me to be enhanced rather than vitiated by the chance obtrusion here and there of his minor failings, all the more pathetic because he regarded some of them as pinnacles of his intellectual prowess rather than indications of his frailty as a human being" (92).

The mad scientist de Selby is a parodic figure composed from various aspects of real and fictional characters, "a broad range of historical and literary idiot-savants," including Einstein and Walter Shandy.[21] O'Brien may have looked for a French-sounding name to imply a connection with Descartes and with Des Esseintes, the eccentric philosopher in J.-K. Huysmans's novel À rebours. He found such a name quite close to home, in the De Selby Quarries, located between Terenure and Blessington, which in his day were still a going concern. An additional reason for the choice of this name for the mad scientist may have been the fact that the chairman of the De Selby Quarries, Walter Conan (1860–1936), was the inventor of the depth charge known as the "Conan fuse," and held patents for many other designs such as a keyless lock, a system for preserving meat, and an index carding system. He suffered a mental breakdown before his death. O'Brien may have read about Conan in the Blackrock College Annuals for 1930 and 1934, which featured articles about his inventions, or he may have come across an obituary that highlighted some of these details.[22] Whatever the

21. Hopper, *Portrait*, 258.

22. This hypothesis, along with much more that cannot be substantiated, is presented by Conan Kennedy in his pamphlet *Looking for De Selby* (Killala, Co. Mayo, Ireland: Morrigan, 1998).

origin of de Selby's name, however, the two main contributors to his character are the popular scientist and philosopher J. W. Dunne and the eccentric aristocrat Des Esseintes from J.-K. Huysmans's novel *À rebours*.

The influence of Dunne's books *An Experiment with Time* and *The Serial Universe* is apparent in de Selby's concern with the nature of time and space, eternity, and human existence; typically, O'Brien takes Dunne's terms literally and has de Selby develop them with his own rigorous but inscrutable logic. Since the narrator of *The Third Policeman* committed murder for de Selby, the otherworld in which his punishment takes place is in fact "a hell-world constructed from the disparate fragments of de Selby's theories,"[23] and hence ultimately a distorted reflection of Dunne's theories. When the narrator grasps what he thinks is the cashbox hidden under the floor of Mathers's house, he notices a change "which came upon me or upon the room, indescribably subtle, yet momentous, ineffable" (23). From that moment on his world becomes unreliable and confused in matters of space and time. He hears a cough behind him that "seemed to bring with it some more awful alteration in everything, just as if it had held the universe standstill for an instant, suspending the planets in their courses, halting the sun and holding in mid-air any falling thing the earth was pulling towards it" (23). The next thing he notices is Mathers sitting in a chair in the room: "How long we sat there . . . looking at one another I do not know. Years or minutes could be swallowed up with equal ease in that indescribable and unaccountable interval" (24). The narrator is then addressed by his soul, whom he calls Joe, for "convenience" (25).

The clues given to the narrator's death are a subtle change in the narrator, the presence of a man we know is dead, and the existence of a separate soul. Moreover, the ordinary laws of nature no longer seem to be valid. The narrator has died—or, to speak with Dunne and de Selby, he has entered the "death dimension." De Selby claims that "human beings are continually moving in only one known direction" (94); if a way can be found of discovering the "second direction," he argues, "new and unimaginable dimensions will supersede the present order," although "death is nearly always present when the new direction is discovered" (95). The idea of death as a different dimension is consistent with Dunne's theory of the serial observer. Dunne claims that *"every Time-travelling field of presentation is contained*

23. Hopper, *Portrait*, 185.

within a field one dimension larger, travelling in another dimension of Time, the larger field covering events which are 'past' and 'future' as well as 'present,' to the smaller field."[24] He also maintains that *"in this respect every time-travelling field is the field apparent to a similarly travelling and similarly dimensioned observer."*[25] Although "the observer is merely your ordinary everyday self, 'here' and 'now,'"[26] at death he may cross the boundary of traveling fields and find himself in another dimension, unbeknownst to himself. Dunne's theory in fact accounts for the existence of a soul, *"whose immortality being in other dimensions of Time, does not clash with the obvious ending of the individual in the psychologist's Time dimension."*[27]

Dunne writes that "we must sleep if we are not to find ourselves, at death, helplessly strange to the new conditions."[28] Ironically, the narrator of *The Third Policeman* cannot tell the difference between the conditions of life, death, and sleep. Unaware that he is already dead, but remembering the murder that led to his present predicament, he tells his soul, "Perhaps the murder by the roadside was a bad dream," to which Joe responds, *"There is nothing dreamy about your stiff shoulders."* Undaunted, the narrator replies that "a nightmare can be as strenuous physically as the real thing" (25–26). The stiff shoulders indicate that guilt is more important in the death dimension than the passing of time, for in the "real-world" dimension the narrator had murdered Mathers some three years before the cashbox-bomb propelled him, too, into the death zone.

The "serial observer" of Dunne's theory manifests itself in *The Third Policeman* in several guises to reveal the void at the heart of all quests for closure. Looking at Mathers, whose eyes are like "mechanical dummies animated by electricity or the like" (24), the narrator feels that behind this eye there might be a real eye, or perhaps "merely another dummy with its pinhole on the same plane as the first one so that the real eye, possibly behind thousands of these absurd disguises, gazed out through a barrel of serried peep-holes" (25). He also wonders if his soul might not be a body inside of him, part of an interminable series of bodies within bodies like the skins of an onion, receding to some unimaginable ultimum: "Was I in turn merely

24. J. W. Dunne, *An Experiment with Time* (1927; reprint, London: Scientific Book Club, 1944), 158.

25. Ibid., 158–59.   26. Ibid., 158.

27. Ibid., 195–96.   28. Ibid., 183.

the interior of the being whose inner voice I myself was? Who or what was the core and what monster in what world was the final uncontained colossus? God? Nothing?" (18). As Keith Booker points out, the serial perspective "can be interpreted either as an argument that there must be a God (because only God can be infinite) or as an argument that the very concept of God as a stopping place for such regressions makes no sense."[29] Serialism also informs Mathers's explanation of life itself as a succession of colored gowns: a person has a particular color—determined by the color of the prevailing winds—and on every birthday is presented with a gown of that color. They are all worn on top of one another, until the color turns black, at which point the person dies. This series is itself part of a series, for when the narrator finds out from Divney at the end of *The Third Policeman* that he is dead and a ghost, just before he starts the cycle anew, his mind "became quite empty, light, and felt as if it were very white in colour" (197). The otherworld in which the narrator finds himself also has a serial aspect; it has another, cyclical "eternity" underneath it which in its turn has a place underneath it "where nobody went before" (140). Indeed, the entire plot of *The Third Policeman* can be seen as one in a series of many, since it "ends" with the narrator embarking again on his hellish journey; in fact, it does not have an ending, for—like the first book by de Selby ever read by the narrator—its final two pages are "missing," in that they repeat instead verbatim the description of the narrator's first entrance into the policemen's parish.

Dunne likens the nature of the series of his theory to "the 'Chinese boxes' type—the type where every term is contained in a similar but larger . . . term."[30] This is the apparent origin of Policeman MacCruiskeen's chests, which fit inside each other in an interminable series, and which to the narrator look as if they were "all the same size but invested with some crazy perspective" (73). A very similar notion, however, can be found in J.-K. Huysmans's *À rebours*. Some time in the late 1930s Niall Sheridan passed his copy of Huysmans's book on to O'Brien, who reportedly "was greatly taken" with it, especially with its protagonist Des Esseintes.[31] The latter eats his

29. Booker, *Menippean Satire*, 60.

30. Dunne, *Experiment*, 158.

31. Niall Sheridan, "Brian, Flann, and Myles *(The Springtime of Genius)*," in *Myles: Portraits of Brian O'Nolan*, ed. Timothy O'Keefe, 51.

meals in a dining room designed like a ship's cabin: "Like those Japanese boxes that fit one inside the other, this room had been inserted into a larger one, which was the real dining-room planned by the architect."[32] This room-within-a-room may also in part be responsible for the design of Fox's police station, which is built inside the walls of Mathers's house, although O'Brien's reading of Heinrich Heine's *Die Harzreise* (which was part of his college curriculum and is the book the student narrator of *At Swim-Two-Birds* keeps reminding himself to buy) may also have contributed to the idea. Heine reports that one of the towers in the town of Goslar "has such thick walls that whole rooms are hewn out in it."[33]

O'Brien borrowed various aspects of *À rebours* for *The Third Policeman*, but adapted them to an Irish country setting. In Huysmans's novel, Des Esseintes's mother, "a tall, pale, silent woman, died of nervous exhaustion. Then it was his father's turn to succumb to some obscure illness when Des Esseintes was nearly seventeen." His father "was almost a complete stranger; and he remembered his mother chiefly as a still, supine figure in a darkened bedroom." Husband and wife met only rarely, exchanging "one or two words at the most, and then the Duke would unconcernedly slip away to catch the first available train."[34] The narrator of *The Third Policeman* relates that "my mother was always in the kitchen. . . . I never saw my mother outside the kitchen in my life," and that "my father and I were strangers and did not converse much" (7). They were all "happy enough in a queer separate way" until first his mother and then his father were "gone" by the time he reached the age of sixteen (8). Projects undertaken by Des Esseintes are also the model for several of de Selby's schemes, as well as for Policeman MacCruiskeen's inventions. To provide the illusion of being on a ship, Des Esseintes inserts an aquarium between the real window in the real house wall and the porthole in his inner dining room, and at times "he would set in action the system of pipes and conduits which emptied the aquarium and refilled it with fresh water."[35] De Selby's house is described as "the most water-piped edifice in the world" (148). Des Esseintes's notion that travel is

32. J.-K. Huysmans, *Against Nature*, trans. Robert Baldick (Harmondsworth, U.K.: Penguin Books, 1959), 33.

33. Heinrich Heine, *The Harz Journey*, in *Poetry and Prose*, ed. Jost Hermand and Robert C. Holub (New York: Continuum, 1982), 133.

34. Huysmans, *Against Nature*, 18.

35. Ibid., 34.

a waste of time and that "without stirring out of Paris it is possible to obtain the health-giving impression of sea-bathing"—by immersing oneself in a bath of salt water, smelling a twist of rope, "consulting a life-like photograph of the casino and zealously reading the *Guide Joanne* describing the beauties of the seaside resort"[36]—has its counterpart in de Selby's illusory journey from Bath to Folkstone by means of "a supply of picture postcards of the areas which would be traversed on such a journey" (51).

Other borrowings from and parodies of *À rebours* include the quality of the landscape, which in Huysmans's novel has an "artificial, made-up appearance"[37] and which in *The Third Policeman* seems to have been "arranged by wise hands" (37). Des Esseintes's "mouth organ," a collection of liqueur casks that allows him to play "internal symphonies to himself" and perform "upon his tongue silent melodies and mute funeral marches,"[38] is translated into MacCruiskeen's diminutive silent piano on which he plays inaudible tunes "in order to extract private satisfaction from the sweetness of them" (75). Des Esseintes's mastery of the grammar of perfumery, "the syntax of smells,"[39] has its equivalent in MacCruiskeen's otherworldly machine "that splits up any smell into its sub- and inter-smells the way you can split up a beam of light with a glass instrument" (139). Even the sensual female bicycle that comes to the narrator's rescue at the end of *The Third Policeman* has its origin in Huysmans. Des Esseintes claims that nature has been outdone by artifice, even to the point where nature's most beautiful creation, woman, is superseded by "an animate yet artificial creature that is every bit as good from the point of plastic beauty":

Does there exist, anywhere on this earth, a being conceived in the joys of fornication and born in the throes of motherhood who is more dazzlingly, more outstandingly beautiful than the two locomotives recently put into service on the Northern Railway?

One of these, bearing the name of Crampton, is an adorable blonde with a shrill voice, a long slender body imprisoned in a shiny brass corset, and supple catlike movements; a smart golden blonde whose extraordinary grace can be quite terrifying when she stiffens her muscles of steel, sends the sweat pouring down her steaming flanks, sets her elegant wheels spinning in their wide circles, and hurtles away, full of life, at the head of an express or a boat-train.[40]

36. Ibid., 36.
37. Ibid., 38.
38. Ibid., 58–59.
39. Ibid., 120.
40. Ibid., 37.

Locomotives become bicycles in O'Brien's book, for they are the appropriate vehicles for riding around rural Ireland; the bicycle, moreover, "is the only vehicle . . . to which man has deigned to concede the attribute of sex,"[41] and as such provides plenty of scope for double entendres—"bicycle" being a colloquialism for "prostitute" and "riding" for sexual intercourse. Even so, steam-engine references also abound in *The Third Policeman:* MacCruiskeen, for example, is "a walking emporium, you'd think he was on wires and worked with steam" (76); his light-mangle resembles "the inside of a steam thrashing-mill" (106); and the underground eternity looks like a "steam-engine" (128).

MacCruiskeen in *The Third Policeman,* an inventor who looks "like a poet" (57), combines the scientific and literary characteristics of Dunne (whose concern is the relationship between life and death) and Huysmans (whose concern is the relationship between reality and fiction). O'Brien's book deliberately blurs the distinction between the factual and the fictitious on all levels of the book, including its two epigraphic "quotations" from de Selby and Shakespeare. The indistinguishableness between the real and the imaginary has its basis in O'Brien's notion that the human mind "is the paramount contemporary mystery but it cannot be investigated as a preliminary to reform owing to the absence of extra-human investigators." The "real" has no existence apart from our perception of the "real," and we cannot step away from our perception. A similar conundrum was recognized by quantum physicists, who realized that the observer of an experiment also inevitably influences the experiment by his act of observation. In *À rebours,* Huysmans, too, is concerned with the relationship between fiction and reality and the inevitable mediation of perception in literary realism:

À rebours and its hero, des Esseintes, pursue with relentless rigor the logic of realism as literary practice—fiction as *truquage,* literary special effects, the manipulation of the reader's senses and desire through language in an effort to elicit the momentary hallucination that there is no difference between the text and the real, no difference between the fiction being recounted, or imagination, and actual events. Des Esseintes withdraws from the world and seals himself off from it in an effort to

---

41. Myles na Gopaleen, *The Hair of the Dogma,* ed. Kevin O'Nolan (London: Hart-Davis, MacGibbon, 1977), 125.

attain perfect control over his reality and to reduce to nothing, within the walls of his house, the difference between imagination and reality, artifice and nature. . . . The manipulation of the reader (des Esseintes) by the author (des Esseintes) or the author's words, which occurs here within the text (in des Esseintes's effort to create a "real fiction"), perfectly duplicates Flaubert's project as a realist: to create a literary reality more credible, more immediate than phenomenal reality.[42]

The logical conclusion is that, if we can "manipulate our own perceptions, we can manipulate our reality."[43] "Turn everything you hear to your own advantage" is one of Sergeant Pluck's five rules of wisdom, but the empirically inclined narrator decides that listening to him is "a waste of time" (60).

The works of Dunne and Huysmans form the main inspiration for the ideas about time and reality in *The Third Policeman*, but just as *At Swim-Two-Birds* proclaims itself to be "largely a work of reference" (25), its successor is also to a large extent a *bricolage* of elements garnered from numerous other texts.[44] Apart from constituting yet another serial element, borrowings and parodies introduce the problem of authenticity, and draw attention to the nature of the policemen's world as a textual construct, even if, to the book's protagonist, everything there seems "real and incontrovertible" (86). The sources of O'Brien's parodies are eclectic and range from scientific treatises to works of literature, myth, the occult, and even popular cinema. For example, Keith Hopper points out that "the story of Quigley the balloon-man evokes images from the 1939 film *The Wizard of Oz*—a film which was released during the writing of *The Third Policeman*. Quigley, like Professor Potts in the film, disappeared over the rainbow in a balloon and lands in a strange country."[45] Indeed, the Tin Man may have been a model for Sergeant Pluck, whose head when struck makes "a booming hollow sound, slightly tinny, as if he had tapped an empty watering-can with his nail" (154). The policemen in *The Third Policeman* also owe a debt

42. Jefferson Humphries, "Decadence," in *A New History of French Literature,* ed. Denis Hollier (Cambridge, Mass.: Harvard University Press, 1989), 786.

43. Ibid., 788.

44. This idea preceded both books. While at UCD, O'Brien and his friends collectively intended to write "The Great Irish Novel," to be entitled *Children of Destiny,* for which "existing works would be plundered wholesale for material"; see Hopper, *Portrait,* 41.

45. Hopper, *Portrait,* 140.

to their counterparts in James Stephens's *The Crock of Gold,* who arrest the Philosopher for a murder he did not commit. The brutal murder of Mathers with a blow of a shovel and his subsequent reappearance with a bandaged head conjures up echoes of Synge's *The Playboy of the Western World,* while the suspicious closeness between Divney and the narrator of *The Third Policeman* may be a take-off from *Melmoth the Wanderer,* as Thomas Shea suggests.[46]

The influence of Heine's *Die Harzreise* can be felt not only in the consciously aesthetic depiction of the landscape—in Heine, the color of the clouds "corresponds harmoniously with the blue sky and the green earth,"[47] while in O'Brien trees are arranged "with far-from-usual consideration for the fastidious eye" (39)—but also in other details. To avoid arousing suspicion, the narrator decides not to ask the policemen directly about the cashbox but to inquire after a stolen American gold watch (the kind of watch Divney used to steal from the customers in his public house). Almost as soon as he has invented this timekeeper he begins to believe that he really does have a gold watch. His need for a watch derives from the strange nature of time in this unfamiliar country, where "today" is really "yesterday" (60), and where it is "always five o'clock in the afternoon" (80). He begins to believe that "if I had not lost my American gold watch it would be possible for me to tell the time" (52). His obsession with the timepiece, his rational mind-set, as well as his inability to perceive that time has stopped for him because he is dead and a ghost, have a counterpart in *Die Harzreise* when Heine encounters the ghost of Dr. Saul Ascher. Referring to Kant's *Critique of Pure Reason* and to the difference between phenomena and noumena, the ghost of the professor "added one syllogism to another and concluded with the logical proof that there is absolutely no such thing as a ghost." He then absentmindedly "took, instead of a gold watch, a handful of worms out of his watch pocket."[48]

Mary Power has argued that Mathers, whose ghost maintains that "No is a better word than Yes" (29), is to some extent based on MacGregor Mathers (1854–1918), the leading theoretician of the Order of the Golden Dawn, an influential occult society founded in London in 1888 with an interest in the

46. Shea, Flann O'Brien's *Exorbitant Novels,* 119.
47. Heine, *Harzreise,* 125.
48. Ibid., 139.

existence of different planes of being. MacGregor Mathers's introduction to *The Kabbala Denudata* discusses the relative values of the negative and positive states. In it, he argues that "the Negative, the Limitless" are superior precisely because "they are ideas which our reason cannot define." In fact, such ideas could only be defined by making them "contained by our reason,"[49] in which case they would no longer fit the definition. O'Brien held similar Wittgensteinian views about the limitations of reason and logic, and the indefinable and the indescribable are, of course, thematically central to *The Third Policeman*. All these parodies introduce a further serial element: nothing in the book is authentic, and everything reflects other "realities," not only within the text, but outside it as well.

The policemen in *The Third Policeman* live in a strange kind of Tír na nÓg and have resided there "for hundreds of years" (35). Indeed, the narrator's sojourn into their realm can be read as an otherworldly journey on a par with those of Bran or Oisín; like these characters, he finds that he cannot return from the Land of Eternal Youth, but must reside forever in the twilight zone. The policemen live in mythical time—the time of eternity—and consequently have the kinds of gifts described in legendary texts. In chapter 3 the narrator quotes de Selby, who has something to say about roads (perhaps an echo of a similar passage in Rabelais, book 5, chapter 26, of *Gargantua and Pantagruel*) and mentions the trick the Celts had in ancient times of "throwing a calculation" upon a road, thereby estimating exactly the number of men who had passed. This is not one of de Selby's strange inventions, but a direct borrowing from Strachan's *Stories from the Táin*, which O'Brien had been required to read during his second year of early and medieval Irish at UCD.[50] According to this text, "Cú Chulainn throws a calculation on the tracks for a long time. . . . 'I have indeed thrown a calculation on them,' he said. 'Eighteen cantreds this,' he said, 'as far as its counting, but the eighteenth cantred is divided among the entire army, so that its counting is confused.'"[51] When the one-legged men are on their way

---

49. Mary Power, "The Figure of the Magician in *The Third Policeman* and *The Hard Life*," *Canadian Journal of Irish Studies*, 8, 1 (1982): 58.

50. See Cathal Ó Hainle, "Fionn and Suibhne in *At Swim-Two-Birds*," in *Conjuring Complexities*, ed. Clune and Hurson, 19.

51. *Stories from the Táin*, ed. John Strachan (1944; reprint, Dublin: Royal Irish Academy, 1944), 23 (my translation).

to rescue the narrator, Fox leaves Pluck the following note: "MADE A CAL-CULATION ON TRACKS AND ESTIMATE NUMBER IS SEVEN. SUBMITTED PLEASE.—FOX" (157). The one-legged men, however, are equally adept at the mythical ruse: there are, in fact, fourteen of them, but they have removed their prostheses and have tied themselves together in pairs to confuse the counting.

The policemen have the ability to see the colors of the winds, another belief that can be found, as Mathers tells the narrator, "in the literature of all ancient peoples" (32). The description of the colors of the winds can be found in the Early Middle Irish *Saltair na Rann* or "Rhymed Psalter." The *Saltair* is a long, rambling text that has not been rendered into English in its entirety, but a translation of the section on the colors of the wind can be found in Eleanor Hull's *The Poem-Book of the Gael* (1912). O'Brien may have perused this text in the course of his research for his master's thesis on early Irish nature poetry, but his version of the colors differs sufficiently from Hull's to suggest that he translated the passage from the Irish himself. Hull's translation reads in part:

> King who ordained them over every void,
> the eight wild under-winds;
> who laid down without defect
> the bounds of the four prime winds.

> From the East, the smiling purple,
> from the South, the pure white, wondrous,
> from the North, the black blustering moaning wind,
> from the West, the babbling dun breeze.

> The red, and the yellow along with it,
> both white and purple;
> the green, the blue, it is brave,
> both dun and the pure white.

> The grey, the dark brown, hateful their harshness,
> both dun and deep black;
> the dark, the speckled easterly wind
> both black and purple.[52]

52. Eleanor Hull, *The Poem-Book of the Gael: Translations from Irish Gaelic Poetry into English Prose and Verse* (London: Chatto & Windus, 1912), 6.

According to Mathers in *The Third Policeman,* "There are four winds and eight sub-winds, each with its own colour. The wind from the east is a deep purple, from the south a fine shining silver. The north wind is a hard black and the west is amber. . . . The sub-winds had colours of indescribable delicacy, a reddish-yellow half-way between silver and purple, a greyish-green which was related equally to black and brown" (32).

The *Saltair na Rann,* a collection of 162 poems written toward the end of the tenth century, is not only a long text, but its author would "take a high place in any literature for sheer incompetence. Like a bad swimmer he puts out tremendous effort in order to travel a few yards, and his splashing and thrashing are an entertainment in themselves."[53] If O'Brien consulted the Irish text, he would have done so in the edition by Whitley Stokes published in 1883, and it is likely that the language would have posed him some problems. The textual minefield surrounding de Selby in *The Third Policeman,* particularly de Selby's "Codex" and the narrator's "Index," may have had its genesis, at least to some degree, in O'Brien's reading of Stokes's *Saltair.* In his preface, Stokes points out a chronological anomaly, namely, that the *Saltair* is attributed to the ninth-century Oengus the Culdee, whose name occurs in l. 8009—"*is me Oengus cele Dé:* I am Oengus the Culdee"—but notes that this must be erroneous because linguistic evidence shows that the text was composed after Oengus's death. Stokes finds parts of the text impenetrable: "Sense here is so completely sacrificed to metrical requirements that these seven poems [CLIII to CLIX] are, to a large extent, unintelligible to me."[54] He concludes the preface by saying that "though several of the words are explained in the Index, it contains so many new vocables as to the meanings of which I am either doubtful or quite in the dark, that I have called it an Index Verborum rather than a Glossarial Index. It will, it is hoped, be useful for future Irish lexicographers."[55]

De Selby's works and their manuscripts, as well as the commentaries on them, characterized as they are by incompleteness, impenetrability, contradiction, and paradox, raise numerous questions concerning the issues of

---

53. *A Golden Treasury of Irish Poetry* A.D. *600 to 1200,* trans. and ed. David Greene and Frank O'Connor (London: Macmillan, 1967), 115.

54. "Preface" to *The Saltair na Rann: A Collection of Early Middle Irish Poems,* ed. Whitley Stokes (Oxford, U.K.: Clarendon Press, 1883), ii.

55. Ibid., vi.

authenticity, essential truth, and interpretation. Together they form a desta-
bilized, serially constructed textual universe that resists closure, although
the narrator's work on de Selby consists of a futile quest for such resolution.
His obsession with the savant began when, at the age of sixteen, he read—
and stole—a first edition of *Golden Hours* "with the two last pages missing"
(9). Subsequently he buys "the complete works of the two principal commentators, Hatchjaw and Bassett, and a photostat of the de Selby Codex"
(11). Eventually, he completes the "definitive 'De Selby Index' wherein the
views of all known commentators on every aspect of the savant and his
work had been collated. . . . In fact it contained much that was entirely new
and proof that many opinions widely held about de Selby and his theories
were misconceptions based on misreadings of his works" (14). He murders
Mathers so that he may "give the 'Index' to the world" (15). The narrator's
own readings of de Selby, then, are implicitly stated to be absolute and true,
although his actual discussions of de Selby are usually inconclusive, and he
devotes more space to the wranglings of the commentators than to the
master himself.

De Selby is the author of books with titles like *Golden Hours, The
Country Album, Layman's Atlas,* and *Rural Atlas,* as well as the aforementioned "Codex." The latter is "a collection of some two thousand sheets of
foolscap closely hand-written on both sides. The signal distinction of the
manuscript is that not one word of the writing is legible" (145). Interpretations of the manuscript vary from "a penetrating treatise on old age" to
"a not unbeautiful description of lambing operations on an unspecified
farm" (145) to "a repository of obscene conundrums" (146). This passage
doubtless owes not a little to O'Brien's reading of Joyce's *Finnegans Wake,*
published a year before *The Third Policeman* was completed; of that book,
Myles na Gopaleen said: "Perhaps the infinity of meaning it can yield to
bold inquirers is to be accounted a virtue—even if the crop be so disparate
as to wear the accidents of fairyland and blasphemy."[56] In *The Third
Policeman* two "commentators" on de Selby claim to possess the only authentic copy of the Codex, one having eleven pages "all numbered '88,' "
while the other has "no page at all bearing this number" (145). The notion
of a forgery without an established authentic model is, of course, problematic, but is further complicated when a third critic, "the shadowy Kraus,"

56. Myles, *Hair of the Dogma,* 154.

publishes a book "purporting to be an elaborate exegesis based on an authentic copy of the 'Codex' with a transliteration of what was described as the obscure code in which the document was written. If Kraus can be believed, the portentously named 'Codex' is simply a collection of extremely puerile maxims on love, life, mathematics and the like, couched in poor ungrammatical English and entirely lacking de Selby's characteristic reconditeness and obscurity" (145). A further commentator, Le Clerque, blurs the issue of authenticity by *pretending* to have read and understood the Codex, and then repudiating his own article. The narrator of *The Third Policeman* concludes that "the position regarding this 'Codex' is [not] at all satisfactory and it is not likely that time or research will throw any fresh light on a document which cannot be read and of which four copies at least, all equally meaningless, exist in the name of being the genuine original" (146). If a proliferation of texts hampers absolute interpretation, so does their absence. Hatchjaw underpins his claim that de Selby was obsessed with mirrors during the writing of *The Country Album* with a reference to "the MS. of some three hundred pages of the *Album,* written backwards." This manuscript, however, "cannot now be found" (64). There is also a lack of "any authoritative record of those experiments with which de Selby always sought to support his ideas" (118).

The authenticity of the commentators on these unstable texts is itself problematized, in order to cast doubt, serially, not only on de Selby's texts and their interpretation, but on the source of the interpretation. One of the narrator's footnotes tells us, for example, that "little is known of Kraus or his life" (118), but that a book by another commentator, Bassett, "contains the interesting suggestion that Kraus did not exist at all, the name being one of the pseudonyms adopted by the egregious du Garbandier to further his 'campaign of calumny'" (119). Hatchjaw, however, is convinced that "the name 'du Garbandier' was merely a pseudonym adopted for his own ends by the shadowy Kraus" (168). Hatchjaw himself is equally difficult to pin down:

Newspaper readers of the older generation will recall the sensational reports of his arrest for *impersonating himself,* being arraigned at the suit of a man called Olaf (var. Olafsohn) for obtaining credit in the name of a world-famous literary "Gelehrter." As was widely remarked at the time, nobody but either Kraus or du Garbandier could have engineered so malignant a destiny. (It is noteworthy that du Garbandier, in a reply to a suggestion of this kind made by the usually inoffensive Le Clerque, savagely denied all knowledge of Hatchjaw's whereabouts on the continent but made the peculiar statement that he had thought for many years that "a similar impersonation" had been imposed on the gullible public at home many years before there was any question of "a ridiculous adventure" abroad, implying apparently that Hatchjaw was not Hatchjaw at all but either another person of the same name or an impostor who had successfully maintained the pretence, in writing and otherwise, for forty years. . . .) (171–72)

The center of truth thus regresses into infinity; the narrator's definitive "de Selby Index" turns out to be a book purporting to disprove the wildly diverging positions of elusive or nonexistent commentators on unreadable texts describing unverifiable experiments conducted by a scientist who suffers from "several failings and weaknesses" (166).

The wisest course in such circumstances may indeed be "that taken by the little-known Swiss writer, Le Clerque," who suggests that the conscientious commentator, "inasmuch as being unable to say aught that is charitable or useful, . . . must preserve silence" (119). This echoes Wittgenstein's famous pronouncement in the preface of *Tractatus Logico-Philosophicus* that "what can be said at all can be said clearly, and what we cannot talk about we must pass over in silence."[57] The narrator's preoccupation with meaning and interpretation leads him to a hell-world where he is confronted with phenomena that exceed logic and the human imagination, and therefore the capacity of human language. Indeed, de Selby's theory of death as a second direction had predicted the indescribable nature of the otherworld, where "unimaginable dimensions will supersede the present order" (95). In other words, the (im)possibilities there are—literally—endless.

MacCruiskeen's otherworldly, invisible spear point "maybe does not exist at all and you could spend half an hour trying to think about it and you could put no thought around it in the end" (69). The narrator finds the policeman's infinitely receding chests "unmentionable" (70), and they "remind" him "of something I did not understand and had never even heard of" (72). The inexpressible alterity of otherworldly objects is paralleled by the indecipherableness of otherworldly sounds, another echo of the "sin" for which the narrator is being punished. When Mathers was hit with the

---

57. Ludwig Wittgenstein, *Tractatus Logico-Philosophicus,* trans. D. F. Pears and B. F. McGuinness (London: Routledge & Kegan Paul, 1961), 3.

spade, he had muttered something like "I do not care for celery" or "I left my glasses in the scullery" before Divney roared at the narrator to "Finish him with the spade!" (16). When MacCruiskeen uses his mangle to "stretch the light," he produces noises like loud shouts "which could not have come from a human throat" (107), and which resemble "commonplace sounds" familiar to the narrator, such as "*Mind the step! Finish him off!* I knew, however, that the shout could not be so foolish and trivial because it disturbed me in a way that could only be done by something momentous and diabolical" (108).

What disturbs the narrator is not so much the possible meaning of the words as the very notion of possibility itself: the world around him, in Bakhtin's words, "loses its finalized quality and ceases to mean only one thing,"[58] and this also has implications for his own being. Mathers tells him that "everything you do is in response to a request or a suggestion made to you by some other party either inside you or outside" (30): in other words, existence and the self are essentially dialogic. That the narrator is, in effect, a split personality is demonstrated by the dialogues he conducts with his own soul, a voice "from deep inside" himself (25) that both argues with him and prompts him into action. The fact that this soul has a name, Joe, whereas the narrator has forgotten his, indicates a reversal of real-world conditions, and points to the primacy of the intangible in the otherworld of the policemen. To the narrator this is profoundly disturbing, for his reading of language and events is consistently monological and therefore at odds with the dialogical nature of his surroundings as well as his own self.

The murder committed by the narrator for the sake of his "definitive" book on de Selby transports him into a hell where language itself "becomes the arena of conflict where Bakhtin's dialogic potential is actualised; a field of play where all utterances resist absolute resolution."[59] After Sergeant Pluck has explained the Atomic Theory, according to which people change into bicycles and vice versa, the narrator is told by his soul, Joe, that "*Apparently there is no limit. . . . Anything can be said in this place and it will be true and will have to be believed*" (86). The limit, however, is precisely what the narrator can *not* say: as Wittgenstein puts it in *Tractatus*, "*the limits of my language* mean the limits of my world." Wittgenstein continues the proposition:

58. Bakhtin, *Dostoevsky's Poetics*, 117.
59. Hopper, *Portrait*, 200.

5.61   Logic pervades the world: the limits of the world are also its limits.

So we cannot say in logic, "The world has this in it, and this, but not that."

For that would appear to presuppose that we were excluding certain possibilities, and this cannot be the case, since it would require that logic should go beyond the limits of the world; for only in that way could it view those limits from the other side as well.

We cannot think what we cannot think; so what we cannot think we cannot *say* either.[60]

In other words, we cannot say what the world does *not* have in it, for if we can put it into words, it is part of the world. The narrator of *The Third Policeman* is "out of this world" as soon as he closes his hand on the cashbox-bomb and is confronted with Mathers's ghost, for he finds it hard "to write of such a scene or to convey with known words the feelings which came knocking at my numbed mind" (24). Time and again he finds himself at a loss for words. When MacCruiskeen shows him objects "of no known dimensions," he finds it an experience "that I could tell nobody about, there are no suitable words in the world to tell my meaning" (135). He therefore does not know what he can say about them: "Simply their appearance, if even that word is not inadmissible, was not understood by the eye and was in any event indescribable" (135).

MacCruiskeen reveals that what makes his impossible experiments possible is omnium—"Some people call it God"—for with even a matchbox of it "you could do anything and even do what could not be described by that name" (111). "Mad" policeman Fox uses omnium to sabotage the work of Pluck and MacCruiskeen in the underground eternity: "that is how I worked the fun with Pluck and MacCruiskeen, . . . they had to run and work like horses every time I shoved the readings up to danger point" (188). Since those readings involve "lumps" (103), it is perhaps significant that Fox's words are also said to come "in thick friendly lumps" from his face (180): the otherworldly machinery is apparently associated with the production of language. Indeed, the underground eternity has a floor like that of "a steam-engine or like the railed galleries that run around a great printing-press" (128). In its circular hall filled with indescribable machinery the narrator hears a sudden burst of "loud frenzied hammering" followed by "silence, then a low but violent noise like passionately-muttered oaths, then

60. Wittgenstein, *Tractatus*, 115.

silence again" (132). The policemen disappear behind the machinery, and soon the hammering begins again, "this time gentle and rhythmical" (132–33). A little later MacCruiskeen produces all sorts of indescribable objects by pressing "two red articles like typewriter keys" (135). De Selby had earlier told us that "hammering is anything but what it appears to be" (144–45), and in this instance it appears that the underworldly machinery is "some kind of cosmic typewriter," and the noises are "the sound of the invisible author, hammering away at his typewriter keys, 'writing' The Parish into existence."[61]

The question is whether the invisible but at times clearly frustrated author is totally in charge of his creation, or whether he is in turn also being manipulated. It is, after all, Fox who appears to the narrator of *The Third Policeman* to have been in charge of the world with the help of four ounces of omnium, "calmly making ribbons of the natural order, inventing intricate and unheard of machinery to delude the other policemen, interfering drastically with time to make them think they had been leading their magical lives for years, bewildering, horrifying and enchanting the whole countryside" (188). The narrator believes Fox's invented world to be the reflection of his inferior reading, "the product of a mind which fed upon adventure books of small boys, books in which every extravagance was mechanical and lethal and solely concerned with bringing about somebody's death in the most elaborate way imaginable" (190). His relief at having escaped the confines of Fox's derivative plot is, however, misguided. As a character in a book *(The Third Policeman)* he believes to be the real world, the narrator is not aware that, serially behind Fox, there may be another manipulator who in turn constructs his plot on the basis of the books he himself has read—books by Huysmans or Dunne, say. There may even be more manipulators behind those authors, serially "receding to some unimaginable ultimum" (118). That ultimum may be God or nothing—the unknowable beyond the grasp of logic or the human imagination. The box of omnium, in that sense, represents truly original—and therefore inhuman—creativity: the ability to invent without depending on preexisting concepts or previously written "plots," that is, the ability to view the limits of the world from "the other side," as Wittgenstein puts it. That box is forever beyond the narrator's grasp: even if he were able to "extend" his imag-

61. Hopper, *Portrait*, 136.

ination (189), his imagination would still be the limit. There are things that cannot be humanly imagined, and things that cannot be put into words. The unknowable is the unnamable. This explains why the narrator cannot name himself: he is a paradox, a living dead man who is simultaneously inside and outside of his own story. He is not named because he cannot logically exist: he is stranger than we, or he, can think, and what we cannot think we cannot say.

As an "engaged" satirist, Flann O'Brien has been accused on occasion of being "occupied, but not committed,"[62] and whatever *The Third Policeman* is, it cannot be described as a sustained satirical critique of Ireland. Bernard Benstock may have a point, however, when he wonders whether hell in *The Third Policeman* is a metaphor for "the rural Ireland of [O'Brien's] time. . . . Sergeant Pluck speaks darkly and menacingly about the County Council as some bureaucratic source for all the evils and shortcomings of the district."[63] It should be remembered that before becoming private secretary to the minister in 1937, O'Brien had been a civil servant in the Department of Local Government, which dealt with loans to local authorities in rural Ireland concerning roads, drains, and the like. Indeed, the play *Faustus Kelly,* written not long after *The Third Policeman,* satirizes precisely such local government, in the form of the Urban Council.

The Third Policeman reflects both O'Brien's desire to escape to some unimaginable otherworld, and his realization that he is forever confined to the world he knows. The otherworld of *The Third Policeman* is strangely disconnected from the real world of 1940 in which O'Brien lived; Hugh Kenner describes the setting as an eerily anachronistic Ireland "from which politics and political awareness have simply been subtracted."[64] Nevertheless, stray, disconnected echoes of the contemporary world can occasionally be perceived. De Selby has constructed a theory of names, according to which certain sound combinations "correspond to certain indices of human race, colour and temperament," making certain physiological "'groups' . . . universally 'repugnant' to other 'groups'" (40); this has an

62. Bernard Benstock, "Flann O'Brien in Hell: *The Third Policeman,*" *Contemporary Literary Criticism,* 47 (1988): 315.

63. Ibid., 315.

64. Hugh Kenner, "The Fourth Policeman," in *Conjuring Complexities,* ed. Clune and Hurson, 65.

echo in Sergeant Pluck's comment, after he has suggested a number of possible names for the narrator, that "only a black man could have a name different to the ones I have recited. Or a red man" (101). De Selby's theory is, however, invalidated by the actions of his own nephew, who "set about a Swedish servant, from whom he was completely excluded by the paradigms, in the pantry of a Portsmouth hotel to such purpose that de Selby had to open his purse to the tune of five or six hundred pounds to avert an unsavoury law case" (40). Keith Hopper suggests such passages "could be construed as a critique of right-wing European movements that espoused social theories" based on race.[65] Beyond these European dictatorships lies America, which is described by the policemen as a place "occupied by black men and strangers" (57) but "a free country" (58); Russia, by contrast, is "a rough land without too much civilisation" (80). Ireland is depicted as a country where the imagination is under siege. Sergeant Pluck relates how Quigley, the balloon man, was threatened with shotguns and hot pokers when he refused to talk about his experiences "in the sky the time he was up inside it," and calls the experience "a terrific indictment of democratic self-government, a beautiful commentary on Home Rule" (159). How such detached statements about the real world are ultimately to be interpreted is an open question. The Sergeant's first rule of wisdom—the rule of thumb of the Menippean satirist—is, after all, "to ask questions but never to answer any" (59).

In many ways, the obliqueness and scarcity of the references to the outside world are themselves an indication of the first stages of O'Brien's "profound experience of social alienation and depression in modern urban Irish society put into quarantine by the Second World War and the isolationist policies of the new Republic."[66] O'Brien's letter to William Saroyan of 14 February 1940 suggests that his main concern at the time was tedium—there's "nothing very new in this town"—and as for the war, "people here have simply forgotten about it."[67] Neutral Ireland during the Emergency became a kind of self-contained otherworld, an insulated cocoon through whose walls the muffled noises of the greater world outside barely penetrated. Although *The Third Policeman* was already completed by early 1940,

65. Hopper, *Portrait*, 189.
66. Kearney, *Transitions*, 84.
67. Hogan and Henderson, "A Sheaf of Letters," 71.

its claustrophobic atmosphere nevertheless reflects some of O'Brien's misgivings and expectations about the effect the Emergency was to have on life in Ireland.

The claustrophobic atmosphere of *The Third Policeman* points to the problematic nature of writing itself, "in that the writer appears to be a prisoner of his own fiction." This condition is also represented in the works of several of O'Brien's contemporaries, in whose writings likewise "there is no exit from the process of writing itself. . . . Narrative becomes for O'Brien, as for Joyce and Beckett, a questioning of its own conditions of possibility."[68] *The Third Policeman*, as a book about what cannot be written, is thus logically a self-defeating exercise. If *At Swim-Two-Birds* was born from a sense "that the only possible life in present-day Ireland is the linguistic," making it "perhaps the most damning indictment of post-independence Ireland in the period,"[69] then *The Third Policeman*, being a book about the unnamable, must literally be a book of the dead.

68. Kearney, *Transitions*, 84.

69. Terence Brown, "The Counter Revival: Provincialism and Censorship 1930–65," in *Field Day Anthology*, ed. Deane, vol. 3, 93.

part five

Mervyn Wall

(1908–1997)

M ervyn Wall was born on 23 August 1908, the third of four children. The Walls lived on income from property they owned in Kilkenny and considered themselves genteel: Mervyn's father was a barrister who had given up his law practice and instead devoted himself to music and travel. Living in a respectable area, Palmerston Road in Dublin, they initially kept four servants, although the number was reduced to one by the time of World War II. The children had a nurse and a governess, and there were musical at-homes and bridge parties. Robert Hogan points out that, because of this urban, middle-class background, "young Wall had little early exposure to the literary and na-tionalist ferment of those fervent years. Irish legends and myths and the whole background of the Gaelic, peasant Ireland were alien to him."[1] Indeed, Wall claims that his childhood home "was full of books that dealt with other lands, and I never heard when young a single place name in Ireland mentioned. All the talk was of Paris, the Italian Lakes, Vienna and Dresden."[2]

Mervyn Wall was educated at Belvedere College, interrupted by a so-journ in Germany from 1922 to 1924, after which he studied for a B. A.

1. Robert Hogan, *Mervyn Wall* (Lewisburg, Penn.: Bucknell University Press, 1972), 19.
2. Mervyn Wall, "Michael Smith Asks Mervyn Wall Some Questions about the Thirties," in-terview by Michael Smith, *Lace Curtain*, 4 (Summer 1971): 80.

degree in literature and philosophy at University College, Dublin. While there, Wall was head of the university dramatic society, and it was his ambition to become a playwright; after graduation in 1928, however, he found himself looking for a more secure form of employment, by no means an easy task during the depression years. In 1934, after working for two years as a clerk in the Agricultural Credit Corporation, Wall entered the Irish civil service, where he had "a dreary enough time . . . for the simple reason that you were with pretty uneducated people. . . . And there was a good deal of bullying, especially in the junior ranks where I was."[3] In the civil service, Wall was bored and unhappy for fourteen years, until he was able to exchange his job at the Department of Social Welfare for that of program assistant at Radio Éireann. In 1957 Seán O'Faoláin invited him to become secretary of the Irish Arts Council, a position he filled until his retirement in 1975. When he died in 1997, eight months after his wife, the violinist and music critic Fanny Feehan, the *Irish Times* characterized him as "a witty, observant, sometimes catty man in a generation famous for its wit," but at heart "a home-loving and industrious man who never sought publicity."[4]

Writers like Liam O'Flaherty, Frank O'Connor, and Seán O'Faoláin have often been credited with voicing the midcentury disillusionment of the generation that had taken an active part in the War of Independence. Although Mervyn Wall was born only a few years after these authors, he saw his own literary generation as essentially different from that of these older writers: "I came along after it [the War of Independence], and my own friends—Denis Devlin, Brian Coffey, Flann O'Brien and all those— we certainly didn't want to hear heroism about Ireland at all. It was a very different world we inherited. All Ireland in 1922 experienced frightful disillusionment."[5] For Wall's generation, which never knew idealism to begin with, the new republic was an antagonistic place "in which there was official and public hostility to literature and the arts. There seemed to be no room in the new State for the intellect or imagination. The atmos-

3. Mervyn Wall, "An Interview with Mervyn Wall," interview by Gordon Henderson, *Journal of Irish Literature*, 11, 1–2 (1982): 8.

4. Brian Fallon, "Mervyn Wall, Novelist and Playwright, Dies Aged 89," *Irish Times*, 20 May 1997, p. 5.

5. Henderson, interview, 11.

phere was oppressive."[6] Censorship became a major issue from the 1920s onward: "We young people were on the side of Yeats and the enlightenment, as it were, and we were aware all the time of this hostility—churchmen were into it and, of course, the Censorship Board itself. Every writer of ability was banned."[7]

During the period 1937–1957 Mervyn Wall's most significant publications were two plays and four novels which, each in their own way, reflect the Irish climate of the time. I have elsewhere discussed the connections between these works and Wall's later novel *Hermitage* (1982).[8] In his writings Wall was able to vent some of the daily frustrations of his life and his job through satire, and this aspect of his writing has generally appealed most to commentators on his work. Both *Leaves for the Burning* (1952) and *No Trophies Raise* (1956) contain satirical elements, but Wall's first two books, *The Unfortunate Fursey* (1946) and *The Return of Fursey* (1948) are his most sustained and accomplished satires, and consequently they will be at the center of the present discussion.

According to Thomas Kilroy,

As a satirist, Wall is particularly interesting as a mouthpiece of that post-Treaty generation which has expressed itself forcibly in some of the work of Patrick Kavanagh, Donagh McDonagh and Myles na gCopaleen. As a satirist, too, he is greater than the others since his satirical output is more consistent and embracing.

Judging by these canons of criticism, Wall's first novel *The Unfortunate Fursey* still remains by far the best. It is a perfectly controlled radical satire. . . . To provide an ideal environment for his satire on the Ireland dominated by petty clergy and bureaucrats, Wall has translated the whole action to the past when Ireland was the "Island of Saints and Scholars."[9]

Robert Hogan, too, thinks that, given a list of Irish satirists, "one of the most honorable names on it must be Mervyn Wall,"[10] but he also sees a danger in Wall's chosen mode of writing:

6. Smith, interview, 84.

7. Henderson, interview, 11.

8. José Lanters, "Unattainable Alternatives: The Writing of Mervyn Wall," *Éire-Ireland*, 27, 2 (1992): 16–34.

9. Thomas Kilroy, "Mervyn Wall: The Demands of Satire," *Studies*, 47 (Spring 1958): 84–85.

10. Hogan, *Mervyn Wall*, 11.

In his novel *Leaves for the Burning,* Mervyn Wall has written a serious realistic novel with many touches of satire; in his novel *No Trophies Raise,* he has written a satiric comedy with some touches of wit, humor, and effectively uncomic sentiment; in *The Unfortunate Fursey* and *The Return of Fursey,* however, he has wedded the manner of satire to the genre of fantasy rather than of comedy. This wedding makes him both interesting and memorable. . . . Fantasy is not, of course, everybody's cup of tea. . . . Satire has never been universally popular either. . . . When the manner of satire, then, is wedded to the form of fantasy, the result is not inevitably a popular success, and that fact may partially explain the relative obscurity of Mervyn Wall.[11]

What Hogan's remarks amount to is that Menippean satire is a much misunderstood genre. It is certainly the case that undeserved obscurity has been the fate not only of Mervyn Wall, but of several of the satirists who are the focus of the present study.

The Unfortunate Fursey began its existence as a short story. Wall explains:

In 1945 I had an attack of pleurisy which kept me at home recuperating for four-and-a-half months. One day my sister on her way to Dun Laoghaire Public Library asked me whether she could get a book for me from there. I replied "Yes, anything about ghosts." . . . She brought me back a book with the title page missing. It was a translation of a book by a French abbé published in Paris in A.D. 1600. I gathered that its title was something like "Of Ghosts, Demons and Similar Matters." It was an account of late Middle Age beliefs in witchcraft and the like. I have never laughed so much, such were the absurdities recorded. For fun I quickly decided to write a short story placing it in Tenth Century Ireland in the monastery of Clonmacnoise. I sent the story to Seán O'Faoláin, editor of The Bell. He refused it, describing it as a "feu d'Esprit." My friend, the novelist Francis MacManus, said to me: "Why not make a novel of it?," which I did.[12]

The short story became the first chapter of *The Unfortunate Fursey,* with only the final sentence altered.

The book about ghosts and demons with the title page missing that gave Mervyn Wall the idea for his story was written by Augustin Calmet (1672–1757), a French Benedictine abbot and author of exegetical and historical treatises, including a *Dictionnaire de la Bible* (1722–1728) and a

---

11. Ibid., 9–10.
12. Mervyn Wall, letter to author, 29 November 1992.

Histoire ecclésiastique et civile de la Lorraine (1728). The book referred to by Wall is considered to be one of the abbot's less important theological works; it was published in Paris in 1746 and its full title is *Dissertations sur les apparitions des anges, des demons & des esprits. Et sur les revenans et vampires. De Hongrie, de Boheme, de Moravie & de Silesie.* The English version of the work was published in London in 1850; it was edited with an introduction and notes by the Rev. Henry Christmas as *The Phantom World; or, The Philosophy of Spirits, Apparitions, &c.* Wall extensively used the material he found in this book in both *The Unfortunate Fursey* and *The Return of Fursey.*

The typescript of the original short story, now with Wall's other manuscripts in the Harry Ransom Humanities Research Center in Austin, Texas, reveals the genesis of *The Unfortunate Fursey.* The story was initially headed "The Haunting of Clonmacnoise." This title was subsequently crossed out, and "Brother Fursey, a novel, by Mervyn Wall," written above it. The word "Brother" was then crossed out, and replaced by the words "The Unfortunate." It is not without poignancy that the satire that became *The Unfortunate Fursey* was handwritten on the reverse of old civil service memos and circulars. The memo on the back of which Wall drafted a summary of chapters 6–11 of his book reveals a glimpse of the almost ludicrous officiousness the author faced on a daily basis:

The serial number allotted to a form I.53 should also be inserted on the copy to be retained at the local office. In addition it will be necessary to indicate on both copies of the form I.53, in the space provided, the serial numbers, allotted in accordance with the instructions in paragraph 51, of the forms I.85 of the consignment to which the I.53 relates. For instance, if the first consignment consists of six bags of envelopes and the second consignment of four, the first form I.53 which will itself be numbered 1, as indicated above, should be endorsed "Forms I.85, Nos. 1 to 6 (inclusive)" and the second form I.53 (No. 2) endorsed "Forms I.85 numbered 7 to 10 (inclusive)."

It is surely ironic—as well as strangely indicative of the double life the author was leading at the time—that Mervyn Wall's subversive digs at the authoritative, monologic language of church and state were written on the backside of civil service memos containing precisely the deadly, unimaginative kind of jargon against which he fulminated in his satires.

chapter ten

"In the Land of Ireland Anything May Happen"

The Unfortunate Fursey

On the surface, the ingredients and many of the details of Mervyn Wall's *The Unfortunate Fursey* are reminiscent of Austin Clarke's 1932 narrative *The Bright Temptation:* Fursey, an innocent medieval monk, is removed against his will from the safe enclosure of his monastery; has strange adventures in the outside world; encounters romance in the person of the farmer's daughter, Maeve, as well as the various obstacles that stand in its way; and ultimately learns that the safe environment to which he longs to return cannot be reclaimed, not just because he himself has changed, but because its idyllic quality was an illusion to begin with. Where Clarke emphasizes the element of romance, however, Wall heightens the satirical comedy, and the result is a very different book. This difference may also have affected the censor. While Clarke's three narratives were all put on the index shortly after they were published (the ban on *The Bright Temptation* remained in effect until 1954), Wall's books were never banned, although they came close to it.[1] *The Unfortunate Fursey* was submitted to the Censorship Board on four occasions, but Wall believed that no action was taken against the book because banning it would have made the censors the laughingstock of the public.[2]

1. Wall recalls: "I went into Eason's, the big bookshop in O'Connell Street, on one occasion, and the manager said to me, 'The theological censor for the diocese called in here and in to the other bookshops, asking them not to stock your book, but we don't allow ourselves to be influenced by that.' Other small shops that sold a lot of Catholic books would be influenced and then wouldn't stock it." Quoted in Carlson, *Banned in Ireland*, 11.

2. Mervyn Wall, letter to author, 29 November 1992.

The Unfortunate Fursey takes place toward the close of the tenth century, and opens when demons invade the monastic settlement of Clonmacnoise, which had until then always been protected from such plagues by the sanctity of its inhabitants. The visitors from the spirit world infesting the monastery are the central Menippean device of Wall's satire, and serve as a catalyst for the development of the plot. Wall borrowed his demonic examples directly from the eighteenth-century writings of the French abbot Augustin Calmet, and this makes them strangely anachronistic and incongruous in the context: these are not the leprechauns and pookas of the Irish folk tradition, but a motley collection of werewolves, poltergeists, vampires, incubi, sylphides, basilisks, and a gargoyle.[3] Apart from being comic and fantastic, the Menippean *mésalliance* of Irish monks and foreign demons creates an extraordinary situation that is subsequently exploited to question assumed truths concerning the nature of good and evil.

In *The Unfortunate Fursey* the haunting of Clonmacnoise rages on for fifteen days, with demons tempting monks and monks muttering exorcisms and throwing holy water, until both parties are thoroughly exhausted; at that point the haunting ceases, but only because the demons have found temporary refuge in the cell of Brother Fursey, whose speech impediment renders him incapable of uttering a word, let alone a prayer or an exorcism, when in a state of excitement or fright. Fursey is an unlikely and reluctant hero who belongs to the category of the wise fool or tragic clown: he "possessed the virtue of Holy Simplicity in such a high degree that he was considered unfit for any work other than paring edible roots in the monastery kitchen, and even at that, it could not be truthfully claimed that he excelled" (11–12).[4] More sinned against than sinning, Fursey in his wide-eyed innocence serves as a foil for the hypocrisy and selfishness of the rest of humanity in general, and of the Irish clergy in particular.

Mervyn Wall claims that he simply looked through a list of Irish saints to find funny names for his characters, and came up with "Fursey," but that he knew nothing of that saint until long after the book was written.[5]

---

3. In the course of the book the gargoyle, possessed of "cute narrowly-spaced eyes and [a] steady dribble of venom from the tongue" (102), is transformed into a minor man of letters, a recurring figure of ridicule in Mervyn Wall's oeuvre.

4. Mervyn Wall, *The Unfortunate Fursey,* in *The Complete Fursey* (Dublin: Wolfhound Press, 1985); all page references in the text are to this edition.

5. Mervyn Wall, letter to author, 29 November 1992.

However, Augustin Calmet discusses the life and career of Saint Fursius in some detail, and it is likely that the choice of name was at least in some measure influenced by Wall's perusal of the abbot's book. Saint Fursey (d. 648) was a visionary who at times would fall into a trance, during which he would see into the spirit world of angels and demons; his visions are "the first of many out-of-body experiences recorded in early Celtic Christianity."[6] During one of these experiences, Saint Fursey learned of "the evils with which God would punish mankind, principally because of the sins of the doctors or learned men of the Church, and the princes who governed the people."[7] Since church and state are the main targets of Wall's satire, the book's protagonist is aptly named, whether deliberately so or not. An additional, perhaps equally unconscious, irony is that "Fursey is apparently a form of the Latin *versutus,* dexterous or cunning."[8]

Like the other satirists of the same period, Mervyn Wall ridicules the dogmatic nature of the medieval Church and its pervasive influence on all facets of life as a means of commenting on the institutions of his own day, while maintaining a critical distance from his targets. In creating his demonic invasion of medieval Ireland, Wall may not have been consciously thinking of the phonetic similarity—pointed out by Declan Kiberd—between "devil's era" and "de Valera,"[9] but his method is nevertheless an economical way of suggesting that the practices and philosophies of church and state in de Valera's backward-looking Ireland were hopelessly outdated, and that the country's insularity and its inhabitants' universal rejection of all things foreign frequently bordered on the ridiculous. Wall's Father Furiosus, a wandering friar who rids the Irish countryside of sin, and who resembles Bec-mac-Dé in Austin Clarke's *The Bright Temptation* in more than one respect, represents this xenophobic attitude when he makes a distinction between native Irish demons, whose chastity "is well-known and everywhere admitted," and foreign demons who "seem to specialise in in-

---

6. Cóilín Owens, "The Mystique of the West in Joyce's 'The Dead,'" *Irish University Review,* 22, 1 (1992): 89.

7. *The Phantom World; or, The Philosophy of Spirits, Apparitions, &c.* by Augustine [*sic*] *Calmet,* ed. Rev. Henry Christmas (London: Richard Bentley, 1850), vol. 2, 232.

8. Owens, "Mystique," 89, note 17.

9. "In the 1920s James Joyce liked to joke that his country was entering 'the devil's era'; and historians now tend to agree that the next three decades were indeed 'the age of de Valera'"; see Kiberd, *Inventing Ireland,* 359.

citing men to lechery" (227). In this context, Fursey's expulsion from the protective enclosure of Clonmacnoise into the wider world outside may be emblematic of Ireland's own emergence from the isolationism of the Emergency period into the realm of international relations. The enclosed space, at the same time safe and stifling, is a recurring image in Mervyn Wall's oeuvre. Lucian Brewse-Burke in *Leaves for the Burning* attempts, unsuccessfully, to liberate himself from his suffocating domestic environment, but the bedroom in which his mother (Mother Ireland?) spends much of her time is "as remote from everyday things as the blue sky, a room which gave the impression of not being real at all, but only a reflection, a scene glimpsed at secondhand. Outside in the harsh world old Europe was falling to pieces. . . . but no tremor from outside disturbed these blue plush curtains."[10] Ireland's emergence from isolation was inevitable, but traumatic. According to F. S. L. Lyons, Ireland during the 1940s was completely cut off from the rest of mankind, "as if an entire people had been condemned to live in Plato's cave. . . . When after six years they emerged, dazzled, from the cave into the light of day, it was to a new and vastly different world."[11] Wall's despondency about his countrymen in the mid-1940s stems from his conviction that the Irish people themselves did not want to be released from their imprisonment: "They wanted a wall around the country to keep out foreign influences. It was a bad atmosphere."[12]

The "sins" of the "princes who governed the people" (the political leaders) and especially of the "learned men of the Church" (the bishops) are as much the focus of *The Unfortunate Fursey* as they were at the heart of Saint Fursey's vision. Not the least of these sins are complacency and pride. The monks of Clonmacnoise are convinced of their own sanctity, and the narrator speculates that "it may have been their presumption in this regard that at last opened the door to the pestilential demons which towards the close of the tenth century thronged to Clonmacnoise from their horrible and shadowy dens" (5). While Abbot Marcus attributes the haunting to the monks' lack of faith, the monks themselves blame their superiors: "'There is a sort of feeling in the monastery,' said Father Crustaceous grimly, 'that our affliction by these fearful demons may be due to a lack of proper sanc-

---

10. Mervyn Wall, *Leaves for the Burning* (New York: Devin-Adair, 1952), 117.

11. Lyons, *Ireland since the Famine*, 557–58.

12. Henderson, interview, 9.

tity in high places'" (11). He may have a point, for the bishop of Cashel, for all his purported humility, lives the good life in a palace much superior to that of even the king, a fact not so surprising given that the latter "is a faithful son of the Church, who never fails to enrich with a tithe of one-third of the spoils of war the abbeys and religious settlements of his kingdom, so that they have grown to an exceeding sleekness, reflecting the highest credit on him" (33–34). Bishop Flanagan is not universally liked and is singularly lacking in grace: "He was spare and stringy, and his Adam's apple was in constant motion in his scraggy throat. His underlip was loose and twitched as he looked at you, but it was not from nervousness, for the way he held his head and the unrelenting gaze of his eyes close placed above the long thin nose, betokened his pride in his exalted rank and his determination to exact from all the respect which was his due. The odour of sanctity was clearly discernible from his breath and person" (27–28). The bishop's reputation as a man of God is surpassed only by that of Father Furiosus, a former wrestler, gambler, and drunkard who eventually saw the light of salvation but could nevertheless not be maintained in any monastery, because his ungovernable temper led him to kill and maim his fellow brethren. A violent nature, however, need not be a religious disadvantage: now a wandering friar and the prime representative of the "Church Militant," Furiosus turns his strong arm against demons and necromancers anywhere, while in passing clearing the lovers from the ditches and the doorways with his blackthorn stick. Bishop Flanagan justifies the friar's temper tantrums by saying that "'God's ways are not our ways,' . . . . 'See all the good that you have been enabled to do'" (29).

The excessive and violent physicality of Father Furiosus's approach to "the hateful passion of love" (30) stands in comic contrast to the physical (but sexual) abstinence he seeks to impose on others. The Church argues that the human body should be accepted in its natural state as it was created by God—except when that natural state involves sexuality and nudity. For this reason, the bishop denounces King Cormac's innovative practice of bathing as evidence of "lax, unrestrained and vicious living," condemns the bathtub itself as a "device of the devil," and the king's attempt to undo God's work by washing off the body's "natural oils and vapours" as impious in the extreme (37). This disavowal of the naked body explains why an unwashed stench surrounds the holiest men of the Church: the "Gentle

Anchorite" whom Fursey encounters on his travels, for example, is "a hideous and dirty-looking apparition, clad in an inadequate piece of sacking, and the odour of sanctity that he shed around him was well-nigh insupportable" (187). The Church's rejection of the life of the body as lascivious and dirty is translated into another, more material form of filthiness. Women, too, are regarded by the Church as a primary source of sexual temptation and hence as inherently evil: when Fursey asks the Gentle Anchorite how he should go about winning the love of Maeve, the daughter of the farmer who fed, clothed, and sheltered him, the holy man cautions him against "the abyss of love" and "the daughters of iniquity" (196), and warns him that his interest in Maeve has brought him to "the brink of Hell" (197). Within the concept of God's natural creation women therefore constitute a problem, so much so that Bishop Flanagan feels compelled to question God's motives in this matter: "'Did it ever occur to you to wonder why God created women?' he asked. 'It's the one thing that tempts me at times to doubt His infinite goodness and wisdom'" (41). That it is not God's concept of nature that is dubious, but the Church's perception of it, never occurs to him. The Devil—the voice of sanity in the topsy-turvy world of satire—explains to Fursey that the clergy's idea of women is not natural at all, but a figment of their imagination: "the clergy's conception of women, both physically and mentally, is a conception of something which doesn't exist in this world." To be sure, the sylphs sent by the Devil to haunt the monks have impossibly voluptuous bodies and exaggerated curves, but only because "to tempt [the clergy] properly and efficiently [the sylphs] must appear to them as they conceive women to be" (141). By condemning the inventions of their own minds, therefore, the clergy ultimately condemn only themselves.

Wall's description of a procession of monks on their way to the witchcraft trial of an old woman known as "the Gray Mare" illustrates the Church's contempt for the life force of the natural creation:

The procession was headed by a column of hooded monks walking two by two and chanting hymns of the most doleful character imaginable. The funereal responses to each sombre anthem filled everyone with mournful thoughts of dissolution and doom. The very birds stopped their play-acting in the trees and huddled together to watch the gloomy train of humans who moved slowly forward as if fatalistically impelled, trampling with unnoticing, indifferent feet the wild pansies and primroses and all the tiny flowering things on the grassy edges of the track. The general body of clergy followed, red-faced, burly men with an occasional gaunt ascetic among them. Close behind came the canons of the Chapter, rotund and mostly out of breath. Father Furiosus walked alone, his blackthorn under his arm, seemingly impatient of the slow pace of the procession. Then, preceded by a choir of youthful ecclesiastics singing *"Ecce Sacerdos Magnus,"* came the Bishop, distributing blessings every few yards to the onlookers left and right. A high cart followed, in which sat the notorious Gray Mare, tied hand and foot. (47)

Like Eimar O'Duffy, Wall uses flowers and birds to represent the beauty and innocence of the natural order, while his depiction of the Church's destructive and uncompromising attitude toward nature is reminiscent of similar portrayals by Austin Clarke. The bishop's pronouncement that "next to women . . . there is nothing more productive of evil than birds" suggests the absurdity of his views on both women and birds: "Birds are inciters to laziness and easy living. They work not, neither do they spin. Their silly singing is a distraction to good men at their prayers and meditations. The very waywardness of birds is an encouragement to man to take pleasure in the deceitful beauty of this world instead of fastening his gaze upon his heavenly home" (43). Even while the monks' procession is in the process of trampling flowers, silencing birds, and branding women as witches, its official seriousness is disturbed by laughter, that liberating counterforce against authority: "Church and State in awful solemnity wound their way in a long, thin serpent under the fresh green of the trees, along the stony track, and across the Maytime fields, while the object of it all sat high above them, grinning and cackling half-wittedly, and to all appearance having the time of her life" (48). The Church is trampling the natural order underfoot, but the witch's laughter is a reminder that nature is about to exact its revenge.

The revenge manifests itself immediately in an outbreak of slapstick panic, one of many such carnival elements in the book, triggered by Fursey's involuntary association with demons and sorcery. As soon as the Gray Mare, bound hand and foot, is flung into the witch-dipping pond, where she immediately sinks to the bottom, Fursey appears on the horizon, leading a "gigantic circus" of "grotesque animals" (45). The solemn gathering of the bishop, the king, and their entourage immediately loses all of its dignity:

Immediate panic ensued. The rope that held The Gray Mare was dropped, and she sank once more to the bottom. Soldiers and people ran blindly in all directions, some in their frenzy were so foolish as to run into the river. Bishop Flanagan was one of the first to fly. He sprang into the royal chariot with such agility and determination that he knocked the unfortunate Cormac out the far side. The Bishop seized the reins and would have left the King behind only for the devotion of two slaves who bundled Cormac back again just as the Bishop made off in crazy career across the fields. Chariots were driven into ditches and gates, and a score of serfs and underlings were trampled underfoot. Father Furiosus made a gallant attempt to stay the panic, until he observed on his left an outflanking movement by a squadron of poltergeists, variegated in hue, but mostly yellow and green; and from seven to nine feet in height. From their drooping shoulders their long arms swung obscenely, the fingers nearly touching the ground. Their faces were creased with unholy smiles. Father Furiosus took one look at this hideous apparition, and jumped into the last chariot. In the space of two minutes there was no one in sight. (53)

When Fursey arrives on the scene, he finds the rope abandoned by the witch-dippers, and when he pulls it, to his amazement "a little old woman tied in a ball, bobbed up on to the surface and came drifting towards him" (56). Fursey rescues the Gray Mare, and with great difficulty carries her on his back to her cottage, where she feeds him with the aid of a magic rope, and cures his limp (the result of an earlier encounter with four poltergeists) by manipulating a wax figure "partly wrapped in a piece of thick brown material similar to the habit he was wearing" (61). Fursey is puzzled, but concludes "that he had lived so long in the cloister that he was quite unaccustomed to the ways of ordinary people, so he carefully suppressed any manifestation of surprise" (62).

Mervyn Wall's satirical method turns the world upside down, a carnival technique of "negation in time and space expressed in forms of the contrary—the backside, the lower stratum, the inside out, and the topsy-turvy."[13] In material terms, grotesque bodily elements suggesting back-to-frontness are inherent in sorcery and devil worship, the main plot ingredients of *The Unfortunate Fursey,* since their practices are based on a material reversal of Christian rituals (such as reciting the Lord's Prayer backward or worshipping the devil's backside). Having rescued the Gray Mare from drowning in the aftermath of the very witch-dipping that had

13. Bakhtin, *Rabelais,* 411.

proven her not to be a witch, Fursey tries to lend a helping hand by attempting, unsuccessfully, to milk her reluctant goat. When the animal keeps turning away from him, he suddenly remembers "the grisly stories that were whispered in Clonmacnoise, of witches and covens, and of the Horned God whom the witches worshipped. What if this were the Horned God in person exacting from him the homage of the posterior kiss?" (75). Similar worries assail Fursey when he spends time with the Gray Mare's neighbor, the sexton and sorcerer Cuthbert. As Fursey and Cuthbert pass the pond in the sorcerer's yard, four ducks belonging to the latter "buried their heads in the inky pool, so that . . . only four sinister sterns were visible pointing heavenwards. Whether they were eating mud off the bottom or whether it was an act of homage to their master, Fursey was unable to say" (103). The posterior is a common image of defiance; when the bishop is ranting about the "depravity of birds," a wagtail on a nearby branch responds by raising his tail and "disclosing to the Bishop's gaze a little feathered backside. He cocked his eye as if to see how the Bishop was taking it, before fluttering away into the trees" (43). Physical reversal is also prevalent when Cuthbert teaches Fursey to fly on a broomstick, an art he wishes to master not because he approves of witchcraft, but because he considers it his only means of escape from sorcery. The first time Fursey takes off, "he was conscious of being suddenly yanked into the air and found himself a moment later in a tree. Cuthbert was standing underneath with set lips contemplating the broken branches and the pink apple blossom which was still fluttering to the ground" (107). The second time, the broom flies out of control, and when told to stop by its frantic pilot, "reared in mid-air, and fell, together with Fursey, into the ducks' pool" (107). The broom is, of course, the traditional witch's symbol,[14] but Bakhtin also mentions it as a carnival element—a symbolic device to sweep out corruption.[15] Fursey's inadvertent transformation from a monk into a sorcerer thus becomes the force by which corruption within the Church is exposed, if not swept away.

In *The Unfortunate Fursey* spatial contrariness is not confined to these

14. "Brooms are a symbol of female domesticity, a tool of every woman, and most witches were women. . . . Another theory holds that the association between witches and brooms goes back to ancient times, when pagans performed fertility rites to induce their crops to grow high"; see Rosemary Ellen Guiley, *The Encyclopedia of Witches and Witchcraft* (New York: Facts on File, 1989), 37.

15. Bakhtin, *Rabelais,* 270.

physical images of topsy-turviness, but extends to the whole of the charac-ters' physical environment, as if the four corners of the globe had secretly and unaccountably shifted positions. Ireland itself appears to be an unsta-ble place devoid of direction, and at times takes on an otherworldly quality:

The road that goes south from Cashel winds crazily; taking little runs over ridges, and curving so as to skirt the irregular boundaries of the farmlands. It is an absurd, switchbacking, Irish road, never straight for more than a hundred paces, encourag-ing the wayfarer with the hope that there may be something unusual and peculiar around the bend or over the brow of the hill. . . . When evening comes and the be-ginning of twilight, the road and countryside become charged with a peculiar opalescent atmosphere as if a faery world had been superimposed upon our own, so that one almost doubts the reality of tree and field; and, according as tempera-ment dictates, either hurries on in terror of what one may meet, or else lingers filled with a sense of wonder and a content that seems to belong to another existence. (159)

The landscape plays strange tricks on Declan, the old man who hires Fursey as a farmhand and with whose daughter Maeve Fursey subsequently, and hopelessly, falls in love:

"Are you going fishing, sir?"
"Yes," replied the old man. "I'm going down to the lake."
"Then you're going in the wrong direction," said Fursey. "The lake is behind you."
The old farmer looked bewildered.
"So it is," he replied at last, and turned back the way he had come. Fursey arose from the stone and fell into step beside him.
"May I ask if you live in the cottage beyond?" he queried.
"Yes," responded the ancient. "That's my house."
"Very convenient having the fishing right at your front door."
The old man looked surprised.
"The lake is at the back of the house," he said. (163)

The back-to-frontness of the countryside may account for the numerous occasions on which Fursey suddenly loses his balance and falls flat on his face—a physical reversal also symbolic of his fall from grace with the official Church.

Fursey's clothes are likewise indicators of a carnivalesque mismatch between the true self and the mask of its surroundings. Condemned to death as a sorcerer by the clergy, Fursey escapes from prison disguised in women's clothes conjured up with the help of Satan. Just when Fursey is scaling the palisade surrounding the town, assisted by a soldier who is under the impression that he is helping a lady elude the unwanted advances of King Cormac, the phantom clothes disappear, exposing Fursey's naked posterior to the startled guard. Fursey regains his modesty by robbing a scarecrow of his rags, and is eventually provided by Declan with a secondhand kilt several sizes too big for him. These incongruous outfits, apart from ensuring that nobody takes the former lay brother seriously, mark Fursey as a marginal character and a misfit, and represent the discomfort he feels with the roles imposed on him by the outside world. At times, a similar dissociation is created between Fursey's spirit and his body. After he has decided to give himself up to the authorities as a sorcerer, Fursey "walked on towards Cashel as if impelled by some force outside himself," his mind being "cold and dead" (184). In the sorcery trial, Father Furiosus distinguishes between Fursey's body and his inner self, arguing that Fursey should be tortured in order to rid him of the demon possessing him, but that this will not harm him: "I won't hurt *you*. I'll only hurt the devil that possesses you" (135).

What *The Unfortunate Fursey* exposes and ridicules most of all is the Church's lack of integrity in the way it argues its case: its fondness of twisting everything to suit its own needs, of what I have earlier in this book called the logic of having your cake and eating it, too. For this purpose, Wall borrows—with some comic exaggeration—the logic and rhetoric of treatises on demonology and witchcraft, such as the book by Abbot Calmet, which strike the modern reader as dubious in the extreme. The notion of "witch-dipping" is an example of such logic: the suspected witch is tied hand and foot and thrown into a pond; if she sinks (that is, if she drowns) she is innocent, but if she floats she is a witch and is subsequently burned at the stake. Either way, of course, she ends up dead. Suspected witches were routinely tortured, nor was a penitential confession of guilt by the accused a way of avoiding such painful treatment before the inevitable execution. Calmet quotes the case of a certain Gaufredi, a high-ranking churchman who was accused of being a sorcerer. Having first been degraded from sacred orders, he was subsequently condemned to make honourable amends one audience day, having his head and feet bare, a cord about his neck, and holding a lighted taper in his hands—to ask pardon of God, the king, and the court of justice—then, to be delivered into the hands of the executioner of the high court of law, to be taken to all the chief places and cross-roads of this city of Aix, and torn with red-hot pincers in all parts of his body; and after that, in the *Place des Jacobins,* burned alive, and his ashes scattered to the wind; and before being executed, let the question be applied to him, and let him be tormented as grievously as can be devised, in order to extract from him the names of his other accomplices.[16]

Fursey finds himself in a similar predicament during his nightmarish trial for sorcery. Hoping to escape torture, Fursey pleads guilty to the crime, only to be told by Father Furiosus that his plea will not be accepted because "his guilt must be proved." But in the event the accused should be found not guilty in the course of the trial, "we will start again at the beginning and accept his plea of guilty" (130).

Throughout the book Fursey finds himself at the receiving end of this form of logic, which ensures that, no matter what the premises of the argument are, the conclusion reached is always the predetermined one most convenient to the powers that be. While the demons are confined to Fursey's cell during their occupation of Clonmacnoise, the other monks salve their conscience about not intervening in their fellow brother's suffering by damning him with praise: they depict Fursey as "a lay-brother so grounded in piety as to be indifferent to their hellish charms. Let us leave well enough alone. Brother Fursey is winning for himself a celestial seat. Would you deprive him of it?" (17). When the demons show no sign of departing, however, the monks have no qualms about expelling Fursey along with his hellish entourage: after all, "is he not a harbourer of demons?" (20). Fursey's first act after his expulsion is to rescue the Gray Mare from drowning following her witch-dipping, after which he spends the night in her cottage. The bishop and Father Furiosus are horrified to hear of this scandalous conduct, and conclude that "the unfortunate woman has been compromised by this blackguard, and that wrong can only be righted by marriage" (68). Earlier, of course, they had accused that same "unfortunate woman" of being a witch and left her to drown. Abbot Marcus agrees that, since he cannot allow Fursey to return to Clonmacnoise, marriage would

16. Calmet, *Phantom World,* vol. 1, 128.

be best, but for a different reason: "you tell me that this woman, tho' not a witch, is nevertheless a great sinner who never goes to mass. Union with such a godly man as Fursey cannot but have a profound effect on her character" (67–68). Either way, whatever the reason, the godly blackguard ends up married to the unfortunate great sinner, at the instigation of the clergy. It is Fursey's forced marriage that turns him into a sorcerer, for just before the Gray Mare is killed by the wizardry of her enemy Cuthbert, six hours after her marriage to Fursey, she manages to breathe her magical ability into her unsuspecting husband during their first, and last, kiss. Fursey is as inept a wizard as he was a monk: his magical ability is limited to producing food by pulling a rope, and he never overcomes his aversion to his familiar, the doglike Albert.

In the inverted universe of *The Unfortunate Fursey,* practitioners of sophistry are not necessarily deluding themselves, and logical thinkers are not necessarily always right. While the bishop is convinced that every suspected witch or sorcerer should be tortured and burned, just to be on the safe side, Father Furiosus favors a more scientific, if dogmatic, method of proof. "Witches . . . may always be destroyed by fire or by drowning" (148), he argues; and because the Gray Mare sinks to the bottom of the pool, proving conclusively that she is not a witch, nothing will subsequently convince the "Church Militant" of the opposite. In fact, Furiosus believes her to be an innocent, saintly woman, and he holds the wicked sorcerer Fursey responsible for her death. The bishop, on the other hand, finds evidence of witchcraft in the most commonplace occurrences: he believes, for example, that King Cormac was bewitched by "enchanted beer." How else could one explain why the king, after consuming six quarts of the brew, was "filled with vague and disagreeable sensations," then began to frolic and shout "the most villainous and the lewdest language that ever man heard" (33), whereupon he collapsed in a stupor and did not recover until the next morning, remembering nothing of his frenzy? Bishop Flanagan is also suspicious of a plague of fleas that invaded Cashel, because "they appeared to make a particular set on me and on the canons of the Chapter; and this impiety, together with their exceeding briskness in evading capture, convinced me that their activities were not of nature, but proceeded from the damned art of witchcraft" (32). Skeptical readers who surmise that the plague of vermin may have had more to do with the bishop's professed lack of personal hygiene than with sorcery are, however, given pause for thought by the activities of the Gray Mare—who, in spite of the logic of Father Furiosus's evidence to the contrary, is indeed a witch. Attacked by a pack of hellhounds conjured up by her enemy Cuthbert, she launches a counteroffensive in the form of enchanted fleas as big as mice: "At first the giant dogs merely stopped occasionally in their career to scratch themselves, but when the fleas had warmed to their work, the hounds retreated precipitately, many attempting the pitiable impossibility of scratching and running at the same time" (77). In such a universe the truth is hard to determine.

In the world of *The Unfortunate Fursey* nothing is straightforward and logical; in fact, if there *is* a logical principle at work, it is that everything inevitably leads to its opposite. It is only in such a carnivalized universe, in which "everything lives on the very border of its opposite,"[17] that a witch of the Gray Mare's caliber can be venerated as a martyr after her death, and have her tomb transformed into a sacred place of pilgrimage: indeed, but for the outbreak of war, "the cause for her canonisation would have been by now well advanced" (173). On the other hand, sanctity can be the direct cause of evil, for the Gentle Anchorite who keeps Fursey company for a while was expelled from his monastery because his piety was a nuisance and his "extreme saintliness was leading [his] brethren into the sins of envy and jealousy" (194). It is because of this principle of carnival ambivalence that every attempt Fursey makes to be a good Christian, to run away from witches and demons, and to return to the safety of Clonmacnoise only leads him deeper into a life of sorcery and "evil," until his only friend in the world, and the only one prepared to defend him against the charge of sorcery, is the Devil himself. Satan is, in fact, alone in perceiving that good and evil depend on each other, and in realizing the ironic futility of any efforts of one side to defeat the opponent:

"I cannot conquer this boyish desire of mine to see monks, anchorites and other holy men startled out of their wits by an apparition, preferably a female one. It affords me the keenest amusement, but it's a vice which is rendering me more ineffective as a demon. While I'm splitting my sides laughing, the gentleman whom I'm tempting, has immediate recourse to prayer and other spiritual weapons, the very last thing which I wish him to do. The net result is that he always wins, and

17. Bakhtin, *Dostoevsky's Poetics*, 176.

when I've recovered from my paroxysm of merriment, I find that there is nothing left for me to do but retire chagrined and baffled." (232)

The rational perspicacity and courteousness of the Devil are features of the topsy-turviness of the satirical universe, and stand in great contrast to the torture-obsessed irascibility of Bishop Flanagan. Bakhtin points out that in carnivalized literature, the Devil, rather than being terrifying or alien, is depicted as a force of material renewal, a "gay, ambivalent figure expressing the unofficial point of view, the material bodily stratum."[18]

As such, the Devil in *The Unfortunate Fursey* represents the life force, and it is in this capacity that he—literally—condemns the bishop for going against the natural order, thereby ironically condemning himself to an eternity in the bishop's company: "Mark my words, . . . when that man finishes his career in this world and gets to Hell, the first thing he'll do is found a Vigilance Society. He'll have us all properly pestered with complaints about the nudity of the damned and the like, as if anyone could expect clothing to survive in that temperature. He'll still be trying to alter the machinery of creation, like he does in this world" (128). Taking advantage of the Church's obsession with sex, the "most heinous of all crimes," the Devil makes the clergy an offer they cannot refuse: in return for their country's immunity from sexual temptation, the priests will "not in future lay undue stress on the wickedness of simony, nepotism, drunkenness, perjury and murder" in their teaching (233). Thus, *The Unfortunate Fursey* implies, the evil of the modern world, as well as the status of the contemporary priesthood, have their origins in a tenth-century bargain with the Devil: "I promise the clergy of this country wealth and the respect of their people for all time. When a stranger enters a village, he will not have to ask which is the priest's house. It will be easy of identification, for it will be the largest house there. I promise you that whenever priests are sought, it will not be in the houses of the poor that they will be found. And as a sign that I will keep my part of the bargain, I will stamp the foreheads of your priesthood with my own particular seal—the seal of pride" (234). The Devil now has the souls of the Irish clergy "in his bag" for all time, but given the paradoxical nature of things he realizes that he himself is worse off than before: the new Irish ecclesiastical character of hell will alienate the other damned, and "before

18. Bakhtin, *Rabelais*, 40.

long Hell will hardly know itself. It will bear an extraordinary resemblance to an Annual General Meeting of the Catholic Truth Society. It's a terrible prospect for a demon of sensitiveness and breeding like me" (234–35).

The notion of a Catholic Truth Society meeting in hell compromises both the nature of that "Truth" and the concept of hell. By his own admission, however, the Devil is the "Father of Lies, Deception and Double-dealing" (230), all of which afford him the greatest pleasure; there is no guarantee, therefore, that his word in any of these instances can be taken for granted. The notion of "truth" itself becomes meaningless in an unstable, topsy-turvy universe in which everything always results in its opposite. To borrow Bishop Flanagan's words, "the truth in the matter is not obtainable" (223). This is also the empirical conclusion reached by Abbot Marcus: the Church may have its univocal truth, its dogma, and its principles, but "in the land of Ireland anything may happen to anyone at any time, and . . . it usually does" (224). However, rather than derailing the Church's one-sided seriousness and intolerance of other viewpoints, this insight actually reinforces it, and it should therefore come as no surprise that, once the Devil has departed after successfully defending Fursey in his sorcery trial and proving him innocent, the clergy unanimously agree that "the only thing that remains to be done, is to burn Fursey" (236). The unfortunate monk is once again forced to resort to his broomstick to make his escape. As Bakhtin points out, for the medieval Church, petrified seriousness was "supposedly the only tone fit to express the true, the good, and all that was essential and meaningful."[19] The more intangible the truth becomes, therefore, the more what is true is solely determined by the seriousness of the tone in which the statement is expressed.

It is this deadly seriousness that creates the authority of church and state, but the truth represented by this authority is hollow, and a matter of form rather than substance. Since the truth, unobtainable as it is, cannot be contested, breaking the seriousness of those in authority is the only way of dethroning them, which is why Bakhtin places such emphasis on laughter, which "liberates not only from external censorship but first of all from the great interior censor; it liberates from the fear that developed in man during thousands of years: fear of the sacred, of prohibitions, of the past, of

19. Ibid., 73.

power."[20] The Devil sees no such liberating prospect for Ireland, however, and advises Fursey to emigrate: "what's wrong with this land is the hard-fisted few that have and hold it. . . . Your countrymen have no real sense of humour as the phrase is understood by other peoples. They never laugh at themselves" (235). This is crucial, for liberating laughter is always "also directed at those who laugh. The people do not exclude themselves from the wholeness of the world. . . . The people's ambivalent laughter . . . expresses the point of view of the whole world; he who is laughing also belongs to it."[21] Mervyn Wall was convinced that the Ireland of the 1940s lacked the prospect of change because the inhibiting factors came from within: "the State and the Church did not have to be active—the people wanted censorship. They wanted it that way."[22] Until they learned to laugh at themselves, the Irish were, as he saw it, unable to belong to the world, and condemned to live in insularity and fear. Condemned to death once more as a sorcerer by the clergy, Fursey takes the Devil's hint, abducts Maeve from the church where she is about to be married to the soldier Magnus, and flies with her to Britain on his broomstick, "the first of many exiles for whom a decent way of living was not to be had in their own country" (241).

20. Ibid., 94.
21. Ibid., 12.
22. Henderson, interview, 9.

chapter eleven

"Think Twice and Do Nothing"

The Return of Fursey

Commentators disagree as to the relative merits of *The Return of Fursey*. Whereas Thomas Kilroy, for example, contends that the book "has all the faults of numerous such sequels, its plot and characters being outrageously overworked, and there is little of the original inspiration,"[1] Robert Hogan argues that, although the cliché says that sequels are never as good as their precursors, "*The Return of Fursey* is nearly so, even when gauged by the high standards of the original; and when it is gauged by its own standards, which are rather different, it is very good indeed."[2] All discussion of quality aside, it is a fact that *The Return of Fursey* is a great deal darker in tone than *The Unfortunate Fursey,* mainly because the sequel virtually lacks the playful carnival ambivalence of affirmation and negation of its predecessor. Moreover, the rather abstract "ultimate questions" of good and evil that were central to the first narrative, while still important in the sequel, are partially displaced by a more personal and serious inquiry into the nature of human happiness—an inquiry that would subsequently come to dominate all of Mervyn Wall's writing.[3] *The Return of Fursey* is dominated by negative overtones of death and destruction, without the complementary component of renewal and rebirth. Robert Hogan is right when he calls the sequel to *The Unfortunate Fursey* "a basically serious book" whose greatest charm is its "ultimate sadness."[4]

The plot of *The Return of Fursey* is a direct continuation of the events of

1. Kilroy, "Mervyn Wall," 85.   2. Hogan, *Mervyn Wall*, 45.
3. For a discussion of this theme throughout Wall's work, see my article "Unattainable Alternatives: The Writing of Mervyn Wall."
4. Hogan, *Mervyn Wall*, 45.

The Unfortunate Fursey. It begins three months after the day when Fursey snatched Maeve from Magnus's side at the altar where they were about to be married, with the arrival of Magnus and Abbot Marcus of Clonmacnoise at the court of King Ethelwulf, in whose kingdom of Mercia the wayward couple are now running a modest grocery shop with the aid of Fursey's limited powers of sorcery. The delegation's mission, to arrest Fursey and bring him back to Ireland for judicial burning at the stake, is only partly successful: the king of Mercia refuses to extradite Fursey and instead places him under special protection, believing that he will be able to use the wizard's abilities to his own advantage. The abbot does, however, manage to convince Maeve that her life with Fursey is not respectable, and that she should return to Ireland with the man to whom she was originally betrothed. Meanwhile, the civil service of Mercia—consisting of one "small, bald-headed man" (1)[5]—informs Fursey that he is "forbidden to quit this territory under pain of His Majesty's displeasure," and that he is required to "perform such duties as may be assigned to [him]" (18). Lonely, despondent, and frightened by the prospect of having to perform magic for Ethelwulf, Fursey decides henceforth to serve only evil, since respectability and virtue have brought him nothing but misfortune and unhappiness. He resolves to return to Ireland, kill Magnus, and win back Maeve, and to ask the Devil to help him accomplish his goals.

It is a characteristic of Menippean satire that it contains dialogues that take place on the threshold separating different planes of existence, and that such dialogues inquire into the nature of existence in terms of life's "ultimate questions." Fursey's conversations with the Devil and other members of the spirit world serve to call into question the relative nature of good and evil. While Fursey was, unsuccessfully, attempting to remain on the side of virtue in the course of *The Unfortunate Fursey,* the official representatives of good (the Church in general and the monks of Clonmacnoise in particular) were under considerable threat from the forces of evil (represented by sorcerers and demons, including Satan himself). Now that, in *The Return of Fursey,* Fursey has decided to join the forces of evil, however, the roles have been reversed, and depravity no

---

5. Mervyn Wall, *The Return of Fursey, in The Complete Fursey* (Dublin: Wolfhound Press, 1985); all page references in the text are to this edition.

longer has the upper hand. To begin his life of wickedness, Fursey appeals to his old acquaintance Satan for assistance in the practices of evil. The Prince of Darkness turns out to be in bad shape: "[T]he dark-complexioned fiend presented the appearance of a very decayed gentleman indeed. His countenance seemed tarnished with malignant vapours and his black cloak was singed and smelt abominably of brimstone. In fact, the Archfiend was a hideous piece of wreckage, very rickety as to his legs, and generally very much in need of repair" (37). The Devil's life has been made a misery, not only by the first Irish ecclesiastical contingent to arrive in hell, but also by the Gentle Anchorite, who turned out to be more than a match for Satan after the latter overconfidently challenged him to a contest. As a result, the Devil vows he will never set foot in Ireland again. Most of the other representatives of evil Fursey encounters are equally unhappy: a vampire complains bitterly to Fursey about the loneliness of his spirit existence, and the sorcerer Cuthbert, having lost his magical books and props after a "pogrom" by the bishop of Cashel, has taken to drink and now lives in a cave in the woods amid other incompetent and self-destructive wizards, one of whom foresees his own future in his crystal ball as "leaping flames of a pyre and a circle of grim-visaged clerics standing around it, apparently chanting a requiem" (149). Fursey is not surprised by this turn of events, knowing as he does that "wherever there was strong religious conviction there was blood-letting and oppression" (127). Wall's satire blurs the distinction between antithetical moral categories: how good is "good" when most of its representatives are in hell, or on their way there? And how evil is "evil" when its representatives are polite, pathetic victims of aggression and bullying? Fursey is directly affected by the confusion surrounding these moral definitions: in *The Unfortunate Fursey,* the harder he had tried to be good, the more closely he had become associated with the forces of evil; in *The Return of Fursey,* the more he decides to dedicate himself to evil, the more the outside world comes to regard him as a saint. The ambiguity with which Wall depicts good and evil creates a moral void in which neither term ultimately has any significance.

In order to dedicate himself fully to works of evil, Fursey decides, Faust-like, to sign a pact with the Devil in his own blood. Mervyn Wall borrowed the details of Fursey's written agreement with Satan directly from Calmet, who provides the example of a man named Michael who sold his soul to

Satan by means of a contract written on two different bits of paper, "one of which remained in the possession of the demon, the other was inserted in Michael's arm, at the same place whence the demon had drawn the blood."[6] The bureaucratic nature of the undertaking clearly appealed to Wall's sense of humor, and when the Devil explains to Fursey that "it has to be in duplicate. . . . One copy is filed in my closet in Hell and the other must be swallowed by you" (47), Wall makes him speak with the petty officiousness of a minor civil servant. In the course of a bout of seasickness during his voyage back to Ireland, Fursey vomits up the document he had ingested at the Devil's instigation, and when Satan subsequently tries to remind him of their pact, Fursey matches him in legalistic formality and absolutely denies that he ever signed anything: "I trust . . . that my mark to the document in question was duly witnessed by a third party. I'm afraid that otherwise it can have no validity. Without the signature of a witness no court on earth or in Heaven would accept it as genuine in the face of my denial" (196). The act of dedicating oneself to evil is thus reduced to a bureaucratic paper transaction, a mere formality without actual substance, that can be invalidated on the grounds of a technicality.

Fursey manages to persuade a band of Vikings to give him passage to Ireland on their ship by pretending to be a powerful sorcerer capable of controlling the winds. To begin his life of depravity, and to get his own back on the monks who expelled him from the monastery, he swears an oath of allegiance to Thor and offers to show the plunderers the way to Clonmacnoise. Fursey's association with the Vikings is incongruous, as is evidenced by his ill-fitting apparel: "Snorro helped him into a corselet of mail and a pair of greaves. It was rather difficult to fit Fursey, who was small and tubby; but Snorro managed it at last, except for the helmet. Even the smallest helmet fell down over Fursey's eyes when he nodded his head, but he found that by throwing his head well back and keeping his eyebrows raised he could keep it in position. Then Snorro girt on him a long, dangerous looking sword, which incommoded Fursey greatly in his walking" (57). If Fursey is out of place on a Viking ship, the Danes in their turn provide Wall with an alien and uncomprehending point of view from which to depict the Irish, a way of "making strange" the object of his satire.

6. Calmet, *Phantom World*, vol. 1, 32–33.

As the Viking ship approaches the Irish shore, Fursey tries in vain to clarify the presence of "meagre, half-naked creatures" on the rocks off the coast.

"They're undoubtedly maritime hermits, who live largely on shell fish," explained Fursey to the intrigued Vikings.

"But do they not live in community?" he was asked.

"No," replied Fursey. "Their love of monastic seclusion is such that they cannot stand the sight of one another," and he made a feeble attempt to explain the nature of sanctity. But the Vikings only shook their heads and made the centuries-old joke common to every Germanic tongue, in which Ireland is called "Irre-land"—the land of the Mad. (66)

Fursey is more familiar with hermits than with raiders, and he is uneasy about the depravity of his shipmates: "One had only to contemplate the fierce aspect of his companions to realise that they were men exposed to all the hurricanes of unbridled passions, and their very proximity was alarming to Fursey. Yet these were the men whom he was helping to lead against his own countrymen and, worse still, against his own kind" (67). If in this passage Wall implies a contrast between depraved Danes and virtuous Irishmen, however, in virtually the same breath he manages to suggest the opposite as well. When the ship passes Ballybunion, Fursey's matter-of-fact description of the vices of "his own countrymen," even those of "his own kind," makes the Vikings appear almost tame by comparison.

"I understand that the dissolute inhabitants are entirely given over to pleasure and vice. It's much frequented in the summer months by members of the lower clergy, who spend their time gaming and in the consumption of strong liquors. It's a notorious centre for cockfighting, dicing and other licentious pursuits."

Even though it was still early afternoon, the night life of Ballybunion was already under way, and one could hear the wicked hum of the settlement, the barking of depraved dogs, the incessant rattling of dice boxes and the indignant howls of drunkards being ejected from taverns because they had no more money. But the dragonship soon left this modern Babylon behind and crept up the estuary of the River Shannon. (67–68)

Fursey's comments say more about human nature than about cultural differences, and it is this wickedness of humanity in general that comes increasingly to dominate Wall's satire. *The Return of Fursey* is ultimately less an indictment of Irish institutions than it is a condemnation of mankind as a whole.

The Shelter for Unemployed Vikings in the Danish city of Limerick in which Fursey spends his first night back on his native soil is a medieval, Scandinavian parody of a contemporary Salvation Army shelter, a charitable institution run on pious principles. The philosophical enquiries of Menippean satire often take place in slum settings among the down-and-out, but if Fursey learns anything in this environment it is that the pagan Vikings are as averse to laughter as are the representatives of the Christian establishment. In the shelter, Fursey is accosted by a drunken Viking named Thorkils, who repeatedly demands to know whether Fursey is laughing at him, and who will not believe the little man's timid assurances to the contrary: "'I knew you were laughing at me,' said the Viking, and raising his great fist he brought it down with all his strength on Fursey's pate" (77).

For Wall, this threatening, humorless figure has great symbolic importance, for he reintroduces him in his novel *Leaves for the Burning* (1952) in the shape of the drunken doctor Thullabawn, who accosts helpless strangers in a similar way.[7] The importance of laughter as a force that undermines authority and liberates the laugher from both external and internal censorship has been addressed before.[8] In Wall's work, however, the characters who are accused of laughing and assaulted in these confrontations are not, in fact, laughing at all: rather, they are overcome with fear. Wall's satires of the late 1940s and early 1950s depict widespread paranoid behavior of a kind that detects ridicule, threat, and insult even when there is none to be perceived: this is the kind of vigilante climate in which censorship flourishes, especially the Irish form of censorship which relied on members of the public (often, in practice, zealous members of the Catholic Truth Society) to bring what they regarded as indecent or obscene literary passages to the attention of the Censorship Board. J. H. Whyte points out that criticism of the Censorship Board's excessive severity began to mount during the 1940s, but that instead of relaxing its methods, the Board react-

---

7. "'If you're laughing at me, it would be better for you that you had never been born. I'd just screw the head off you as I've done to many a better man.' 'I haven't been laughing at you,' said the little man faintly"; *Leaves for the Burning*, 131.

8. See Bakhtin, *Rabelais*, 94.

ed by becoming "even stricter, and the number of books banned . . . reached a peak during the years 1950–55, when it averaged over six hundred a year."[9]

The Return of Fursey ridicules the Censorship Board's zeal in the figure of the monastic Censor, who "had been appointed by the Synod of Cashel to visit every monastery in Ireland and search the libraries for written matter offensive to morals," and whose principal qualification for the post "was that each of his eyes moved independently of the other, a quality most useful in the detection of double meanings" (82). He commits to the flames all manuscripts that do not pass his touchstone—his mother, who is to him "the type of the decent, clean-minded people of Ireland," but who is also completely illiterate: "Whenever I'm in doubt about a word or phrase, I ask myself would such word or phrase be used by her" (83). This method means that virtually all texts are condemned: Greek and Latin manuscripts such as Ovid's *Metamorphoses* go up in smoke, and even the Old Testament, which the Censor, in the language of the 1929 Censorship Act, "had denounced as being in its general tendency indecent" (82), does not escape the flames.[10] The monastic Censor enthusiastically burns the great books of Western civilization, but Wall's fictional account is in fact barely a satirical exaggeration of the censorship reality that existed in Ireland in the 1940s and 1950s: many of the authors whose books were banned (Gide, Sartre, Hemingway, and Steinbeck, to name but a few[11]) were among the most important in modern literature, and even works "that had an imprimatur from the Archbishop of Westminster and were chosen as the selection of the Catholic Book Society of the United States" were banned in Ireland.[12]

Book burning is often denounced in common parlance as a "medieval" practice, and in the Middle Ages Ovid was indeed often among the casualties on the pyre,[13] but the practice is, of course, by no means unknown in

9. Whyte, *Church and State*, 315.

10. The Censorship of Publications Act of 1929 provided for the banning of publications that were "in . . . general tendency indecent or obscene" (part 2, section 6).

11. See Whyte, *Church and State*, 315.

12. Henderson, interview, 11.

13. For a medieval example of a burning of Ovid's *Ars Amatoria*, see Marie de France's "Guigemar": "The walls of the chamber were covered in paintings in which Venus . . . was skilfully depicted together with the nature and obligations of love. . . . In the painting Venus was shown as casting into a blazing fire the book in which Ovid teaches the art of controlling love

authoritarian, repressive societies in the modern world. Nazi Germany had its share of book burnings, but so, on a different scale, did Mervyn Wall's Ireland. Wall himself believes that the copies of Joyce's *Dubliners* and *Portrait* he bought as a young man were burned by his father.[14] Copies of Brinsley MacNamara's *The Valley of the Squinting Windows* were also ritually disposed of in this way on more than one occasion: Benedict Kiely recollects that "a local butcher burned the book, and an old lady went into the house and said, 'Thank God, the trouble's over now. The book's burned.' I think that's a lovely medieval attitude."[15] Edna O'Brien's second novel, *The Lonely Girl,* underwent a similar fate after its publication in 1962: "There were a few copies of it burned in the chapel grounds. It all belongs to the Middle Ages, don't you think?"[16] The most heartrending instance of this kind is perhaps the experience of the old couple known as the Tailor and Ansty, whose humorous stories were recorded by Eric Cross: "Three priests appeared at their little cottage one day and forced that dying old man to go on his knees at his own hearth and burn the only copy he had of his own book."[17] The incendiary attitude of the clergy is satirized in Seán O'Casey's play *Cock-a-Doodle Dandy* (1949), in which a bonfire is made of dangerous reading material, including a book called "*Ulisississies,* or something."[18] In *The Return of Fursey* Wall makes his medieval Censor the ultimate incinerator. When the plundering Vikings set fire to Clonmacnoise, it only takes him a moment to take advantage of the situation: emerging from the manuscript room after a hard day's work of chasing innuendoes, he "cast one glance at the raging fires which threatened the whole settlement; then he returned and set fire to the library" (89). The sight of his "sub-human visage" has meanwhile caused even the Vikings to retreat in alarm.

The monks of Clonmacnoise survive the Viking attack and manage to hide their gold and their manuscripts because they are warned in time by

and as excommunicating all those who read this book or adopted its teachings." See *The Lais of Marie de France,* trans. Glyn S. Burgess and Keith Busby (Harmondsworth, U.K.: Penguin Books, 1986), 46.

14. As he states in a letter to Julia Carlson, quoted in her *Banned in Ireland,* 10.

15. Benedict Kiely, interview with Julia Carlson, in Carlson, *Banned in Ireland,* 28.

16. Edna O'Brien, interview with Julia Carlson, in Carlson, *Banned in Ireland,* 72.

17. Frank O'Connor, "Frank O'Connor on Censorship," in Carlson, *Banned in Ireland,* 156.

18. Seán O'Casey, *Cock-a-Doodle Dandy,* ed. David Krause (Washington, D.C.: The Catholic University of America Press, 1991), 102.

"a small man in armour and wearing the horned helmet of a Viking" (84–85), in whom they fail to recognize their former companion. Fursey realizes that his action has saved Clonmacnoise from spoliation by the Vikings, and that living a life of iniquity may be harder than he had anticipated, but he is determined to persevere, spurred on by his love for Maeve. To win her affections with the aid of a love potion, and to become evil enough to murder her husband, Magnus, Fursey seeks out the sorcerer Cuthbert, now an outlaw in much reduced circumstances. The sorcerer suggests that Fursey be initiated at the Witches' Sabbath on May Eve in order to make his wickedness official. The details of such a Sabbath are found in the pages of Calmet.

> People are carried thither, say they, sitting on a broom-stick, sometimes on the clouds or on a he-goat. . . .
>
> The demon, their chief, appears there, either in the shape of a he-goat, or as a great black dog, or as an immense raven; he is seated on an elevated throne, and receives there the homage of those present in a way which decency does not allow us to describe. In this nocturnal assembly they sing, they dance, they abandon themselves to the most shameful disorder; they sit down to table, and indulge in good cheer; . . . they find the viands devoid of savour, and quit the table without their hunger being satisfied. . . .
>
> When they are admitted for the first time to the sabbath, the demon inscribes their name and surname on his register, which he makes them sign.[19]

Wall borrows heavily from his source but elaborates on the grotesque details and at the same time provides the "shameful disorder" of the Sabbath with an incongruously bureaucratic infrastructure: "'Broomsticks to be parked by the lakeside on the left,' shouted a tall man in black" (162). Fursey dutifully parks his broom, stables his familiar in the designated place, dances in a circle around a man in a goat-costume while swinging a cat by its tail, and then joins the other sorcerers for the night's supper. The witches' banquet Fursey is forced to attend can be regarded as the ultimate grotesque meal:

> Men whom he had known as courteous, dapper sorcerers were guzzling food with an air of frenzy, their beards and hair awry, their faces scratched and their clothes torn to shreds. . . .

19. Calmet, *Phantom World*, vol. 1, 110.

Fursey was a man who enjoyed food, and his eyes nearly fell from his head when he saw what he was expected to eat. There were huge dishes on the table loaded with strings of entrails, carrion and putrid garbage. The black-clad attendant had set up a brazier beside the table, and when anyone seemed diffident about consumption of the food placed before him, he was immediately threatened with red-hot iron plates. To convince the delinquent that he was in earnest, the attendant directed attention to a leg-crushing machine in the background. (165–66)

A banquet of entrails, carrion and garbage has a topsy-turvy quality about it, and as such has the potential of being a triumphant feast of renewal in which life feeds on death, demonstrating, in Bakhtin's terms, the constant unfinished character of the world. Mervyn Wall is no Rabelais, however, and the banquet in *The Return of Fursey* is neither celebratory nor accompanied by festive laughter. For Fursey, who is revolted by the meal, it is a purely negative experience, but he half-heartedly resolves to go through with the initiation ceremony. When he pays homage to the goatman and is questioned about the evil deeds he has perpetrated, Fursey begins to cry with fear. Since no wizard or witch can weep, his weakness exposes him as an impostor, whereupon the goatman whips him savagely until he howls with pain, after which he is expelled from the Sabbath.

Having failed in his endeavor to become a fully fledged wizard, Fursey is equally unsuccessful in achieving his objective of winning back Maeve with the aid of a magical love philter. The love potion is left by Cuthbert to brew in a bucket overnight while he and Fursey are attending the Witches' Sabbath, but when Fursey returns from his unsuccessful journey he is just in time to see the final drops of the liquid disappear down the gullet of the cow he had charitably rescued from starvation some time previously. The consequences are predictable: "She extended her broad, rough tongue and licked his ear. . . . There could be no doubt about it: the light in her eye was an amorous one" (174). The crossing or erasing of boundaries between human and animal is a grotesque notion, and Wall uses the comic infatuation of beast with man to point up the misguided nature of Fursey's obsession with Maeve. The amorous cow makes a mockery of Fursey's love quest and functions as a distorting mirror, magnifying both his own foolish infatuation and the less attractive qualities of the object of his desire. The besotted animal follows Fursey around for a while, until her mooing becomes so plaintive that she leaves Fursey no other option than to destroy her. Her demise foreshadows not only the failure of Fursey's plan to regain Maeve, but also the death of his love for life as a whole. Fursey learns no lesson from the substitution of an infatuated cow for his idealized beloved, however, other than that sorcery may not be the best course of action to achieve his goal.

Fursey rids himself of his sorcerous spirit by reversing the method by which he acquired it from the Gray Mare: he breathes it into another person. He finds a willing recipient in a rustic prophet of extreme piety, who is absolutely certain that for this charitable act he will be greatly rewarded in heaven—an arrogant conviction in which he turns out to be sadly mistaken. The prophet is surprised and upset to find himself in hell after he dies, but he should have known better, for he had himself diagnosed the paradox inherent in Christian charity: "To be unselfish in these matters one would have to give without hope of recompense. Only those who do not believe in an after-life, can be truly unselfish" (185). Fursey is now himself again, but he is no longer the timid little lay brother of *The Unfortunate Fursey*, and the concepts of heaven and hell have lost their meaning for him. Demons can no longer tempt or frighten him: "I have suffered so much terror and affrightment from your like during the past year that I can gaze on the worst that Hell can produce, quite unappalled" (192–93). Neither can he pray, for that would amount to hypocrisy: "He had lost his simple faith, and he knew that it was gone for ever" (199). Fursey has come to the cynical conclusion that the choice between the binary opposites of good and evil is meaningless, that "the golden rule in life is to think twice and do nothing" (194), and that everything can be twisted to serve his own interests. He is thus able to tell the Devil that he is giving up his wicked ways and "going in for virtue in future" (195), while at the same time steeling himself in his resolve that "no matter what punishment might await him, he would kill Magnus and have Maeve" (199). In acquiring the art of doublespeak, Fursey has become like his tormentors in *The Unfortunate Fursey*, who persecuted him with "the charitable intention of securing the safety of his immortal soul by burning him on a pyre" (9). Fursey has no qualms, for example, in promising an unpleasant, grubby little boy a handsome reward for delivering a belligerent message to Magnus, and then fulfilling his promise by smiling benignantly while giving the boy "a couple of unmerciful skelps" with a big stick until the child flees down the road, howling for his mother (210).

For Fursey, the pursuit of Maeve equals the pursuit of happiness, but the undertaking is compromised from the very beginning, for even in the days when he was living in Mercia and still had Maeve he had not been happy:

He was thinking of the strangeness of things, of his own hatred of adventure and his longing for the quiet and safety that went with marriage and a little piece of land. . . . Then he remembered that he had sat like this under a tree in Britain and looked about him at a scene in which everything was in harmony except himself. In those days he had possessed woman and house and land, and such share of wealth as he needed. Yet he had felt himself an outsider. He had not been content: he had been a man of property sitting under a tree aware of his possessions and of the beauty of the world in which he moved; but he had not been content. His friend the molecatcher was a philosopher and might have been able to explain these things; but they had taken the molecatcher and hanged him from his own roof-tree. (206–7)

At that time he had come to the conclusion that happiness is not so much a positive condition as it is "the absence of unhappiness" (19). However, "happiness" and "unhappiness" are relative terms dependent on perceptions of good and bad, and since *The Return of Fursey* depicts a moral void in which the clear distinction between good and evil is problematized, happiness gradually comes to be defined as absence itself: it consists in what you do not have, no matter what that may be, and is therefore forever out of reach. When Fursey was living with Maeve, he found that "a woman fussed by her household duties is a different sort of creature altogether from the girl one remembered standing beside a lake with the wind blowing through her hair" (13); but after Maeve has gone back to Magnus, Fursey remembers "a Maeve who turned on him a gaze that was sweet, kind and understanding, a woman who spoke but little (and then only when spoken to), but who stood slender and graceful, her face demurely aglow with love for her lord and master" (156). Rather than being enemies, Magnus and Fursey are alter egos who find themselves in similar predicaments: the one who does not have Maeve wants her to complete his happiness; but the one who lives with her longs for the life he led before she came along. Fursey need not murder Magnus to win back Maeve, for Magnus is perfectly willing to give him his wife, having "grown weary of that woman's apron strings" (230). Magnus concocts a plan with which Fursey wholeheartedly agrees: the soldier will go back to Mercia and join the king's army, leaving Fursey in charge of the house, and after a month he will have a message sent home stating that he has been killed in battle. Maeve will mourn for six months, after which she will consent to marry Fursey. Before the plan can be executed, however, it is thwarted by Maeve's announcement that she is expecting a child. Although Magnus seems uncertain as to the cause of the pregnancy and expresses suspicion at its timing—"I wouldn't be surprised if it's all on purpose," he tells his friend (232)—he has the advantage over Fursey, whose union with Maeve was never consummated, because, as he confessed to the Devil, "we both had a good Irish Catholic upbringing, and we don't know how" (44). Rather than representing a new beginning, the baby constitutes a dead end for Fursey and Magnus, who come to the conclusion that Maeve's new allegiance has made them both superfluous: "for all she cares the two of us may go and drown ourselves" (233). Magnus regrets that marriage means the end of adventure, but Fursey already knows that "adventure is not all that the writers of romance would have us believe" (99). If there are choices in *The Return of Fursey,* they are always between a rock and a hard place, without the option of a satisfactory compromise.

Fursey cannot stay with Maeve and Magnus, but neither can he go back to Clonmacnoise. Abbot Marcus offers to give him back his old position, paring edible roots in the monastery kitchen, but Fursey realizes that he has outgrown that limited existence: "I've seen the world, and bitter and cruel as it is, I belong there now" (212). Fursey is eternally torn between opposite states of being: when he is by himself, he is lonely and reflects that "it was a terrible thing to have no one to talk to" (102), but when he has company, he cannot help thinking that "if only man were absent . . . how beautiful the world would be!" (155). The only time Fursey feels truly happy and in tune with the world and mankind is paradoxically when he is in a state of transience on board the Viking ship, suspended between two worlds, surrounded by strange runic inscriptions and grotesque carved ornaments, and listening to a skaldic recital in a language he does not understand.

Fursey's dilemma has no solution, and his fate at the end of *The Return of Fursey,* like that of Cuanduine at the end of Eimar O'Duffy's trilogy, is appropriately left unresolved, as the "negligible figure" of Fursey wanders off in the direction of "unknown lands in the south" against the backdrop of "the vast night sky" (234). In fact, Mervyn Wall's outlook on life is generally very similar to the view expressed by his fellow satirist almost two decades earlier. At the end of *Asses in Clover,* O'Duffy predicted that mankind, an experiment of the gods that had gone badly wrong, would destroy itself through its stupidity and wickedness. By the end of *The Return of Fursey,* Wall's misanthropy has reached similar proportions, and this despondency about humanity comes to dominate all his subsequent writings. "I can't write optimistically about human beings,"[20] he told one interviewer in 1982; "from the beginning of time human beings have been stupid. It's the one thing that has been constant. I do propose writing a new novel about the very fact that the creation of man was an error and possibly God some time will replace him."[21] Wall never wrote that book. The final novel of his career is *Hermitage* (1982), in which the protagonist finds sanctuary from life's impossible choices in prison, where he writes his life's story: "You always know what's coming next. You don't have to make decisions. You have no responsibility."[22] A sardonic comment elsewhere by the author of these words confirms the suspicion that the sentiment expressed by his character is not purely fictitious, and that the satirist is subtly aware of the symbiotic relationship, even the complicity, that always exists between a repressive regime and the critical writer who is both persecuted and inspired by it: "The best thing for a writer would be the solitude conferred by a long gaol sentence. If we had an enlightened government, this could be arranged. Look what it did for John Bunyan and Cervantes."[23]

20. Henderson, interview, 18. 21. Ibid., 17.
22. Mervyn Wall, *Hermitage* (Dublin: Wolfhound Press, 1982), 351.
23. Smith, interview, 86.

Afterword

The Republic of Ireland officially came into existence on Easter Monday, 1949. The early postwar period had brought a remarkable expansion in industrial production and employment, but a structural lack of efficiency and organization meant that this ground to a virtual halt in the early 1950s. The unrelieved bleakness of the following decade is summed up by John A. Murphy: "This was a period of unprecedented gloom and depression. No longer could the state of the economy be attributed to colonial misgovernment or wartime restrictions. Economic growth was non-existent, inflation was apparently insoluble, unemployment rife, living standards low, and emigration approaching 50,000 a year, a figure not far below the birth rate. Even some who were securely employed threw up their jobs to seek a new life in countries which held out brighter prospects for the future of their families."[1] The preoccupation of satirists in the 1940s and early 1950s with text and meaning was indicative of their growing concern during these years with issues relating to censorship and freedom of expression. This censorship had been, at least in the early years, "an attempt to translate into reality the puritanism that often goes with revolution—to establish . . . that the new Ireland should shine like a good deed in a naughty world,"[2] but this idealistic effort had turned increasingly sour. Censorship of publications reached its peak in the years 1950–1955, with an average of over six hundred books banned per year. Generally speaking, Menippean satire thrives in periods of cultural turmoil and political upheaval; these, however, were times of stagnation. The satirical trend in Irish writing, so prevalent in the first decades after the Treaty, petered out in the early 1950s.

Three of the Menippean satirists discussed in this study were still alive

---

1. Murphy, *Ireland in the Twentieth Century,* 142.
2. Lyons, *Ireland since the Famine,* 686.

in the 1950s. Mervyn Wall's *Leaves for the Burning* was published in 1952. It provides a rather depressing account of life in Ireland in the 1940s and early 1950s, and the satirical element, if present, is much reduced. Wall himself liked to think that the book gave an exact picture of Ireland as it was in the middle of the twentieth century, reflecting the rule of the philistines and the end of idealism. The plot of his subsequent book, *No Trophies Raise* (1956), explores the clash between spiritual values and crass business practices. On the one hand, Wall invites us to share his indignation at the trampling of spiritual values by commercial boots; on the other hand, he shows that the defenders of these values are themselves unworthy of our praise, given their spinelessness and general inertia. Wall appears to suggest more and more strongly that the sense of stagnation in Ireland in the decade following the Emergency was as much the result of the paralysis of its people as it was its cause.[3]

Flann O'Brien wrote no major satirical works after the publication of *An Béal Bocht* in 1941, but diverted his satirical powers into the column he wrote, as Myles na Gopaleen, for the *Irish Times*. It ran for more than twenty-five years (1940–1966), but it, too, became less playfully satirical as the years went on, relying less heavily than before on wordplay and nonsense devices and becoming less inclined to undermine its own seriousness.[4] O'Brien wrote three stage plays in 1943: *Faustus Kelly, The Insect Play* (after Čapek), and the one-act comedy *Thirst*. Thereafter, nothing appeared until the publication of *The Hard Life* (1961) and *The Dalkey Archive* (1964), and both of these lack what Bakhtin calls the "experimental fantasticality" characteristic of the earlier Menippean satires.

Austin Clarke, too, was largely silent during the first half of the 1950s and wrote no more narrative satires. Since the somber poems of *Night and Morning* (1938) he had published "a series of not very satisfactory verse-plays" but little else.[5] Then came a newfound poetic strength in *Ancient Lights* (1955), a volume with which he "emerged from silence in sudden, full-fledged humanitarian rage. . . . In Clarke's new poetic voice, certainly by the time he was writing the poems in *Flight to Africa* [1963], nothing was

3. See Lanters, "Unattainable Alternatives."
4. See Lanters, "'Still Life' versus Real Life," passim.
5. Thomas Kinsella, "Austin Clarke," in *The Macmillan Dictionary of Irish Literature,* ed. Robert Hogan (London: Macmillan, 1980), 157.

unsayable."[6] These poems had a definite satirical dimension—but satire in the sense of invective rather than unresolved dialogue—and Clarke attacked specific instances of abuse of power by the Catholic Church and the government. His last poetic theme before his death in 1974 was "a cheerful sensuality . . . , poetry as pure entertainment, serene and full of life."[7]

By the end of the bleak 1950s, circumstances changed. In 1958 T. K. Whitaker presented his program for economic development, which was implemented by the administration of Seán Lemass; it offered solutions to the economic impasse and ushered in a period of unprecedented growth and change. Unemployment fell, emigration was reduced, and morale was strengthened. In 1962, Irish television began broadcasting; it opened the country to ideas and influences from outside, fueled controversy and debate, and contributed greatly to the modernizing process. The Censorship of Publications Act was revised and relaxed—but not abolished—in 1967, when many previously banned books were released and any newly imposed ban was limited to a period of twelve years. Menippean satire had become a thing of the past: Irish writers turned away from addressing matters of public and social interest, focusing instead on the personal and the psychological. Even when they dealt with the legacy of the past—repression, emigration, disillusionment—the spotlight fell on the effect of such circumstances on the individual, rather than on the circumstances themselves.[8] An irreversible turning point had been reached, and after decades of conservatism and censorship "there began in the 1960s a new frankness of discussion, a spirit of positive self-criticism, a liberalisation of religious thinking . . . , an increase in intellectual maturity, and a rejection of paternalism."[9] The nation had come of age.

6. Ibid., 159–60.   7. Ibid., 161.

8. See Maurice Harmon, "Generations Apart: 1925–1975," in *The Irish Novel in Our Time,* ed. Patrick Rafroidi and Maurice Harmon (Villeneuve-d'Ascq, France: P.U.L., 1975–1976), 49–65.

9. Murphy, *Ireland in the Twentieth Century,* 145.

Selected Bibliography

Adams, Michael. *Censorship: The Irish Experience*. University: University of Alabama Press, 1968.

Anelius, Josephus. *National Action: A Plan for the National Recovery of Ireland*. Dublin: Gaelic Athletic Association, December 1942.

Asbee, Sue. *Flann O'Brien*. Boston: Twayne, 1991.

Bakhtin, M. M. *The Dialogic Imagination: Four Essays*. Translated by Caryl Emerson and Michael Holquist. Edited by Michael Holquist. Austin: University of Texas Press, 1981.

———. *Problems of Dostoevsky's Poetics*. Translated and edited by Caryl Emerson. Minneapolis: University of Minnesota Press, 1984.

———. *Rabelais and His World*. Translated by Hélène Iswolsky. Bloomington: Indiana University Press, 1984.

Barth, John. *The Floating Opera*. New York: Bantam Books, 1972.

Benstock, Bernard. "Flann O'Brien in Hell: *The Third Policeman*." *Contemporary Literary Criticism*, 47 (1988): 315. First published in *Bucknell Review*, 27, 2 (1969): 67–78.

Bergin, O. J. "Poems Attributed to Gormlaith." In *Miscellany Presented to Kuno Meyer*, edited by Osborn Bergin and Carl Marstrander, 343–69. Halle, Germany: Max Niemeyer, 1912.

Blain, Virginia, Patricia Clements, and Isobel Grundy, eds. *The Feminist Companion to Literature in English: Women Writers from the Middle Ages to the Present*. New Haven, Conn.: Yale University Press, 1990.

Booker, M. Keith. *Flann O'Brien, Bakhtin, and Menippean Satire*. Syracuse, N.Y.: Syracuse University Press, 1995.

Boyd, Ernest. Review of *King Goshawk and the Birds*, by Eimar O'Duffy. *New York Herald Tribune*, 31 October 1926, p. 5.

Briant, Keith. *Passionate Paradox: The Life of Marie Stopes*. New York: W. W. Norton, 1962.

Brown, Terence. "The Counter Revival: Provincialism and Censorship, 1930–65." In *The Field Day Anthology of Irish Writing*, edited by Seamus Deane, vol. 3, 89–93. Derry, Northern Ireland: Field Day, 1991.

———. *Ireland: A Social and Cultural History, 1922 to the Present*. Ithaca, N.Y.: Cornell University Press, 1981, 1985.

———. *Ireland's Literature: Selected Essays*. Mullingar, Ireland: Lilliput Press, 1988.

Burgess, Glyn S., and Keith Busby, trans. *The Lais of Marie de France*. Harmondsworth, U.K.: Penguin Books, 1986.

Calmet, Augustine [*sic*]. *The Phantom World: or, The Philosophy of Spirits, Apparitions, &c.* 2 vols. Edited by Rev. Henry Christmas. London: Richard Bentley, 1850.

Carlson, Julia, ed. *Banned in Ireland: Censorship and the Irish Writer.* Athens: University of Georgia Press, 1990.

Clark, John R. *The Modern Satiric Grotesque and Its Traditions.* Lexington: University of Kentucky Press, 1991.

Clarke, Austin. *The Bright Temptation: A Romance.* 1932. Reprint, Dublin: Dolmen Press, 1965.

———. *The Collected Poems of Austin Clarke.* Introduction by Padraic Colum. New York: Macmillan, 1936.

———. *A Penny in the Clouds: More Memories of Ireland and England.* 1968. Reprint, Dublin: Moytura Press, 1990.

———. *Selected Poems.* Edited with an introduction by Thomas Kinsella. Portlaoise, Ireland: Dolmen Press, 1974.

———. *The Singing-Men at Cashel.* London: George Allen & Unwin, 1936.

———. *The Sun Dances at Easter.* London: Andrew Melrose, 1952.

———. *Twice Round the Black Church: Early Memories of Ireland and England.* 1962. Reprint, Dublin: Moytura Press, 1990.

Clissmann, Anne. *Flann O'Brien: A Critical Introduction to His Writings.* Dublin: Gill and Macmillan, 1975.

Clune, Anne, and Tess Hurson, eds. *Conjuring Complexities: Essays on Flann O'Brien.* Belfast: Institute of Irish Studies, 1997.

Colum, Padraic. "Darrell Figgis: A Portrait." *Dublin Magazine,* 14, 2 (1939): 22–31.

Costello, Peter. *The Heart Grown Brutal: The Irish Revolution in Literature, from Parnell to the Death of Yeats, 1891–1939.* Dublin: Gill and Macmillan, 1977.

Costello, Peter, and Peter van de Kamp. *Flann O'Brien: An Illustrated Biography.* London: Bloomsbury, 1987.

Cronin, Anthony. *No Laughing Matter: The Life and Times of Flann O'Brien.* London: Paladin, 1990.

Cronin, John. *Irish Fiction, 1900–1940.* Belfast: Appletree, 1992.

Cross, Tom Peete, and Clark Harris Slover, eds. *Ancient Irish Tales.* 1936. Reprint, New York: Barnes and Noble, 1969.

Deane, Paul. "The Death of Greatness: Darrell Figgis's *The Return of the Hero.*" *Notes on Modern Irish Literature,* 3 (1991): 30–36.

Deane, Seamus. *Strange Country: Modernity and Nationhood in Irish Writing since 1790.* Oxford, U.K.: Clarendon Press, 1997.

———, ed. *The Field Day Anthology of Irish Writing.* 3 vols. Derry, Northern Ireland: Field Day, 1991.

Denman, Peter. "Austin Clarke: Tradition, Memory, and Our Lot." In *Tradition and Influence in Anglo-Irish Poetry,* edited by Terence Brown and Nicholas Grene, 63–78. Totowa, N.J.: Barnes and Noble, 1989.

Devlin, Joseph. "The Politics of Comedy in *At Swim-Two-Birds.*" *Éire-Ireland,* 27, 4 (1992): 91–105.

D'haen, Theo. "Popular Genre Conventions in Postmodern Fiction: The Case of the Western." In *Exploring Postmodernism,* edited by Matei Calinescu and Douwe Fokkema, 161–74. Amsterdam: John Benjamins, 1987.

Duncan, Lilian, trans. and ed. *Altram Tige Dá Medar. Ériu,* 11 (1932): 184–225.

Dunn, John J. "Darrell Figgis: A Man Nearly Anonymous." *Journal of Irish Literature,* 15, 1 (1986): 33–42.

Dunne, J. W. *An Experiment with Time.* 1927. Reprint, London: Scientific Book Club, 1944.

Duszenko, Andrzej. "The Joyce of Science: Quantum Physics in *Finnegans Wake.*" *Irish University Review,* 24, 2 (1994): 272–82.

Eglinton, John. "Dublin Letter." *Dial,* March 1921, pp. 332–35.

———. "Dublin Letter." *Dial,* August 1923, pp. 179–83.

———. "Irish Letter." *Dial,* May 1927, pp. 407–10.

Elliott, Robert C. *The Power of Satire: Magic, Ritual, Art.* Princeton, N.J.: Princeton University Press, 1960.

Esty, Joshua D. "Flann O'Brien's *At Swim-Two-Birds* and the Post-Post Debate." *Ariel,* 26, 4 (1995): 23–46.

Fallon, Brian. "Mervyn Wall, Novelist and Playwright, Dies Aged 89." *Irish Times,* 20 May 1997, p. 5.

Farnon, Jane. "Motifs of Gaelic Lore and Literature in *An Béal Bocht.*" In *Conjuring Complexities: Essays on Brian O'Nolan,* edited by Anne Clune and Tess Hurson, 89–109. Belfast: Institute of Irish Studies, 1997.

Feeney, W. J. "Eimar O'Duffy's 'A Military Causerie.'" *Journal of Irish Literature,* 10, 3 (1981): 91–108.

Figgis, Darrell. *The Gaelic State in the Past and Future.* Dublin: Maunsel and Co., 1917.

———. *The House of Success.* Dublin: Gael Co-Operative Publishing Society, 1921.

———. *Recollections of the Irish War.* Garden City, N.Y.: Doubleday, Doran and Co., [1927].

——— [Michael Ireland, pseudonym]. *The Return of the Hero.* London: Chapman & Dodd, 1923.

———. *The Return of the Hero.* New York: Albert and Charles Boni, 1930.

———. *Sinn Fein Catechism.* Dublin: Kiersey, [1918?].

Flower, Robin. *Catalogue of Irish Manuscripts in the British Museum.* Vol. 2. London: Trustees of the British Museum, 1926.

———. *The Irish Tradition.* 1947. Reprint, Oxford, U.K.: Clarendon Press, 1978.

Foster, John Wilson. *Fictions of the Irish Literary Revival: A Changeling Art.* Syracuse, N.Y.: Syracuse University Press, 1987.

Foster, R. F. *The Apprentice Mage, 1865–1914.* Vol. 1 of *W. B. Yeats: A Life.* Oxford, U.K.: Oxford University Press, 1997.

Frye, Northrop. *Anatomy of Criticism: Four Essays.* Princeton, N.J.: Princeton University Press, 1957.

Greene, David, and Frank O'Connor, trans. and eds. *A Golden Treasury of Irish Poetry A.D. 600 to 1200.* London: Macmillan, 1967.

Guiley, Rosemary Ellen. *The Encyclopedia of Witches and Witchcraft.* New York: Facts on File, 1989.

Haldane, J. B. S. *Possible Worlds and Other Papers.* New York and London: Harper and Brothers, 1928.

Halpern, Susan. *Austin Clarke: His Life and Works.* Dublin: Dolmen Press, 1974.

Harmon, Maurice. *Austin Clarke, 1896–1974: A Critical Introduction.* Totowa, N.J.: Barnes and Noble, 1989.

————. "The Era of Inhibitions: Irish Literature 1920–1960." In *Irish Writers and Society at Large,* edited by Masaru Sekine, 31–41. Gerrards Cross, U.K.: Colin Smythe, 1985.

————. "Notes towards a Biography." *Irish University Review,* 4, 1 (1974): 13–25.

Heine, Heinrich. *The Harz Journey.* In *Poetry and Prose,* edited by Jost Hermand and Robert C. Holub, 115–73. New York: Continuum, 1982.

Hogan, Robert. *Eimar O'Duffy.* Lewisburg, Penn.: Bucknell University Press, 1972.

————. *Mervyn Wall.* Lewisburg, Penn.: Bucknell University Press, 1972.

————, ed. *The Macmillan Dictionary of Irish Literature.* London: Macmillan, 1980.

Hogan, Robert, and Richard Burnham. *The Art of the Amateur, 1916–1920.* Dublin: Dolmen Press, 1984.

————. *The Years of O'Casey, 1921–1926: A Documentary History.* Newark: University of Delaware Press, 1992.

Hogan, Robert, and Gordon Henderson, eds. "A Sheaf of Letters." *Journal of Irish Literature,* 3, 1 (1974): 65–92.

Hopper, Keith. *Flann O'Brien: A Portrait of the Artist as a Young Post-Modernist.* Cork, Ireland: Cork University Press, 1995.

Howes, Craig. "Rhetorics of Attack: Bakhtin and the Aesthetics of Satire." *Genre,* 18 (Fall 1986): 215–43.

Hull, Eleanor, trans. *The Poem-Book of the Gael: Translations from Irish Gaelic Poetry into English Prose and Verse.* London: Chatto & Windus, 1912.

Humphries, Jefferson. "Decadence." In *A New History of French Literature,* edited by Denis Hollier, 785–88. Cambridge, Mass.: Harvard University Press, 1989.

Huysmans, J.-K. *Against Nature.* Translated by Robert Baldick. Harmondsworth, U.K.: Penguin Books, 1959.

Imhof, Rüdiger. "Two Meta-Novelists: Sternesque Elements in Novels by Flann O'Brien." In *Alive-Alive O! Flann O'Brien's At Swim-Two-Birds,* edited by Rüdiger Imhof, 160–90. Dublin: Wolfhound, 1985.

Jeffares, A. Norman. *Anglo-Irish Literature.* Dublin: Gill and Macmillan, 1982.

Kearney, Richard. *Transitions: Narratives in Modern Irish Culture.* Manchester, U.K.: Manchester University Press, 1988.

Kelly, Eamonn. *Sheela-na-Gigs: Origins and Functions.* Dublin: Country House/National Museum of Ireland, 1996.

Kennedy, Conan. *Looking for De Selby.* Killala, Co. Mayo, Ireland: Morrigan, 1998.

Kenner, Hugh. "The Fourth Policeman." In *Conjuring Complexities: Essays on Flann O'Brien,* edited by Anne Clune and Tess Hurson, 61–71. Belfast: Institute of Irish Studies, 1997.

Kiberd, Declan. *Inventing Ireland: The Literature of the Modern Nation.* London: Jonathan Cape, 1995.

Kiely, Benedict. *Modern Irish Fiction: A Critique.* Dublin: Golden Eagle Books, 1950.

Kilroy, Thomas. "Mervyn Wall: The Demands of Satire." *Studies,* 47 (Spring 1958): 83–89.

Knott, Eleanor, and Gerard Murphy. *Early Irish Literature.* Introduction by James Carney. London: Routledge & Kegan Paul, 1966.

Lanters, José. "Eimar O'Duffy's *Cuanduine Satires.*" In *Troubled Histories, Troubled*

Fictions: Twentieth-Century Anglo-Irish Prose, edited by Theo D'haen and José Lanters, 129–40. Amsterdam: Rodopi, 1995.

————. "'Still Life' versus Real Life: The English Writings of Brian O'Nolan." In *Explorations in the Field of Nonsense*, edited by Wim Tigges, 161–81. Amsterdam: Rodopi, 1987.

————. "Unattainable Alternatives: The Writing of Mervyn Wall." *Éire-Ireland*, 27, 2 (1992): 16–34.

Leslie, Shane. *Saint Patrick's Purgatory: A Record from History and Literature*. London: Burns Oates and Washbourne, 1932.

Longford, the Earl of, and Thomas P. O'Neill. *Éamon de Valera*. Boston: Houghton Mifflin, 1971.

Lowe-Evans, Mary. *Crimes against Fecundity: Joyce and Population Control*. Syracuse, N.Y.: Syracuse University Press, 1989.

Lyons, F. S. L. *Ireland since the Famine*. London: Fontana, 1973.

Mac Lochlainn, Alf. "Eimar O'Duffy: A Bibliographical Biography." *Irish Book*, 1, 2 (1959–1960): 37–46.

McMullen, Kim. "Culture as Colloquy: Flann O'Brien's Postmodern Dialogue with Irish Tradition." *Novel: A Forum on Fiction*, 27, 1 (1993): 62–84.

MacNeill, Eoin, ed. *Duanaire Finn: The Book of the Lays of Fionn*. Vol. 1. London: Irish Texts Society, 1908.

Malone, Andrew E. "Darrell Figgis." *Dublin Magazine*, 1, 2 (1926): 15–26.

Marlowe, Christopher. *Doctor Faustus*. In *The Literature of Renaissance England*, edited by John Hollander and Frank Kermode, 348–99. New York: Oxford University Press, 1973.

Masi, Michael, trans. *Boethian Number Theory: A Translation of the* De Institutione Arithmetica. Amsterdam: Rodopi, 1983.

Mays, J. C. C. "Brian O'Nolan: Literalist of the Imagination." In *Myles: Portraits of Brian O'Nolan*, edited by Timothy O'Keeffe, 77–119. London: Martin Brian and O'Keeffe, 1973.

Meehan, Donnchadh A. "Of Four Fantasies." *Irish Bookman*, 3, 1 (1948): 11–24.

Mercier, Vivian. *The Irish Comic Tradition*. Oxford, U.K.: Oxford University Press, 1962.

————. "The Satires of Eimar O'Duffy." *Bell*, 12, 4 (1946): 325–36.

Mitchell, Arthur, and Pádraig Ó Snodaigh, eds. *Irish Political Documents, 1916–1949*. Dublin: Irish Academic Press, 1985.

Murphy, John A. *Ireland in the Twentieth Century*. Dublin: Gill and Macmillan, 1975.

na gCopaleen, Myles (pseudonym of Brian O'Nolan). Review of *The Sacred River: An Approach to James Joyce*, by L. A. G. Strong. *Irish Writing*, 10 (January 1950): 71–72.

na Gopaleen, Myles (pseudonym of Brian O'Nolan). *The Best of Myles*. London: Picador, 1977.

————. *Further Cuttings from Cruiskeen Lawn*. Edited by Kevin O'Nolan. London: Hart-Davis, MacGibbon, 1976.

————. *The Hair of the Dogma*. Edited by Kevin O'Nolan. London: Hart-Davis, MacGibbon, 1977.

Nagy, Joseph Falaky. *Conversing with Angels and Ancients: Literary Myths of Medieval Ireland*. Dublin: Four Courts Press, 1997.

———. *The Wisdom of the Outlaw: The Boyhood Deeds of Finn in Gaelic Narrative Tradition.* Berkeley and Los Angeles: University of California Press, 1985.

O'Brien, Flann. *At Swim-Two-Birds.* 1939. Reprint, Harmondsworth, U.K.: Penguin Books, 1967.

———. *Stories and Plays.* Harmondsworth, U.K.: Penguin Books, 1974.

———. *The Third Policeman.* London: Hart-Davis, MacGibbon, 1967.

O'Casey, Seán. *Cock-a-Doodle Dandy.* Edited by David Krause. Washington, D.C.: The Catholic University of America Press, 1991.

Ó Conaire, Breandan. "Flann O'Brien, *An Béal Bocht* and Other Irish Matters." *Irish University Review,* 3, 2 (1973): 121–40.

O'Curry, Eugene. *Lectures on the Manuscript Materials of Ancient Irish History.* Dublin: William A. Hinch and Patrick Traynor, 1878.

O'Daly, John, trans. and ed. *Laoithe Fiannuigheachta; or, Fenian Poems.* Dublin: Ossianic Society, 1859.

———, ed. and trans. *Laoithe Fiannuigheachta; or, Fenian Poems.* Second series. Dublin: Ossianic Society, 1861.

Ó Drisceoil, Donal. *Censorship in Ireland, 1939–1945: Neutrality, Politics, and Society.* Cork, Ireland: Cork University Press, 1996.

O'Duffy, Eimar. *Asses in Clover.* London: Putnam, 1933.

———. *King Goshawk and the Birds.* London: Macmillan, 1926.

———. *The Spacious Adventures of the Man in the Street.* London: Macmillan, 1928.

O'Grady, Standish H., trans. and ed. *Silva Gadelica: A Collection of Tales in Irish, with Extracts Illustrating Persons and Places.* Vol. 2, *Translation and Notes.* London: Williams and Norgate, 1892.

Ó Hainle, Cathal. "Fionn and Suibhne in *At Swim-Two-Birds.*" In *Conjuring Complexities: Essays on Flann O'Brien,* edited by Anne Clune and Tess Hurson, 17–36. Belfast: Institute of Irish Studies, 1997.

O'Hara, Patricia. "Finn MacCool and the Bard's Lament in Flann O'Brien's *At Swim-Two-Birds.*" *Journal of Irish Literature,* 15, 1 (1986): 55–61.

O'H[egarty], P. S. Obituary for Eimar O'Duffy. *Dublin Magazine,* new series, 10, 3 (1935): 92.

O'Keeffe, J. G., trans. and ed. *Buile Suibhne (The Frenzy of Suibhne): Being the Adventures of Suibhne Geilt. A Middle-Irish Romance.* London: Irish Texts Society, 1913.

O'Keeffe, Timothy, ed. *Myles: Portraits of Brian O'Nolan.* London: Martin Brian and O'Keeffe, 1973.

O'Looney, Bryan, trans. and ed. *The Land of Youth.* Dublin: Ossianic Society, 1859.

O'Malley, Ernie. *Army without Banners.* 1937. Reprint, London: Four Square Books, 1961.

O'Nolan, Kevin. "The First Furlongs." In *Myles: Portraits of Brian O'Nolan,* edited by Timothy O'Keeffe, 13–31. London: Martin Brian and O'Keeffe, 1973.

Ó Nualláin, Ciarán. *The Early Years of Brian O'Nolan/Flann O'Brien/Myles na gCopaleen.* Translated by Róisín Ní Nualláin. Edited by Niall O'Nolan. Dublin: Lilliput Press, 1998.

O'Toole, Mary A. "The Theory of Serialism in *The Third Policeman.*" *Irish University Review,* 18, 2 (1988): 215–25.

Owens, Cóilín. "The Mystique of the West in Joyce's 'The Dead.'" *Irish University Review,* 22, 1 (1992): 80–91.

Palmeri, Frank. *Satire in Narrative: Petronius, Swift, Gibbon, Melville, and Pynchon.* Austin: University of Texas Press, 1990.

Plato. *The Republic.* 2nd ed. Translated with an introduction by Desmond Lee. Harmondsworth, U.K.: Penguin Books, 1974.

Power, Mary. "The Figure of the Magician in *The Third Policeman* and *The Hard Life.*" *Canadian Journal of Irish Studies,* 8, 1 (1982): 55–63.

Power, Patrick C. *The Book of Irish Curses.* Dublin and Cork: Mercier Press, 1974.

Rafroidi, Patrick, and Maurice Harmon, eds. *The Irish Novel in Our Time.* Villeneuve-d'Ascq, France: P.U.L., 1975–1976.

Shea, Thomas F. *Flann O'Brien's Exorbitant Novels.* Lewisburg, Penn.: Bucknell University Press, 1992.

Sheridan, Niall. "Brian, Flann and Myles *(The Springtime of Genius).*" In *Myles: Portraits of Brian O'Nolan,* edited by Timothy O'Keefe, 32–53. London: Martin Brian and O'Keeffe, 1973.

Spencer, Andrew. "Many Worlds: The New Physics in Flann O'Brien's *The Third Policeman.*" *Éire-Ireland,* 30, 1 (1995): 145–58.

Stephens, James. *The Crock of Gold.* 1912. Reprint, London: Macmillan, 1928.

Stokes, Whitley, ed. *The Saltair na Rann: A Collection of Early Middle Irish Poems.* Oxford, U.K.: Clarendon Press, 1883.

———, trans. and ed. *The Tripartite Life of Patrick, with Other Documents Relating to That Saint.* Part 1. London: HMSO, 1887.

Stopes, Marie Carmichael. *Contraception (Birth Control): Its Theory, History, and Practice. A Manual for the Medical and Legal Professions.* London: John Bale, Sons/Danielsson, 1924.

———. *A New Gospel to All Peoples: A Revelation of God Uniting Physiology and the Religions of Man.* London: Mothers Clinic/Arthur L. Humphries, 1922.

———. *Radiant Motherhood: A Book for Those Who Are Creating the Future.* New York and London: G. P. Putnam's Sons/Knickerbocker Press, 1921.

———. *Wise Parenthood.* London: G. P. Putnam's Sons, 1918.

Strachan, John, ed. *Stories from the Táin.* 1944. Reprint, Dublin: Royal Irish Academy, 1976.

Tapping, G. Craig. *Austin Clarke: A Study of His Writings.* Dublin: Academy Press, 1981.

Vonnegut, Kurt. *Breakfast of Champions.* New York: Dell, 1974.

Wall, Mervyn. "An Address." *Journal of Irish Literature,* 11, 1–2 (1982): 63–79.

———. *The Complete Fursey (The Unfortunate Fursey and The Return of Fursey).* Dublin: Wolfhound Press, 1985.

———. *Hermitage.* Dublin: Wolfhound Press, 1982.

———. "An Interview with Mervyn Wall" (Conducted by Gordon Henderson). *Journal of Irish Literature,* 11, 1–2 (1982): 3–18.

———. *Leaves for the Burning.* New York: Devin-Adair, 1952.

———. "Michael Smith Asks Mervyn Wall Some Questions about the Thirties." *Lace Curtain,* 4 (Summer 1971): 77–86.

———. "A Nightmare of Humour and Horror." *Hibernia,* September 1967, p. 22.

Welch, Robert. "Austin Clarke and Gaelic Poetic Tradition." *Irish University Review,* 4, 1 (1974): 41–51.

————, ed. *The Oxford Companion to Irish Literature.* Oxford, U.K.: Clarendon Press, 1996.

Wessel-Felter, Maryanne. "Darrell Figgis: An Overview of His Work." *Journal of Irish Literature,* 22, 2 (1993): 3–24.

Wittgenstein, Ludwig. *Tractatus Logico-Philosophicus.* Translated by D. F. Pears and B. F. McGuinness. London: Routledge & Kegan Paul, 1961.

Whyte, J. H. *Church and State in Modern Ireland, 1923–79.* 1971. 2nd ed. Dublin: Gill and Macmillan, 1980.

Index

Unauthorized Versions: Irish Menippean Satire, 1919–1952 was designed and composed in Minion with Kaufmann display by Kachergis Book Design, Pittsboro, North Carolina; and printed on 60-pound Writers Offset and bound by Thomson-Shore, Inc., Dexter, Michigan.